Group Work Around the Globe:
Creating transformative connections
in challenging times

Proceedings of the XXXVIII and XXXIX International Symposium
of the International Association for Social Work with Groups, New
York City, New York, USA, June 15-18, 2016 and June 7-10, 2017

Group Work Around the Globe
Creating transformative connections
in challenging times

Edited by
Christine Wilkins, Mark Doel, Sari Skolnik,
John Genke, and Lorrie Greenhouse Gardella

w&b
MMXVIII

© Whiting & Birch Ltd 2018
Published by Whiting & Birch Ltd,
Forest Hill, London SE23 3HZ
ISBN 9781861771452
Printed in England and the United States by Lightning Source

Contents

The XXXVIII and XXXIX International Symposium
of the International Association for Social Work with Groups, New
York City, New York, USA, June 15-18, 2016 and June 7-10, 2017

Acknowledgements vii

Tribute ix

About the Editors xi

The Contributors xiii

Introduction xxv

2016 Sumner Gil Memorial Plenary Panel
*Theses on working with refugees in Germany: Considering the
experiences of Louis Lowy*
Klaus-Martin Ellerbrock Translated by Quirina Busch
with introduction by Lorrie Greenhouse Gardella (Chair) 1

2017 Sumner Gil Memorial Plenary Panel
*Children of War in Ukraine: Exploring the trauma of war through
collective creative writing in literary workshops*
Olga Derkachova ....
with introduction by Lorrie Greenhouse Gardella (Moderator) 10

Discovering social work and social groupwork through objects
Mark Doel 21

Creative Strategies for Working with Diversity in Challenging Times
Sarah LaRocque, Melissa Popiel, William Pelech, David Este,
David B. Nicholas, and Christopher Kilmer 37

Making Group Theories Real: A brief cultural exchange activity
that translates theory into experience
Donald G Jordan and Daphne Henderson 62

All education is group work:
Group work in education in challenging times
Hilda Baar-Kooii 79

The VAWA/U Visa Self Prep Course: Socio-political and organizational influences on an interdisciplinary legal and social work group model for immigrant survivors of intimate partner violence
Martha L. Garcia and Diana Halperin 99

"Putting it out on the table:" Exploring the impact of difference in group work through the experience of a male group worker in an all-female member group
Kyle T. Ganson..116

Who cares for the caregivers of the elderly? Strength-based groups and diversity considerations
Thelma Silver and Linda McArdle...126

Practicing gratitude: Reflections on a community-based group in a supportive housing setting
Patricia Ki and Adina Muskat 136

Māori student perceptions of group work in their social work degree
Donna Guy 149

P.re.turn: Group practice approach for working with citizens returning from prison
Thomas Kenemore, Brent In, and Sr. Hien Nguyen 171

A conversation begins: Using teach-ins to begin a dialogue about racial justice
Samuel R. Benbow 192

Passing the baton: Revitalization of an IASWG chapter
Maria Gandarilla, Cheryl D. Lee and Mei Kameda............................... 206

Shifting contexts: Transforming and sustaining professional identities using group work
Mary Wilson and Deirdre Quirke...219

Team-based learning: A classroom approach for teaching group work skills
Kristina Lind...237

Teaching appreciation for differences via intergroup dialogue (IGD)
Carolyn Gentle-Genitty, Corinne Renguette, and Dan Griffith.........251

Welcome the stranger: Group work and hospitality in a fearful era
Lorrie Greenhouse Gardella..265

Index...277

Acknowledgements

Association for the Advancement of Social Work with Groups, Inc.
XXXVIII Annual International Symposium
New York City, New York, June 15-18, 2016
Symposium International Honoree:
Urania Glassman
Symposium Local Honorees:
Hélène Filion Onserud
John Genke
Bellevue/NYU Program for Survivors of Torture
Cancer Care
Sanctuary for Families
Symposium Co-Chairs
Christine Wilkins , Sari Skolnik, and John Genke
IASWG Conference Planner
Emily Wilk

Association for the Advancement of Social Work with Groups, Inc.
XXXIX Annual International Symposium
New York City, New York, June 7-10, 2017
Symposium International Honorees:
Ginette Berteau
Shirley Simon
Symposium Local Honorees:
Jennifer Clements
Robina Niaz
Stephanie Stolzenbach
Jorūnė Vyšniauskytė-Rimkienė
Rainbow Heights Club
Symposium Co-Chairs
Christine Wilkins, Sari Skolnik, John Genke, and Alexis Howard
IASWG Conference Planner
Emily Wilk

Acknowledgements

Many thanks for the support and assistance to past Dean Lynn Videka, past Interim Dean James Jaccard, and all the faculty and staff of New York University for opening their doors wide open to the IASWG 2016 and 2017 Symposia. Thanks also to Ben Sher and Jenna Adolph of the Office of Global and Lifelong Learning, Kathryn Leslie of the Residential Life & Housing Services, Richard Tom, Milton Sarmiento and their teams of NYU Kimmel Center Operations – these symposia could not have happened without your hard work and dedication.

Much appreciation to all those who helped make the two New York City symposia possible. Sincere gratitude to Greg Tully for his valuable input, guidance and oversight – as IASWG President and native New Yorker, he went over and above the call of duty to make the two symposia a success. Tremendous appreciation to Emily Wilk, IASWG Conference Planner, for her tireless work and organizational talent – we could not have done this without her. Thanks to Dana Grossman Leeman who as Symposium Chair kept us on track and focused on the tasks at hand. Thanks for the efforts of the New York City Planning Committee whose hard work and support is greatly appreciated. Thanks also to the student volunteers from the various schools of social work, and the many IASWG Board members who were supportive and helpful throughout the process.

Thank you to the many authors in this volume who contributed their scholarly writing. Much appreciation to you all for being part of this project.

And lastly, a special thank you to David Whiting, our publisher. Without his guidance and support we could not have developed and produced this volume.

Tribute

This volume is dedicated to the many individuals, especially children who are suffering around the globe as a result of violence, discrimination, injustice, and displacement. And to those who strive to build bridges not walls.

And to Steve Kraft and Robert Salmon, both natives of New York, who died peacefully on April 27, 2016, and May 11, 2016 respectively.

Steve was a loving husband to his wife Aura, a beloved father, grandfather, and together with his wife, a foster parent of 22 children. Steve was a dedicated social worker who always championed group work. He served troubled teens, and worked in substance abuse, child welfare, mental health and other areas. Steve was a talented teacher, who served as field instructor, adjunct assistant professor and taught group work courses. Steve was a productive lawyer and IASWG Board Legal Counsel for decades. Steve was a member of IASWG for many years. He was co-founder, along with Catherine Papell, of the IASWG Long Island Chapter. In 2009, Steve was elected as IASWG President, and he served in this role until 2012. Steve enjoyed supporting many IASWG chapters, and visited several including the German, Lithuanian, European and Francophone Chapters.

Steve connected warmly and passionately with many, and his joie de vivre was truly inspiring. As IASWG President he was charismatic and dedicated. His love for social group work, and his commitment to the mission and values of IASWG, including the power of mutual aid, the importance of international outreach and development, and the need for global diversity and connection, were evident to anyone who had the pleasure to know him. He is deeply missed.

Robert (Bob) Salmon is survived by his loving wife Sheila, children, and grandchildren. As a social work academic, Bob's significant contributions to gerontology, social work administration, and social group work have influenced group work practice globally. While at Hunter College School of Social Work, Bob was a beloved classroom professor and faculty colleague for many IASWG members. A prolific writer, Bob published five books, and over fifty articles and chapters, many about group work practice.

Bob was a cherished longtime member of IASWG. He was a popular symposium presenter. He was an active IASWG Board member, and served on the Executive Committee for nine years.

Bob contributed his superior scholarship and generous service to

IASWG for many years. He had a great many IASWG friends who dearly cherished his collegiality. Bob's bright mind, warm spirit, positive attitude, and strong commitment to group work will always be cherished.

Steve and Rob, we miss your precious presence, wisdom, and love for social group work. Forever in our hearts.

About the Editors

Mark Doel, Ph.D., MA (Oxon), CQSW, is Professor Emeritus in the Centre for Health and Social Care Research at Sheffield Hallam University, England. He is a registered social worker with twenty years of direct practice experience with communities, specializing in group work. He has been a social work teacher and trainer, a head of school, writer and researcher. Doel leads training workshops, largely in the fields of groupwork and practice education. He continues to be an External Examiner for social work programmes and doctoral candidates. He is the Vice-President of the International Association for Social Work with Groups (IASWG). Doel has extensive experience in Russia and Eastern Europe and he is honorary professor at Tbilisi State University, Georgia. Doel has published widely, including 21 books, most recently Social Work in 42 Objects (and more), and Rights and Wrongs in Social Work: Ethical and practice dilemmas.

Lorrie Greenhouse Gardella, JD, LMSW, ACSW, is Associate Professor of Social Work and MSW Program Coordinator at Southern Connecticut State University in New Haven, Connecticut, USA. Gardella was introduced to group work as a settlement house volunteer, and she served as a consultant in children's law before beginning her academic career. She has held leadership positions in various national social work associations, such as President of BPD, Board of Directors of CSWE, Chair of NASW Legal Defense Fund, and other positions; and she currently serves as a member-at-large on the IASWG Board of Directors. Gardella's research interests include social work history; social work with immigrants, migrants, and refugees; and religion and social work practice. Upon request of the IASWG German Chapter, she is preparing a German edition of her last book, The Life and Thought of Louis Lowy: Social Work through the Holocaust (Syracuse University Press, 2011).

John Genke, LCSW-R, has served on the IASWG Board since 2010 as the Representative of NYC's Red Apple Chapter where he is also Co-Chair. He is a member of the Symposium Planning Committee and a coordinator of IASWG's Group Work Camp. From 2003 to 2010, John taught group work at Hunter College School of Social Work where he earned his MSW degree. He retired in 2012 from Services and Advocacy for GLBT Elders (SAGE) and is currently in private practice. His published articles include: "HIV and Older Adults" in The Journal of Long Term Home Health Care; "Resistance and Resilience: Older Gay Men Aging with Chronic Illness" in The Journal of Gay and Lesbian Social Services, and "How leading a workshop can be a real eye-opener" in the UK journal Groupwork. He has also reviewed books for Social Work With Groups.

Sari Skolnik, Ph.D., LCSW, is an Assistant Professor at Wurzweiler School of Social Work, Yeshiva University. Her teaching areas include advanced clinical practice, social work practice theories, and group work. Her clinical experience extends more than twenty-five years with a focus on interpersonal trauma, domestic violence, and group work. Additionally, she is a certified psychodramatist and facilitates psychodrama groups for victims of domestic violence. Skolnik has presented both nationally and internationally on topics related to group work, psychodrama, and teaching social work practice. She is on the board of the International Association for Social Work with Groups.

Christine Wilkins, Ph.D., LCSW, is the Advance Care Planning Program Manager at NYU Langone Health, and Adjunct Faculty at NYU Silver School of Social Work. She has taught core clinical social work courses and advised students for the past 18 years. She has presented nationally and internationally on clinical social work, social group work, advance care planning, program development, domestic violence, and palliative care. She was co-chair for the 2016 and 2017 IASWG International Symposium in New York City. She served as member-at-large on the IASWG and NASW-NYC Board of Directors, and is currently IASWG Symposium Committee co-chair.

The Contributors

Hilda Baar-Kooij, MA, is an Ed.D. student in the Department of Education at Sussex University (UK) and a licensed group worker. As a trained teacher and group worker, she has worked extensively to promote skills development and knowledge about group work in education. Teachers work with groups of children in a classroom but that does not necessarily mean that they facilitate group work. Baar-Kooij has extensive experience in group work that includes international canoeing trips in Eastern Europe that she organized from 1982 (the last years of the Cold War) to 1998. In the past year Baar-Kooij has been working with two schools that are committed to changing their educational system. With a focus on social pedagogy, Baar-Kooij has been facilitating group work with children and teachers that have resulted in very motivated children, personal growth, satisfied teachers and happy parents. Her research has focused on promoting group work knowledge and skills among teachers by helping them address situations of bullying, cyber bullying and conflicts stemming from cultural differences.

Samuel R. Benbow, D.Ed, MS, is an Associate Professor in the Department of SocialWork and Gerontology at Shippensburg University of Pennsylvania. He holds a BS in Social Work, an MS in Counseling: Student Personnel, from Shippensburg University of Pennsylvania, and a D.Ed in Administration and Leadership from Indiana University of Pennsylvania. He has spent the past 28 years serving as an educator, social work practitioner, trainer and workshop presenter nationally and internationally. Professional areas of focus are college student development, retention and persistence of Black males in secondary education, multicultural education, team building and group work education. Additionally, Benbow serves as Co-Chair of the Membership Committee, and the Pennsylvania Chapter Representative of the IASWG Executive Board. He is also an executive board member on several social service organizations in South Central Pennsylvania.

Olga Derkachova, DPS, is a Doctor of Philological Sciences. She is an Associate Professor in the Department of Pedagogy at Vasyl Stefanyk Precarpathian National University in Ukraine. As a professor of language, she uses the creative writing method to work with classroom groups of school children who experience war in the country.

Derkachova is also a writer, with two novels and five collections of short stories to her credit, as well as a volunteer in the military.

Klaus-Martin Ellerbrock, Soz.arb/Soz.paed, graduated in 1979 with a Social Work Degree from the University of Kassel. He completed training in social work with groups at IBS in Aachen under the direction of Georg Nebel and Heinz Kersting, and training in supervision under the direction of Heinz Kersting and Delia Anton. He has worked with children and youth in a municipal youth center, and with elderly persons at a community center in a suburb of Cologne. In 2006 he held the position of "Sozialraumkoordinator" working in community organizing. Since 2014, Ellerbrock has been working in the "Center for Integration" of the city of Cologne, providing consultation to migrant organizations. He was elected president of the German chapter of IASWG in 2012. One of the most important activities that he has organized is the conference at the TH-Köln in November 2015, where the book by Lorrie Greenhouse Gardella (2011), The Life and Thought of Louis Lowy: Social Work through the Holocaust was presented. Since 2015, Ellerbrock has served as guardian of a minor refugee boy from northern Iraq.

David Este, Ph.D., MSW, is a professor in the Faculty of Social Work at the University of Calgary. The majority of his research has focused on different aspects of the immigrant/refugee experience in Canada. He has also been involved in research studies that have examined the health and well-being of people of African descent in Canada, assessed HIV/AIDS service utilization by African newcomers in Calgary, and African Canadian contributions to Canadian social welfare history. David is co-author of one book, co-editor of three volumes, and has published several journal articles and book chapters focused on issues related to immigration and diversity.

Maria Gandarilla, BSW, MSW, currently works as a hospice and palliative care social worker in Southern California. She has facilitated and co-facilitated several groups throughout her career, including teen parenting support groups, psycho-educational groups, parent advocacy groups, and talking circles with elementary aged children. Gandarilla has also served and participated on several task oriented groups including the YMCA of Greater Long Beach Community Development Branch, Board of Managers, the IASWG International Board, and the CSULB Social Work Alumni Group, to name a few. Gandarilla has served as an elected board member to the IASWG Southern California Chapter and has held multiple leadership positions, including Chair, Co-Chair, and Marketing and Membership Chair.

Kyle T. Ganson, LCSW, LICSW, is a clinical social worker in private practice in Kittery, Maine, adjunct instructor at Simmons College and the University of New England, and a Ph.D. student at Simmons College.

Martha L. Garcia, Ph.D., teaches in the Social Work Program at Marist College. She is an educator and engaged practitioner in New York and Oregon. She was faculty and Director of Social Work at CUNY School of Law where she became interested in interdisciplinary collaboration. She has worked in a variety of settings and capacities. She was: Executive Director of the Violence Intervention Project, for survivors of domestic violence in the Latino community; Director of Immigrant Programs at the Committee for Hispanic Children and Families and developed popular education program models including the first educational film in Spanish about Domestic Violence, Dolores. She was a founding member of the Network for Undocumented Women, served on the Board of Directors of the Center for Immigrant Rights and became the Director of Program Development for the organization. She is a psychotherapist and organizational consultant to Legal Services of New York.

Carolyn Gentle-Genitty, Ph.D., Assistant Vice President for University Policy and Director of the University Transfer Office at Indiana University. Gentle-Genitty has engaged in over a decade of leadership and received the Diversity Excellence award in 2017 for advancement of diversity efforts on her campus. Gentle-Genitty has won local and national awards for engagement with students and academic advising and mentoring coupled with awards for teaching excellence. She has over 18 years of higher education teaching experience and excels in management, leadership, human behavior theory and social work practice. She has combined this expertise into her current work with Intergroup Dialogue. Her leadership and innovation is highly sought after to respond to challenges globally. She was recently named a World Change Leader by IATDP. She is the lead author on the book Group-based Knowledge and Skills: Steps to Competency.

Daniel Griffith, JD, is Director of Conflict Resolution and Dialogue Programs at IUPUI and directs initiatives focused on facilitating dialogues, public forums and other communication processes involving issues of social justice and civil discourse. He is also associate faculty at IUPUI where he teaches graduate and undergraduate courses in organizational leadership, human resources, diversity, and alternative dispute resolution and negotiation. An attorney and mediator, Griffith specializes in mediating employment, management and higher education disputes and training lawyers, HR professionals, and managers in mediation, negotiation, communication, and dialogue skills. Griffith is co-author of The Conflict Survival Kit: Tools for Resolving Conflict at Work (2nd ed.), published by Pearson Education, Inc., and writes monthly articles on workplace topics for HigherEdJobs.com, an on-line job and recruitment source. Griffith holds a BA degree in English from DePauw University, and a JD degree from the IU Robert H. McKinney School of Law.

Donna Guy, MEd, BASS (Social Work), is a registered social worker and Native of New Zealand. Following an elite sports/coaching career, she experienced a significant spinal injury which required a change of life direction. Also at this time Guy was a single mother raising three young children. To provide a future for her children she enrolled in a social work degree, graduating in 2004. Guy went on to complete her Masters in 2017. She has practiced in a range of social work/counselling fields, including adventure therapy, health, and community development projects supporting oppressed and marginalized communities. Currently Guy is employed as a lecturer in a large New Zealand Polytechnic Institution. Her research interests include experiential group work practice, social work education, social change, and community development.

Diana Halperin, LCSW, has over twenty-five years experience as a social group worker. Informed by her training in the performing arts, as well as a decade of experience as a community theatre artist utilizing people's life stories toward therapeutic and community building goals, she is a specialist in activity-based and non-deliberative group practice. She has designed and facilitated group programs with many communities throughout New York City, including monolingual Spanish and bilingual groups, older adults, immigrant teenagers, and World Trade Center workers after the September 11th attack. She has taught, written, and presented about social group work. Currently working with public interest attorneys, she develops group work programs to support immigrants' rights and advocacy and to cultivate community leadership. Halperin is a candidate in the Institute for Contemporary Psychotherapy's psychodynamic psychotherapy program and has a private practice.

Daphne M. Henderson, Ph.D., MSSW, received her Ph.D. in social work in 2004 and an MSSW in 1998 from the University of Texas at Arlington. She received a BSW in 1997 from Texas A&M University-Commerce. Henderson has worked in various fields of practice including medical, child welfare and mental health. She is currently interim chair for the Department of Behavioral Sciences and associate professor in the Social Work Program at The University of Tennessee at Martin. Prior to coming to UT-Martin, she was an assistant professor in the Department of Social Work at East Tennessee State University. Her teaching interests include: social work practice and cultural diversity. Henderson's research interests are in the areas of mental health, cultural diversity, and family functioning.

Brent In, MSW, is a doctoral student at the Loyola University Chicago: School of Social Work. He received his MSW from the University of Illinois-Chicago, Jane Addams College of Social Work, and Bachelors in Psychology from the University of Illinois, Urbana Champaign. He is also a retired Senior United States Probation Officer with 23 years of service. Primary duties included supervising high-risk and high-security cases. He also developed the Workforce Development Committee and the Offender Employment Training program for the federal probation office. In addition, In worked as a Medical Social Worker at the Cook County Department of Corrections for 19 years. Primary duties included conducting intake assessment and case-management, and providing individual and group therapies, for the psychiatric detainees. In's research interests are in psychological factors that contribute to successful reentry; mental illness and crime; community corrections; and evaluation of evidence based and faith based reentry programs.

Donald G. Jordan, LMSW, is an Assistant Professor of Social Work at The University of Tennessee at Martin, teaching individual and group practice courses as well as social policy, justice, research, and spirituality courses. He also has a small clinical practice working with children and adults at a local community mental health center, and has worked with groups through drug treatment courts, inpatient units, and grief groups for those who have lost loved ones to homicide. His most recent publication is: "The risks and rewards of speed: Restorative retelling compressed into a three-day retreat," in Death Studies. He enjoys occasional blogging at mosthopeful.com, spoiling everyone else's children, traveling as often as possible, and laughing until his stomach hurts.

Mei Kameda is a graduate-level social work student at California State University, Long Beach and a working social work professional in the geriatric field. Kameda has worked in the geriatric field in facility and community-based settings, long-term care, providing services to family caregivers, and mental health services. Kameda's field of interest is patient-centered care in the medical model, end of life care, caregiver support, and intergenerational group work.

Thomas Kenemore, Ph.D., currently teaches master's level courses in the School of SocialWork at Loyola University Chicago, and taught a course in Loyola's doctoral program for several years. He recently retired from fourteen years of teaching in the Master of Social Work Program at Chicago State University. He received a Doctor of Philosophy degree and a Master of Arts degree from The University of Chicago School of Social Service Administration, and a Master in the Arts of Teaching degree from Oklahoma City University. His research interests include a focus on social justice, particularly understanding of citizens returning from prison to their communities. He is currently conducting an evaluation of a reentry mentoring program for Safer Foundation, and an evaluation of a pilot program with Chicago Coalition for the Homeless providing housing for individuals with criminal backgrounds. He recently completed an evaluation of a mindful meditation program for individuals incarcerated in Cook County Jail. He previously studied victims of police torture and the experiences of individuals engaged in successful reentry. He evaluated a trauma-informed program for urban youth at Chicago State University, and conducted a study of experiences of school personnel in working with youth exposed to violence. He served as Editor of the Child & Adolescent Social Work Journal for eighteen years.

Patricia Ki, BFA, DTATI, MSW, RSW, is an art therapist and registered social worker in Toronto, Ontario, Canada. She is a graduate of the Ontario College of Art & Design, Toronto Art Therapy Institute, and York University. She currently works as a counsellor in the supportive housing program for women living with mental health and/ or substance use issues in Toronto, and has been working in the areas of trauma and women's mental health since 2010. She offers individual counselling and facilitates group programming, using expressive arts, mindfulness-based practices, and narrative therapy framework. Ki works from a trauma-informed, feminist, and harm reduction approach in direct practice, program development and research. Her research interests focus on the intersections between psycho-medical discourse, community-based mental health services, and gender inequities. She is interested in using arts-based practices to increase inclusiveness and diversity in service development, research, policy change, and advocacy, with the aim of contributing to changes in the mental health system that embrace rather than pathologize difference.

Christopher Kilmer, BSW, RSW, is a Research Coordinator in the Faculty of Social Work at the University of Calgary, Central and Northern Alberta Region. He brings experience in a variety of qualitative and mixed-method research designs, as well as qualitative interviewing, focus group facilitation, qualitative data analysis, and survey design. Kilmer's areas of current research include: exploring the use of diversity in group work practice, quality of life for individuals with disabilities and their families, lived experience of service users, health service access and use, patient- and family-centred care, stakeholder engagement, and neurodevelopmental disability with a focus on autism spectrum disorder.

Sarah LaRocque, MSW, RSW, is a Ph.D. candidate in the Faculty of Social Work at the University of Calgary, researching a group training method in practica. She is also a clinical social worker in private practice, specializing in group therapy and the treatment of Borderline Personality Disorder. LaRocque is a co-editor of the 2014 IASWG Symposium Proceedings, and has published several journal articles on groups.

Cheryl D. Lee, Ph.D., MSW, is Professor Emeritus at California State University, Long Beach School of Social Work. She has been teaching group work for eighteen years, started a group work club at the university, and recently co-authored a group work text and instructor's manual entitled Inclusive Group Work published by Oxford University Press. She was on the International IASWG Board for six years and chaired the Southern California Chapter of IASWG for many years. She was Co-chair of the international IASWG symposium on the Queen Mary in Long Beach, California in 2011. She is on the editorial board of Group Work and has many group work publications.

Kristina Lind, Ph.D., LICSW, is Associate Professor and Chair of the Social Work Department at Plymouth State University in Plymouth, New Hampshire. She is a member of IASWG and has initiated a new chapter of IASWG for Northern New England.

Linda McArdle, MSW, is retired from the University of Akron School of Social Work in Akron, Ohio. She is on the Executive Committee of the Northeast Ohio Chapter of the International Association for Social Work with Groups. Her direct work experience includes hospital social work where she worked in rehabilitation, geriatric and cardiac care. She also has experience teaching group work at the undergraduate and graduate levels, and has presented extensively on group work.

Adina Muskat, RSW, is a registered social worker and graduate of University of Toronto Factor-Inwentash Faculty of Social Work. Muskat began her social work career working with youth with learning disabilities, mental health and behavioural challenges in both community and residential summer camp settings. She has held positions in community-based hospital settings working with adults struggling with obesity and related socio-emotional challenges. Muskat is currently a counsellor and team lead of a supportive housing program for women living with mental health and/or substance use challenges in downtown Toronto. Throughout her career, Muskat has consistently found group work to be the highlight of her practice as a means of facilitating meaningful, rewarding and effective opportunities for mutual support and community-building.

Sr. Hien Nguyen, MSW, MA, is a third year doctoral student at Loyola University Chicago, School of Social Work. She graduated from Boston College with master degrees in Social Work and Pastoral Ministry, and from Stone Hill College with a Bachelor degree in Psychology. She has more than four years experience in pastoral, school and mental health settings, working with diverse populations in Vietnam, Boston and Chicago. She worked for a year as a Volunteer in Prison ministry in Boston with Vietnamese inmates. Sr. Nguyen is interested in serving Asian families and serves as a therapist for families and youths. Her research interests include spirituality, interventions in social work practice, and marriage.

David Nicholas, Ph.D., RSW, is an Associate Professor in the Faculty of Social Work at the University of Calgary, Central and Northern Alberta Region. He is the author of over 120 peer-reviewed research publications, with a focus on wellbeing and quality of life in social services. He has been a PI on major grant funding from federal and provincial sources. He brings extensive experience in multi-method research methodology, graduate-level teaching, and an extensive clinical and administrative background in the fields of social work and health. Increasingly, Nicholas has focused his research in areas of systems development and organizational practices.

William Pelech, Ph.D., MSW, currently holds an appointment as Full Professor in the Faculty of Social Work at the University of Calgary. Pelech has conducted research and practice group work and currently holds a major national tri-council grant, which focuses on how practitioners utilize diversity in their group work practice. He has been a co-principal investigator on a major CIHR grant relating to intergenerational trauma among First Nations people and a national research project, which developed a virtual community of practice for practitioners and caregivers for individuals who experience fetal alcohol spectrum disorder. Pelech also pioneered the BSW Virtual Learning Circle, a blended BSW program and was presented the Killam Award for Innovation in Education for this work. In 2016, he was also awarded the University of Calgary Teaching Excellence Award for Educational Leadership.

Melissa Polpiel, MSW, is a Ph.D. candidate in the Faculty of Social Work at Wilfrid Laurier University researching impacts on access to social determinants of health experienced by family/friend episodic carers over time. Prior to her current program, she worked on policy issues related to income support and employment access for people living with unpredictable episodic illnesses, including HIV. In that context, she provided education and policy supports to employers in various sectors. Presently, she approaches diversity-related research with a lens to connect research, education, and policy, applied to practice.

Deirdre Quirke, BSS, MA, DASS, CQSW, is a graduate of Trinity College Dublin and University College Dublin. She occupied a joint appointment with the School of Applied Social Studies at University College Cork and Brothers of Charity (Southern Services) as Principal Social Worker and Student Unit Coordinator. Her research interests include disability, supervision, and creative practice curricula within the European social group work context. Her career in social work in Ireland has spanned more than three decades and a variety of contexts, namely in the areas of medical social work, statutory child care, child and adolescent mental health and more recently disability. Since her retirement in 2013, Quirke has taken on the role of Professional Tutor in the Master of Social Work programme at University College Cork. She also teaches group work in the Advanced Diploma in Fieldwork Practice and Supervision at the Universities in Cork and Galway.

Corinne Renguette, Ph.D., is Program Director and Assistant Professor of Technical Communication at Indiana University Purdue University Indianapolis (IUPUI). In addition to her doctorate in Applied Linguistics, she holds certificates in Technical Communication and in Teaching English to Speakers of Other Languages. Her background in industry helps her foster experiential learning classroom collaborations with industry partners. She has taught face-to-face, online, and hybrid courses in Linguistics, Technical Communication, and English for Academic and Specific Purposes (engineering, technology, legal, apprenticeship trade), and her research areas include assessing learning and learning technologies, user experience, teacher training, health literacy, and intercultural technical communication.

Thelma Silver, Ph.D., LISW-S, is Professor in the Department of Social Work, Youngstown State University, Youngstown, Ohio. She is on the Executive Committee of the Northeast Ohio Chapter of the International Association for Social Work with Groups. She has 40 years of direct social work experience with individuals, and groups, especially in the areas of life transitions and mental health. She also has experience in teaching group work, both at the undergraduate and graduate levels.

Mary Wilson, Emeritus, Ph.D , B.Soc.Sc, CQSW, Diploma in Social Work, is attached to the Bachelor of Social Work (BSW) programme at the National University of Ireland, Cork. Her research and publications are reflective of her teaching and practice interests, notably using group work in the professional training of social workers. She also engages in work with service users and volunteers to create more empowering forms of service delivery. Her research interests include creativity in professional formation, including the professional and pedagogical implications in teaching and learning; social group work, and gate keeping the profession.

Introduction

In these challenging times where war, despair and insecurity reign around the globe, social group work emerges more than ever as a ray of hope. These proceedings present a compendium of articles from authors from many countries: Canada, Germany, Ireland, Lithuania, Netherlands, New Zealand, Ukraine, United Kingdom, and the United States, highlighting the global identity of social group work and the diversity of the IASWG members. The eighteen chapters represent the valuable work that so many group workers internationally facilitate with such commitment and dedication. These chapters are the result of the scholarship shared at the 38th and 39th Annual International Association for Social Work with Groups (IASWG) Symposia.

The 38th Annual IASWG Symposium, held in 2016 at New York University, New York City, New York, USA, was dedicated to group work across the globe. And the 39th Annual IASWG Symposium, held in 2017, also at New York University, New York City, was devoted to group work in the challenging times we face. New York City's ethnic and cultural diversity and its vibrant mix of world influences made it a natural site choice for these two symposia.

New York City's Ellis Island is a stark reminder of the many individuals who years ago left their countries of origin to build a better life for themselves and their families. Today, too, so many are fleeing from their home countries to escape war and violence, often to end up in poorer neighboring nations. As home to the United Nations, New York City reminds us of the value of global diversity and our responsibility to think and serve not only those close to us but to also reach across borders to contribute to a better world for all. New York City's many bridges also remind us of the valuable work that we all strive for – group work that promotes transformative connections and helps build bridges, not walls.

The opening events at both symposia were scholarly, raw with the realities that our world today holds, and inspiring with excellent testimonies to the value of group work. Greg Tully, President of IASWG, Lynn Videka, past Dean, and Dr. Diane Grodney of NYU Silver School of Social Work, Dana Grossman Leeman, and the New York City Symposium Planning Committee welcomed the participants. And as the evening progressed, many old connections were rekindled, and new friendships formed.

We were fortunate to be able to hold not one but two consecutive symposia at New York University, right in the center of New York City; and with the feedback received from the first, we were able to make changes and improve participants' experiences at the second symposium. The many presentations, poster sessions, plenary sessions, and the world café were inspiring, thought provoking, but more than anything a reminder that the power of social group work knows no borders.

This double volume of the 2016 and 2017 IASWG Symposia was challenging and rewarding to produce. Working on this volume also brought to life for us the many inspiring moments, the wonderful opportunities to learn from and with one another, and to celebrate as one. The plenaries, presentations, workshops and institutes offered valuable opportunities for global group work sharing and learning. The chapters in this volume reflect the diversity and eclectic work of group workers around the globe.

In Chapter One, we are honored to present the 2016 Sumner Gill Memorial Plenary Panel introduction by Lorrie Greenhouse Gardella titled: "Welcoming Newcomers: Social Group Work with Immigrants, Migrants, and Refugees." She explains that although the current refugee crisis in Europe is unprecedented in scope, there are many similarities with the refugee crisis that followed the Second World War. She reminds us about the important work of Louis Lowy, a Jewish war refugee, Holocaust survivor, and social group worker. Lowy's teachings on the value of human worth and dignity, the power of groups, and on the imperative of political engagement with and on behalf of our clients, echo the value of social group work in these challenging times.

Klaus-Martin Ellerbrock, a plenary speaker on the 2016 Sumner Gill Memorial Plenary Panel, further highlights the life and work of Louis Lowy, and provides a reflection on the current work with refugees in Germany. He outlines a thought provoking description of the challenges faced by refugees in Germany today and social work's role, with Lowy's life and central messages as a backdrop.

Lorrie Greenhouse Gardella's introduction to the 2017 Sumner Gill Memorial Plenary Panel describes today's global refugee crisis and the many children who end up alone in their journey to safer grounds. Gardella emphasizes the long-lasting effects of such trauma on children, and how social group work provides an opportunity for a safe space, a social base for building hope, and a bridge to the future.

Olga Derkachova, a writer and a professor of language, tells us about her work with "Children of War in Ukraine", as the plenary speaker for the 2017 Sumner Gill Memorial Plenary Panel. She explains how she used collective creative writing in the Ukrainian language (which, in this primarily Russian-speaking area, her students did not trust could be expressive) to help primary school children in Kramatorsk — an important industrial center in eastern Ukraine — confront and deal with the trauma they experienced for almost a year and a half while the region was at war with Russia. She describes the theory behind this approach to dealing with trauma and how it developed, then gives us several examples of the kinds of exercises she used with these children and how these exercises helped the children come to terms with their fears and suffering.

Mark Doel presents the outcomes from an experimental project, Social Work in 40 Objects for his speech in the 2017 Joan K. Parry Memorial Plenary. This international project involves participants from 24 countries and considers the possibilities of Objects as a means to understand the complexities and ambiguities of social work and social groupwork. The project was an attempt to evoke a professional identity through Objects in contrast to lengthy texts and dry definitions. He also considers the group process in a virtual project of this nature.

Sarah LaRoque and her colleagues consider the various dimensions of diversity in the group context, both within and between groups. They point to the fact that relatively little research has been undertaken to consider the effects of diversity on therapeutic processes in groups. In this article, the authors consider a model for working with diversity in order to better respond to diversity within groups. The research process is described, with further phases yet to be concluded. This article focuses on the first phase, the experiences of 24 group workers relating to diversity in groups, and the authors explore seven themes that emerged. An illuminating vignette highlights the findings from the research. In particular, diversity is considered as relational, that is, as something that exists between people (their relationship to and with one another), and not as a quality in an "other".

Donald G. Jordan and Daphne Henderson introduce the reader to an experiential learning activity designed to help students with group work concepts like identity and diversity, and to develop cultural competence. The BaFá BaFá activity provides students who have come from a monoculture with the opportunity to experience a different culture first hand. The authors explore the effects when students play out the roles and values of two strongly contrasting cultures, the Alphas and the Betas. The frustrations of entering these cultures and communicating across them mirror the identities, challenges and power relationships experienced in the 'real world'. The authors detail the process of using this activity, the framework for debriefing with the participants, and the location of this activity in helping students to find 'the soul of the profession'.

Hilda Baar-Kooij, a teacher and group worker emphasizes the importance of group work in primary schools in the Netherlands, and the need to help teachers learn this important skill. She describes her action research study that focused on a primary school classroom and on helping the students own responsibility for their problems that emerged from their interactions in WhatsApp. She demonstrates the effectiveness of group work as a strategy for promoting behaviour change through experiential learning strategies. She highlights the impact not only on the students' behaviour, but explains that through forming a collaborative relationship with the teacher of the class, she was also able to help him develop a strategic plan for change. Baar-Kooij outlines the relevant theories, citing both group work and educational frameworks.

Martha L. Garcia and Diana Halperin give us an in-depth presentation of an interdisciplinary (legal/social work) group model that grew out of the Violence Against Women Act (VAWA) of 1994. The model was designed to help female immigrant survivors of intimate partner violence become active participants in their legal immigration cases. The paper tells the detailed story of how this model was created and developed by legal and social work faculty and students in legal clinics at the City University of New York School of Law, and how it went through several iterations until it was finally tried out in 2015 at a public interest legal services agency to see if it could work outside of a university setting. The paper further explores how socio-political and organizational contexts have affected the development, implementation, and adaptation of this group model and how the current political climate has challenged its ability to maintain its intended purpose.

Kyle T. Ganson uses his experience as a male group worker in an all-female eating disorder group to point out how taboo topics in the group — in this case, the descriptive difference between worker and members — can impact the work of the group if they are not discussed. He looks at the theory behind this practice and how the group worker can help the group address it; and he uses his own group as a case example.

Thelma Silver and Linda McArdle ask Who Cares for the Caregivers of the Elderly? With a large majority of older people wishing to grow old in their own homes, the authors consider the issues facing older people and their families when trying to realize their aspiration to age "in place." The authors review existing knowledge in the North American context, in particular the potential for groups that include different families and family members (multifamilies) using psychoeducational approaches. They chart the success of these approaches with different and diverse population groups and call for further research into their potential for helping older people who want to age in place, whilst also meeting the needs of their caregivers.

Patricia Ki and Adina Muskat's focus on the concept of gratitude, with particular reference to support for women who have experienced trauma, mental health issues or substance use. They describe the components of a group programme for women living in a supportive housing program in Canada, including art-based activities (like photography) and body-based ones (such as walks and mindfulness). The group aimed to connect the women not just to one another, but to resources and services outside the supportive housing building. The authors describe the group's life, the value of a strengths approach, and the creativity that the group encouraged amongst the participants, illustrated in many ways including a concluding group mural.

Donna Guy interrogates the assumption that group work is an effective teaching approach by enquiring whether her Maori students agree. In an interpretative study using a mixed method approach, she presents some surprising results, not least the ambivalence and mixed feelings that Maori students express about group-based learning on their Applied Social Science course in Aotearoa, New Zealand. We learn important lessons about challenging generalisations about Maori (and indeed any) indigenous culture. Guy considers key concepts in Maori culture, and finds them congruent with group learning approaches; however, group experiences were only positive if a sense of trust and belonging had been established. Guy's paper helpfully gives strategies for successful group-based learning, not just with Maori and other indigenous groups, but universally.

Kenemore, In and Nguyen present an innovative group practice that seeks to reverse the poor reentry outcomes of returning citizens. 'P.RE. TURN', is a conceptual process aimed at overcoming oppression and facilitating movement toward liberation. It recognizes the importance of a consistently supportive ecological context during the reentry process, a psychologically transcendent narrative, and a facilitative relational stance by those who help.

Sam Benbow describes "Teach-in about Racial Justice," an event organized by the Social Work and Gerontology Department at

Shippensburg University in response to a student's racist comments on Facebook. Benbow describes the historical roots and goals of the "teach-in" concept, and details how this event was designed and implemented by him and his colleagues. Using social group work and mutual aid, the teach-in event created a safe space for honest and sincere dialogue among students and faculty about race relations.

Gandarilla, Lee and Kameda present a case study of the International Association for Social Work with Groups, Southern California chapter. The authors examine the Southern California Chapter's leadership and planning, and outline how these factors impacted its revitalization and development. Lessons learned are highlighted, and suggestions for future study are presented.

Mary Wilson and Deirdre Quirke highlight the underuse of social group work in continuous professional development in Ireland. Wilson and Quirke present research which was undertaken with two groups of field instructors-in-training, and provides a new perspective on using group work for sustainable continuous professional development. Text and context are explored for their meanings and application in fieldwork instruction.

Kristina Lind explains that while the use of groups is on the rise for baccalaureate level social workers, opportunities for acquiring group skills in BSW and MSW group-specific courses are on the wane. The challenge for social work educators is in finding ways of teaching group work skills outside of an actual group work course. One such opportunity is through a team-based learning pedagogy. This chapter provides both a description of the team-based learning process and adaptations to the model as a means of promoting an experiential platform for the acquisition of group work skills.

Carolyn Gentle-Genitty, Corinne Renguette, and Dan Griffith present inter-group dialogue (IGD) as an effective way to teach appreciation for differences. They argue that the skills promoted by IGD can help participants gain awareness and foster action, and can help educators teach appreciation for differences, integrate the model into their courses, and measure the outcomes. They describe the components of the IGD four-stage model and discuss how this can help inform teaching.

Lorrie Greenhouse Gardella discusses group work and hospitality in a fearful era. She argues that group work and hospitality are complementary approaches to social justice that mediate between "us" and "them." In an era of rising populism, nationalism, and fear, the profession of group work and the value of hospitality promise to welcome the stranger, to nurture hope, and to propel people forward. Although hospitality has inspired group workers since settlement houses welcomed the immigrant poor, hospitality is a challenging value that opens the boundaries between professional and personal life. Gardella explores the potential for group work to serve as a hospitable profession.

We hope you will enjoy reading these chapters, and that they help to illuminate your own group work practice.

2016 Sumner Gil Memorial Plenary Panel

Theses on working with refugees in Germany:

Considering the experiences of Louis Lowy

Klaus-Martin Ellerbrock
Translated by Quirina Busch

Introduction by
Lorrie Greenhouse Gardella (Chair)

Hello everyone and welcome to the Sumner Gill Memorial Plenary international panel, "Welcoming Newcomers: Social Group Work with Immigrants, Migrants, and Refugees." Let me begin by thanking the Board of Directors and the Symposium Planning Committee for supporting the proposal for this session, with particular gratitude to Greg Tully, Mark Doel, and Dana Leeman Grossman who helped in planning throughout the year; and to Christine Wilkins, Emily Wilk, and Joyce Webster for making this session possible. Thank you, above all, to our panelists for your contributions to social work with groups and your generosity in sharing your insights with us tonight.

Before introducing our panel, I will try to set the stage with a brief historical reflection. We practice social work today in the context of a global refugee crisis. According to the United Nations Refugee Agency, today's global refugee population is at the highest level ever recorded (UNCHR, 2016, p. 13). By the end of 2015, "65.3 million persons were forcibly displaced worldwide as the result of persecution, conflict, generalized violence, or human rights violations" and the flow of distressed migrants continues with no end in sight (UNCHR, 2015, p.1). While more than one million distressed migrants made their way to Europe from Middle Eastern and African countries, most displaced persons – the other 59 million – found themselves in poorer countries closer to home. By contrast, the United States admitted under 70,000 refugees in 2014, the latest figures available (UNCHR, 2017).

All this data, yet we understand very little. We know from history that we will not be able to measure the scope or impact of the global refugee crisis for generations to come. In this sense, the global refugee crisis seems timeless and endless. We have seen it all before: the perilous journeys; the closed borders; the commerce in human smuggling; the inhumane detention camps; the deportations; the illusory protections of international law or human rights. The United Nations High Commissioner for Human Rights has compared the challenges of refugee crisis for Europe today with the refugee crisis that followed the Second World War (UNCHR, 2015). What then might we learn from refugees of the World War II era?

In researching a biography of the social group worker and gerontologist Louis Lowy, I learned that Lowy was himself a Jewish war refugee who remembered surviving the Holocaust as the formative experience of his career (Gardella, 2011). After the war, Lowy led a community of 800 other survivors to a displaced persons camp in Deggendorf, Germany, that was being established by UNRRA, the United Nations Relief and Rehabilitation Administration, for so-called "stateless and non-repatriable Jews" (Mankowitz, 2002). Louis Lowy had no social work education at the time; he had been a philosophy student before the war. Nonetheless, as the elected leader of the displaced persons camp, he created groups – cultural, educational, and political groups – as the means for individual and community rehabilitation (Giere, 1998). As he later wrote, "Groups provide what the ego needs, hope and the sense of a future" (Lowy, 1985, p. 291).

Lowy became a fierce and fearless advocate for the displaced persons camp. He joined with the indigenous leaders of other displaced persons camps to advocate for the right of Jewish war refugees to represent themselves before the U.S. Military and other world powers (Gringauz, 1947). "Social statesmanship," he later taught, is an essential dimension of a social work career (Lowy, 1960).

As with colleagues of every generation, Lowy's experience as a refugee led to his calling as a social worker (Wieler & Zeller, 1995). As our panelists explore promising practices in social group work with immigrants, migrants and refugees, I will listen for practices that promote Lowy's teachings on the value of human worth and dignity, on the power of groups, and on the imperative of political engagement with and on behalf of our clients.

And now it is my privilege to introduce our panelists:

- *Bini Araia, Manager of Assisted Voluntary Return at North of England Refugee Service and founder of the nonprofit, Investing in People and Culture in Middlesbrough, England*
- *Maeve Foreman, Assistant Professor in Social Work in the School of Social Work and Social Policy at Trinity College, Dublin*
- *Padraic Stanley, Program Coordinator for Health Promotion and Disease and Prevention at Rush University Medical Center in Chicago, USA. and*
  Klaus-Martin Ellerbrock, President of the German Chapter of IASWG and social worker in the Municipal Center for integration of Cologne, Germany (by video)

Theses on working with refugees in Germany:

Considering the experiences of Louis Lowy

Klaus-Martin Ellerbrock
Translated by Quirina Busch

The following theses were developed keeping in mind the so called "refugee crisis" in Europe but at the same time, considering the experiences of Louis Lowy, as Lorrie Greenhouse Gardella describes them in her book, *Life and thought of Louis Lowy: Social Work throughout the Holocaust* (Gardella, 2011). At the end of the Symposium "Living / Surviving in Groups" on November 19, 2015 in Cologne, Germany, where Professor Gardella's book was discussed, I had the chance to ask the chairman of the Cologne Refugee Council about the role that *hope* plays in working with refugees in their accommodations. His answer was quite shocking to me, as he said: "In this kind of accommodation – where hundreds of people are housed together for months at a time – people cannot have any hope!"

The central and most important message of the heritage of Louis Lowy is that group work can only be emancipatory and resource-orientated when it is based on hope and love for each other. It is only through hope that human beings can be empowered in a crisis situation to be in charge of their own lives.

The context of the so called "refugee crisis"

1. At the moment, with over 60 million people on the run, the world is experiencing the most severe Refugee Crisis since World War II (UNCHR, 2016). Many different reasons cause people from various countries to leave their homes, such as suppression and disrespect of human rights, wars, and catastrophes. We have to keep in mind that the politics of rich countries, including Germany, contribute to uprooting people and withdrawing their livelihoods by disrupting local economies. This happens by exploitation of spacious areas, eviction of smaller farms by multinational agricultural companies, and arms trade with regimes that are very often unstable and disrespectful towards human rights. People are uprooted also through destabilizing military interventions in various countries and through climate change that has been caused by the doctrine of constant growth. Out of this understanding, the German Chapter of IASWG does not consider it a generosity of German politics to have taken in about 1/60 of the world's refugees during the last year. It was Germany's profit-orientated politics that led to the refugee crisis, and it is now Germany's obligation to pay.

2. Germany has taken in many refugees in comparison to other European countries, and many people still see Germany as their destination. The country is experiencing a culture of warm welcome and a broad commitment of the citizens like never before (Le Blond & Welters, 2016). And yet, this development of an intercultural and open-minded society cannot happen without resistance and setbacks.

3. The policies of European countries aim to reduce the number of migrants in Europe and Germany. This is happening by closing parts of the so called "Balkanroute," by differentiating between economic refugees and refugees as defined by the 1951 Refugee Convention, by declaring unsafe states to be "safe countries of origin," and by a massive intensification in the practice of deportation (*BBC News*, 2016, March 4; *BBC News*, 2016, March 8; *BBC News*, 2016, March 9). All of these actions undermine the asylum law, and fall behind the standards of the 1951 Refugee Convention. The current conditions for refugee accommodations in Greece prove this point (Tolis, 2016).

4. *Refugee politics as "divide and rule".* Since autumn of 2015, the

media attention to right-wing extremist, populist, and racist minorities has caused a competition between refugees and the less advantaged parts of our society. The current refugee crisis accentuates the deficits in social, housing, health, security, and education policies, because the ongoing austerity policy in Germany has led to a reduction of resources for infrastructure. Especially in the area of public housing, neo-liberal policies have led to a shortage of affordable housing, which is endangering the poorer parts of the population. Instead of appropriately increasing the governmental resources by raising the taxes for those who profit from our globalized economy, the German government insists on continuing the path of austerity. The consequence is an aggravated competition between the poor, that is, between those who long have been excluded from economic and social participation, and the refugees.

5. *Changes in social work caused by immigration.* In the wake of reconstruction after World War II and reunification, German society has grown into a multicultural society of immigrants. A relevant part of society is affected by people's own migration experiences, including the development of organizations that were formed by migrants themselves. When social work started being professionalized, methods were developed for the self-organization of residents of poorer districts. The same can be observed in social work with migrants. In self-organized migrant organizations we can find many different approaches, which revive practices of community organizing, and social group work once again. Social group work has to use and strengthen the structures of the migrant organizations.

6. In the history of social work in Germany we can find various examples of emigration and exile. Professor Joachim Wieler specifies these in his book, *Emigrant Social Workers: Portraits of Social Workers Who Were Exiled after 1933* (Weiler & Zeller, 1995). He describes the difficult experiences of the new United States citizens who acted as social workers, although their European credentials were not acknowledged. Gaining acceptable credentials was a process full of barriers. Today we experience a quite similar process in Germany. Social work is currently marked by a lack of professionals from migrant populations, yet there are no real efforts to offer migrants opportunities to gain qualifications in social work practice. Very often migrants work in precarious employment and precarious organizations.

Meanwhile, social work has the tendency to not recognize the fact that these working conditions are being perpetuated by our own profession.

Requirements and demands of social work with refugees

7. Refugee work is currently lacking resources. The placement of newcomers in mass housing is an intolerable violation of their rights, which causes hopelessness and depression amongst the refugees. It is not acceptable to crowd in 200 or more people in a gym for weeks and sometimes months without any privacy. These situations can only be handled by hiring security guards, during which time all possibilities of self-organization are suppressed. Under these circumstances social workers are unable to activate the client's resources but instead end up serving as police. In the balance between the social work functions of "helper" and "controller," social workers become agents of control (IFSW, 2012).

8. Social workers and especially social group workers are supposed to act in the interests of those who are seeking protection. That means that social workers have to use their knowledge and skills to empower clients and to encourage self-organization and self-representation. This may not always be possible due to the severe conditions mentioned, but in that case, social work has to demand and advocate for appropriate standards.

9. Empowerment and resource orientation in social work with refugees means involving them in developing concepts and planning sustainable integration, for they are experts of their own needs. Making hope possible and encouraging self-determination has to become a focus in social group work. Louis Lowy described it as essential for his work in the Deggendorf Displaced Person Center to establish an office for emigration. The practical work of providing identity documents, offering language courses, dealing with countries which would offer a destination for emigrants, all of this contributed to strengthening and encouraging the "displaced persons" (DP) community. Encouragement today cannot be achieved only by warm words. It needs organizing of structures and activities that make it clear that the "displaced persons" are able to work on and towards their own future. Therefore the

priority task of social group work is to create conditions in which encouragement can grow.

Social group work and civic commitment

10. Considering group work in the historical context of a broad civic commitment also means that group work needs to focus on the volunteers. Group work therefore has to support the development of intercultural competences, to accompany volunteers in the process of defining their own roles, and to help overcome phenomena like paternalism, the helper syndrome, or cultural colonialism. Significant voluntary and civic engagement should be strengthened in collaboration with the many organizations that stand up for refugees. Civic engagement is a basis for opening society for a culture of diversity and tolerance. It is important to recognize and name the challenges that come along with this kind of engagement. These may be tendencies towards paternalism, incapacitation, and distinctions between "us" and "them." Welcome initiatives evolve out of principles of self-organization in which the knowledge of group processes and methods of social group work is very helpful.

11. Conflicts are completely normal in everyday social life. They cannot be avoided in a welcoming society and anyway that should not be the aim. Social group work has a conceptual framework on how to deal with conflicts in a constructive way.

12. The current social discourse demands that refugees be taught the values of a democratic and enlightened European society. As reasonable as this argument may be, it creates a feeling of "us" and "them" in the relationship between group workers and refugees that leaves behind the possibility of a relationship at "eye-level." Group work needs the courage to negotiate new values as a group. The values of a democratic and enlightened society can only be the result of a negotiation process. Social group work can specifically initiate and moderate these processes in the direct environment of the refugees. This is already happening in refugee meeting centers and programs.

Conclusion

Louis Lowy himself was a survivor of the Holocaust and inhabitant of a displaced persons camp. As chairman of the self-government committee in the Deggendorf Displaced Persons Center, he served the interests of his fellow survivors. At the same time he was always affected himself. Acting for the inhabitants of the displaced persons camp, he was simultaneously community-organizing and advocating for self-determination. He combined social work in everyday life and political lobbying. These activities were characterized by relationship building, love for other people, respect towards their resources and needs, and the conviction that a better world would be possible. In a larger context, it meant attending to the political dimensions of the prevailing circumstances. Otherwise the efforts to create hope could end up as appeasement.

Considering the current migration flows, social group work can contribute to building a society of diversity. If group work takes this perspective seriously and consequently uses empowerment and encouragement, group workers will become agents of this historical process.

References

BBC News (2 ns route. Retrieved from: http://www.bbc.com/news/world-europe-35760534.

Gardella, L. G. (2011). *The life and thought of Louis Lowy: Social work through the Holocaust*. Syracuse, NY: Syracuse University Press.

Giere, J. (1998). "We're on our way, but we're not in the wilderness." In Berenbaum, M. & Peck, A. J. (Eds.), *The Holocaust and history: The known, the unknown, the disputed, and the reexamined* (pp. 699-715). Bloomington: Indiana University Press.

Gringauz, S. (1947, Dec.). Jewish destiny as the DP's see it. *Commentary* 4(6), 501-509. Retrieved from: http://www.commentarymagazine.com/viewarticle.cfm/jesih-destiny-as-the-dps-see-it-466.

IFSW (2012). Statement of ethical principles. International Federation of Social Workers. Retrieved from: http://ifsw.org/policies/statement-of-ethical-principles/

Le Blond, J. & Welters, G. (2016, Oct. 5). Refugees and asylum seekers sign up to offer warm welcome in Germany. United Nations High Commission on Human Rights. Retrieved from: http://www.unhcr.org/en-us/news/stories/2016/10/57e92aa24/refugees-asylum-seekers-sign-offer-warm-welcome-germany.html.

Lowy, L. (1960). Social work and social statesmanship. *Social Work* 5(2), 97-104.

Lowy, L. (1985). *Social Work with the aging: The challenge and promise of the later years* (2nded.). Prospect Heights, IL: Waveland Press.

Mankowitz, Z. W. (2002). *Life between memory and hope: The survivors of the Holocaust in occupied Germany*. Cambridge: Cambridge University Press.

Tolis, C. (2016, Dec. 8). UNHCR moves 1100 tents, beating first snows of winter. United Nations High Commission on Human Rights. Retrieved from: http://www.unhcr.org/en-us/news/latest/2016/12/5849349a4/unhcr-moves-1100-tents-beating-first-snows-winter.html.

UNHCR (2015) *Global trends: Forced displacement in 2015*. Retrieved from: http://www.unhcr.org/576408cd7

UNCHR (2016). Figures at a glance: Statistical yearbook 2016. United Nations High Commission on Human Rights. Retrieved from: http://www.unhcr.org/en-us/figures-at-a-glance.html.

UNHCR (2016). *Global trends: Forced displacement 2016*. Retrieved from: http://www.unhcr.org/en-us/statistics/unhcrstats/5943e8a34/global-trends-forced-displacement-2016.html

UNHCR (2017, March). *UNHCR resettlement handbook: Country Chapter USA*. Retrieved from: http://www.unhcr.org/en-us/protection/resettlement/3c5e5a764/unhcr-resettlement-handbook-country-chapter-united-states-america.html?query=U.S. refugees 2014

Wieler, J. & Zeller, S. (Eds.), (1995). *Emigrierte Sozialarbeit: Portraits vertriebener Sozialarbeiterinnen nach 1933 [Emigrant social workers: Portraits of social workers who were exiled after 1933]*. Frieburg, Germany: Lambertus.

Children of War in Ukraine:
Exploring the trauma of war through collective creative writing in literary workshops

Olga Derkachova

Introduction by
Lorrie Greenhouse Gardella (Moderator)

Children throughout the world live in the social environment of war, and war is the only environment that they know. In the global refugee crisis, a crisis without end, some children flee war or violence by escaping to other regions or other countries. They travel with or without their families, as with children from Latin America who seek the relative safety of the United States. The fighting may end, the children may survive, but they do not leave the memory of loss or the trauma of war behind.

In Ukraine, today, one million children live in a conflict zone; 19,000 children live in peril of land mines; and 12,000 children live in towns where the sounds of warfare are constantly heard. In the words of our keynote speaker tonight, a major challenge for Ukrainian society is the attempt to adapt the children of war to a normal life.

Psychoanalyst Dori Laub famously wrote: "A home can never be a home again after trauma, and an erased relationship can never provide safety" (Laub, 1998, p. 799). It is only through the empathy of listeners that survivors can bridge unspeakable memories with words.

Social group work offers opportunities for speaking the unspeakable and for being heard, for forming empathic relationships, and within those relationships, for realizing the possibility of home. By sharing memories – and by creating the memory of memories – groups provide safety in the present, a social base for building hope, and a bridge to the future.

Group work transcends national and disciplinary boundaries. Social workers are enriched by the insights and experiences of group workers from other countries and other fields, such as education, social pedagogy, and the creative arts. We are therefore particularly grateful to our speakers tonight.

Our keynote speaker is Dr. Olga Derkachova, Associate Professor in the Department of Pedagogy at Vasyl Stefanyk Precarpathian National University in Ukraine. As a professor of language, Dr. Derkachova uses the method of creative writing to work with groups of school children who are experiencing war. Dr. Derkachova is also a volunteer in the military.

Our respondent, Dr. Jorune Vyšniauskytė-Rimkienė, is the Vice Dean and Academic Coordinator for the Faculty of Social Sciences at Vytautas Magnus University in Kaunas, Lithuania. Her professional interests include social work education, social skills training and technology research, and social work with groups and families. She is an IASWG Board member and Chapter Representative for the IASWG Lithuania Chapter, a chapter she helped to create in 2012.

Reference

Laub, D., 1998. History, memory, and truth: Defining the place of the survivor. in Berenbaum, M. & Peck, A. J. (Eds.), *The Holocaust and history: The known, the unknown, the disputed, and the reexamined* (pp. 799-812). Bloomington: Indiana University Press.

Children of War in Ukraine:
Exploring the trauma of war through collective creative writing in literary workshops

Olga Derkachova

Introduction

According to statistics one million Ukrainian children live in a conflict zone; 19,000 children live in areas where they can suffer from mine explosions; and 12,000 children live in towns where weapons are being fired regularly. A major challenge for Ukrainian society today is the attempt to help *children of war* readapt to a normal life. All of them need special care.

Tragically, civilians in Ukraine are increasingly affected by war, many of them children and youth. Although experiences of war and other severe political conflicts often produce long-lasting trauma, it is important to ask what can be done to minimize the effects of exposure to war (Fernando Ch., Ferrari M., 2013). Creative writing in groups is one way to do this.

Theory

The term 'psychiatric trauma' first appeared in the scientific literature at the end of the 19th century. Sigmund Freud wrote that every event connected with fear and pain could have a traumatic influence:

> Any experience which calls up distressing affects such as those of fright, anxiety, shame or physical pain may operate as a trauma of this kind; and whether it in fact does so depends naturally enough on the susceptibility

of the person affected (as well as on another condition which will be mentioned later). (Freud, 2004, p. 6)

The trauma of war is a constant presence in Ukraine. It is our collective trauma. The war is still going on and it is crucial to help people in post-war territories to come back to normal life. Children are the most vulnerable population in these territories because the adults are either not ready or do not want to talk about the war. Creative writing can be a perfect way to get people to talk about it without any pressure. Using such a creative approach in a group setting helps children feel safe enough to open up their inner world and reveal their fears.

This kind of creative writing differs from the kind done by professional writers. It uses the group to help the members access their creativity. In doing so it offers them the possibility of seeing the creative process from the inside, to understand how it works. It can make use of literary texts to create a new ending to a well-known story or to create a new hero and put him into a familiar tale. It can also be used to create original stories.

Creative writing was developed in British primary schools starting around 1950. By the early 1980s it had become part of the curriculum for all primary schools there.

By the late 1960s term creative writing was commonly used to describe children's personal, free writing. Teachers of the 1950s and 1960s rarely used the term autobiographical writing. It is writing that released the younger child's inner creativeness. A more or less official pedagogy of creative writing in schools has to be considered in relationship to the post-war expansion of adult education, the development of the worker-writers and community publishing movement. Self-writing was also used as part of the ethical preparation of intending teachers. It seems rather to have emerged in the schools after the Second World War (McGuigan, 1997, p.111-114).

Creativity is a very important resource for human beings, especially in times of war. It helps people face the trauma of war and talk about the fears and other feelings it brings up for them. This is especially true for children of war.

Creative writing can be done either individually or in a group, but with children group-writing is the preferred choice. Mark Doel has written about the importance of groups and collective work thus:

Despite the rhetoric of individualism and personal freedom, most of the evidence points to the dependency that human beings have on each other and the extremely sociable nature of our species ... We have a strong inclination to group a random selection of individuals and individual things, making connections where there are probably none ... a collection of individuals can suddenly and serendipitously transform into a mutual aid group, whilst a group of people brought together for the specific purpose of group membership might nevertheless result in a collection of individuals (Doel, 2012, p.132).

Collective creative writing helps children:

- to know what others do;
- not to be afraid to create;
- to get quick results;
- to work in a group;
- to be more open
- to talk freely, without self-censorship.

Collective creative writing explores the territory of painful experiences, rather than establishing distance from pain, and identifies the trauma.

Figure 1. Contrasting children's attitudes to creative writing individually and in groups

Self-writing	Group-writing
I do not like to write and do not want to write	There is a person who will write down everything that we create
I am not a writer, so why should I write something	We are not writers, we just play at being writers
It takes a lot of time to write something myself	We do it quickly when we do it in a group
I am not sure if what I do is not stupid	Who cares if it's stupid, we do it together
My text is just my text	Our group text is great

In our work with children, we used 'the spiral of inquiry':

Figure 2. Spiral of inquiry (Timperley, Kaser & Halbert, 2014)

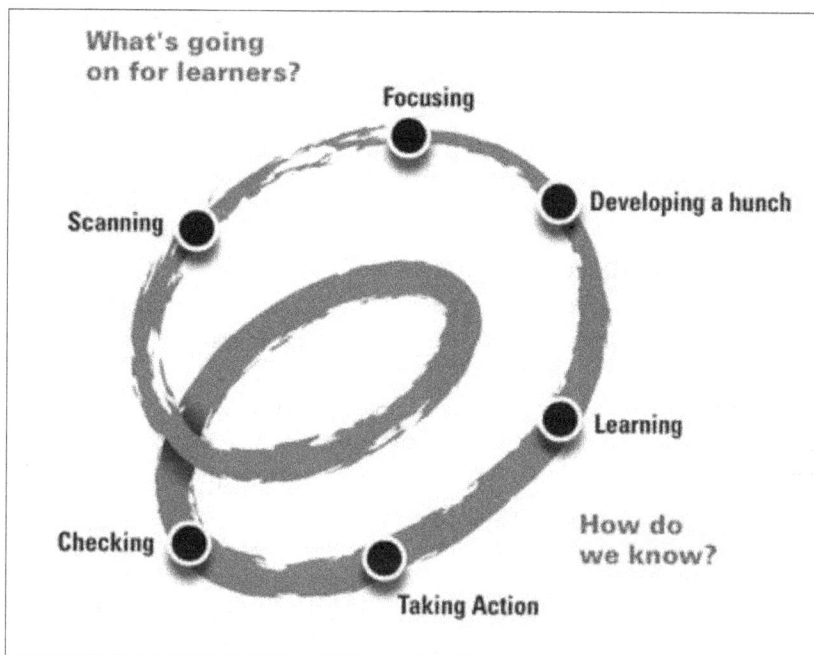

1. Scanning: we place the most emphasis on our observation of the young writers and whether they are ready to work or just play.
2. Focusing: to select the most important thing, which is *how* to create.
3. Developing a hunch: to 'taste' some secrets of creation.
4. Learning: new knowledge about literary text and process.
5. Taking action: not being afraid to make a mistake.
6. Checking: to see what has resulted.

Mary Lee Marksberry (1963) notes that creative writing requires: keeping records of significant experiences; sharing experience with an interested group; and free individual expression. This contributes to mental and physical health. One of the most important benefits of creative writing is the free exchange of ideas between the pupils and their writer-teacher:

Through dialogue, the teacher is no longer the-one-who-teaches, but who is himself taught in dialogue with the students, who in turn while being taught also teach ... In this process, arguments based on 'authority' are no longer valid; in order to function, authority must be on the side of freedom, not against it (Freire, 1970/1982, p.67).

Dialogue and conversation helped children to become active in what we were doing.

Practice

I would like to describe in more detail the experience of working with primary school children in Kramatorsk, an important industrial center located in the Donetsk region of eastern Ukraine. On April 12, 2014, the city was occupied by pro-Russian militants. After months of fighting Kramatorsk came back under Ukrainian control on July 5, 2014. Living under the conditions of war for so many months created serious trauma in every child. Creative writing helped to throw light on their fears and transform them into text.

One of the main problems was language. Kramatorsk is mostly Russian-speaking. Children were not sure that their Ukrainian language would be adequate to create something great, so we discussed in the Ukrainian language what we would do and how we would do it. We used re-writing with additional writing to show the children that they could indeed do it in the Ukrainian tongue. After that, we worked with new-writing techniques (Teaching ideas).

Examples of rewriting and additional writing exercises

1. Writing traditional stories from a different point of view
Tale "Riaba the Hen"
Children were asked to tell this story from the hen's, grandma's, grandpa's, mouse's and egg's point of view. Pupils made a play, where the egg was scared of its future death, the mouse was thinking how to kill, the grandpa thought how to protect the egg.

2. Designing a New Room
Tale "The Glove"
Tasks:
* Count everybody who lives in the glove;
* How many rooms can the glove hold?

Figure 3. Collective creative writing

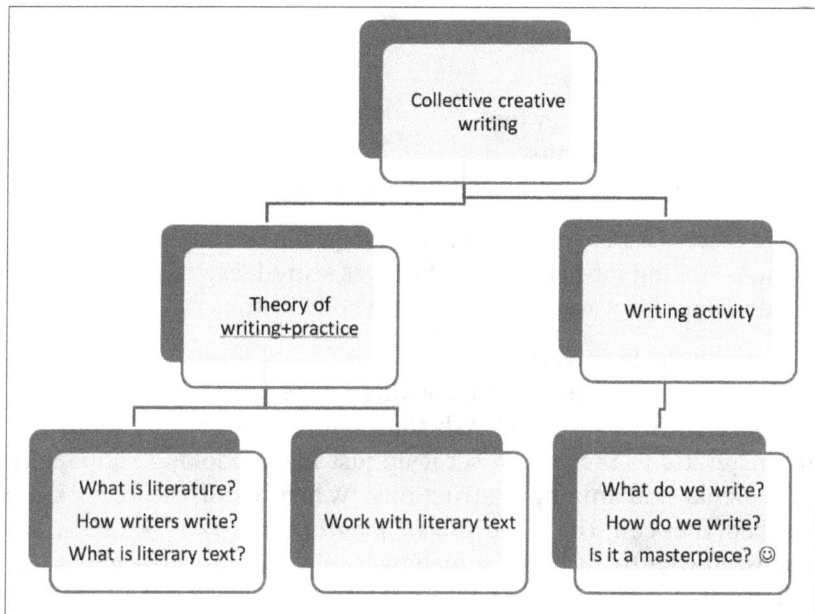

- Describe your room: you are a mouse, a frog, a bunny, a fox, a wolf, a bear.
- How do you feel living in your new place?
- Answering these questions, children told about their own experiences of losing their old homes and getting new ones, about the fears this brought up and about their wishes to hide in the glove.

3. New Adventures of The Bun

The Bun is the hero of one of the most well-known folk tales in Ukraine. Activity: Read the story through with the children. Discuss the main characters, and ask the children to produce a new adventure for a main hero. This could be a tale, a poem, or a picture. Doing this, the children made a story of how the Bun ran away from his enemies, how he was afraid that somebody would kill him. Then the Bun met Ukrainian soldiers who saved him.

These exercises helped children to open up to their creative possibilities and to understand that it is possible to talk about their experiences of the trauma of war in the Ukrainian language.

Examples of new-writing exercises

1. Missing Person
Activities:
1. Describe a person;
2. Describe where they live;
3. Describe their habits;
4. Write a story about this person, sentence by sentence.

We created a story about a girl who stayed in the city alone and how she was looking for her parents. She was scared, crying, but then she decided not to cry and she found everybody from her city.

2. Recipes for Inspiration
Activity: Ask children about a cooking recipe. Can we do something like that with inspiration? Ask the children to make a recipe for an 'inspiration'. They could set it up just like a cooking recipe with ingredients and mixing instructions. When all of the recipes are finished, they could be made into an *Inspiration Recipe Cook Book*. We discussed whether war can somehow inspire, how to write about war and whether it ought to be written about.

3. Group Mascot Activity
Task: take a small soft toy which will become the group mascot. Together as a group, choose a name for the mascot and discuss its background: where it comes from, its friends and family, its likes and dislikes. Our mascot was a pig who came back from war and lived a normal life after that.

4. Using Objects
Task: Take an object and create a story about its adventure. We used a gun which didn't want to kill anybody.

Results

Collective creative writing consists of the theory and practice of writing. Children gained knowledge about the main structural components of a literary text and how to model a character and a plot. They worked with existing literary texts such as well known tales and changed some of the details. After that we tried to write something absolutely new.

The products of our activity were songs and tales. Writing them together, we chose places of action, heroes, and their adventures. All of the children talked and wrote using the Ukrainian language, everybody wanted to be a part of this creative activity. The main topic was a journey somewhere and the return home. Animals, children and soldiers were the main heroes.

Children talked about themselves through our texts and stories. War and peace were both present there. Children "tried not to kill anybody", talked about destroyed homes and coming back to the place and time where and when everything was fine.

Conclusions

Ukrainian children are connected with their age-mates when they work together in school as students in classroom groups, and the classroom group connection with their schoolmates helps the children to make friendships, and to universalize for one another that they are part of a nation at war.

> "Time does not heal trauma. A child must be helped to express suffering and to confront bad memories, with the support and guidance of an empathetic and informed adult. The very act of talking or writing about, or even acting out, traumatic events is a way for a child to begin healing and start on the road to recovery" (The Trauma of War, UNICEF).

Teaching children how to explore their feelings and struggles through collective creative writing in literary workshops is one way to help them. Discussing war texts, and writing about war topics, or interpreting well-known texts through the war-context helps them express their fears to one another about what they are mutually experiencing. Creative writing about war in a workshop group helps the children of Ukraine to freely express themselves, contributing to improvements in their mental health.

References

Building Collaborative Teaching As Inquiry Teams Using Spirals. In http://blog.core-ed.org/blog/2015/06/building-collaborative-teaching-as-inquiry-teams-using-spirals-of-inquiry.html

Caruth, C. (1996) *Unclaimed Experience: Trauma, Narrative, and History.* JHU Press.

Doel, M. (2012). When group is not a group? In *Groups: Gateways to growth.* (pp. 129-138). London: Whiting and Birch Ltd.

Fernando, C, and Ferrari, M. (2013) *Handbook of Resilence in Children of war.* New York : Springer.

Freire, P. (1970/1982). *Pedagogy of the Oppressed.* Translated by Myra Bergman Ramos. New York: Continuum Publishing.

Freud. S. and Breuer, J. (2004) *Studies in Hysteria.* Translated by Nicola Luckhurst. Hadrmondsworth: Penguin.

Marksberry, M. L. (1963) *Foundation of Creativity.* Harper›s Series on Teaching. New York ; London: Harper & Row.

Mc Guigan, J. (editor) (1997) *Cultural Methodologies.* Sage.

Talking to Children about War and Terrorism. In http://www.nctsn.org/nctsn_assets/pdfs/edu_materials/talk_children_about_war.pdf

Talking With Children About War and Violence In The World. In https://www.teachervision.com/historic-wars-military-action/talking-children-about-war-violence-world

Teaching ideas. In http://www.teachingideas.co.uk/writing-fiction/creative-writing-ideas

The Trauma of War. In https://www.unicef.org/sowc96/7trauma.htm

Discovering social work and social groupwork through objects

Mark Doel

This plenary speech presents the outcomes from an experimental project, Social Work in 40 Objects. It considers the possibilities of Objects as a means to understand the complexities and ambiguities of social work and social groupwork. The project was an attempt to evoke a professional identity through Objects in contrast to lengthy texts and dry definitions.

Objects from the project are introduced and the groupwork elements that powered the experiment are explored. The international flavour of the project reflected IASWG's growing internationalism and the global nature of groupwork. Even so, these questions remain: To what extent are Objects locally and culturally specific? What does this experiment tell us about the power of Objects? Might 'Object Work' be used in direct practice with groups? These questions and others were explored with the help of some of the IASWG members who joined in this project by proposing their own Objects for the collection.

The project is published as a book, *Social Work in 42 Objects (and more)*, with proceeds benefiting street children in Delhi, India, through an NGO, TARA Children's Centre.

What follows is a lightly edited version of the presentation and reflects the informal style of the keynote.

Abstract nouns

Social work is an abstraction made manifest as professional practice. We cannot point to any 'thing' and say, "There's a social work." As an abstraction it is open to several interpretations and therein lies its ambiguity. I see this flexibility as a strength; it reflects the reality of the uncertainty in social workers' daily practice, and the need to embrace rather than control this uncertainty. It is important to distinguish uncertainty from vagueness.

Abstract nouns carry dictionary definitions. For example:

Obsolescence (n): the process of becoming obsolete; falling into disuse or becoming out of date.

An alternative way of accessing the sense of an abstraction is to objectify it:

There is no guarantee that this pile of out-of-date transformers will unfailingly conjure the word *obsolescence*. However, as a visual illustration of what obsolescence might look like, perhaps it is capable of conveying a more immediate understanding?

Starting at the other end, we could first view an object, or set of them, then ask what abstraction it might represent:

Does the notion of *order* come to mind?

Order (n): the arrangement or disposition of people or things in relation to each other according to a particular sequence, pattern or method.

Social work has a definition formulated by the International Federation of Social Workers and the International Association of Schools of Social Work:

Social work is a practice-based profession and an academic discipline that promotes social change and development, social cohesion, and the empowerment and liberation of people. Principles of social justice, human rights, collective responsibility and respect for diversities are central to social work. Underpinned by theories of social work, social sciences, humanities and indigenous knowledge, social work engages people and structures to address life challenges and enhance wellbeing. (IFSW/IASSW, 2012)

What, then, would an image of social work look like? This is difficult, not least because social work is *contested* – there are several conceptions of what it is, and these are not necessarily wholly compatible with each other. Even so, we instinctively feel that if we could illustrate social work, it could have a more powerful impact on the wider public than wordy definitions.

Clarkson's Box

Slavery is another abstract noun, one that carries an oppressive weight of unspeakable feelings. In the midst of the *40 Objects* experiment I happened on the house (now museum) of the anti-slavery campaigner, William Wilberforce. In the museum was a box of artefacts collected by Thomas Clarkson. He travelled widely, displaying these objects to show his audiences the paraphernalia of slavery. In addition to the shocking tools used to enforce slavery on the sea journeys, he surprised his audiences by exhibiting things *created* by slaves, carved objects of great beauty that his audiences could handle and wonder at, to feel directly connected to another creative human being.

Though it is Wilberforce who has achieved the historical recognition through his parliamentary achievements abolishing the slave trade

(1807) and slavery in the British Empire (1833), it is the unsung Clarkson who won over hearts and minds via his Box of objects. Where Wilberforce was the policy maker, I like to think of Clarkson as the social worker and, in the skilfull way he addressed and engaged his audiences, the groupworker.

Evocative objects

Collecting objects to tell a story is not novel, though it has experienced a revival. Neil MacGregor (2012) narrated the history of the world through 100 objects chosen from the archives of the British Museum, then told through several short radio programmes; Fintan O'Toole (2013) has reflected on a nation's identity through his collection of 100 Irish objects. Sherry Turkle (2011) invited individuals from many walks of life to choose an object which each found evocative and to relate why and how. "We think with the objects we love; we love the objects we think with," she wrote; and "objects are companions to our emotional lives, a provocation to thought" (Turkle 2011: 5).

We can all relate to the idea of an evocative object:

These are my wife's and my teddy bears. I still treasure my teddy bear from a 1950s childhood; I don't derive my identity from this bear and I could survive its loss, but the early attachment and its continuity as a keepsake in my life are significant, something that helped the transition from an awareness of *me* to one of *not-me* (Winnacott 1953). Even in cultures that do not have teddy bears, the idea of an early infant object that accompanies you through the life journey is universal.

Whole cultures are known through their objects – artefacts that in some instances might be the only way in which we now understand anything about them, even their very existence. One such object, a spiral design from a *Trypillian pot*, was proposed for the 40 Objects collection. If anthropologists from a post-apocalyptic future were seeking evidence of the nature, even existence, of a social work tribe, what might this be?

Objects to evoke social work

"Artefacts, objects and paraphernalia and their relationship to social work practice and identity have attracted little attention in social work despite their ubiquity in all aspects of our lives," wrote Helen Scholar (2016) in a paper on the neglected paraphernalia of social work practice. The concrete presence of objects in everyday social work is a reality often ignored; freed from their taken-for-grantedness, could they throw social work into sharper relief, to the benefit of our own professional identity, and for a wider public that is largely uncomprehending?

In the face of widespread misapprehension of what social work is and what social workers do ('child-snatching'), could *a box of Objects* increase public awareness and confidence, harnessing support for social work like Clarkson did for the anti-slavery campaign? Further, could the social work profession understand itself better by leaving behind dusty definitions and long textbook narratives to discover more direct truths through a collection of Objects?

These thoughts led me to establish an experimental website, *socialworkin40objects.com*, which invited anyone with an interest in social work to propose an object and to write why. The blog is still active and, to date (2017), over 140 people from 24 countries have participated.

Six stories

Let's meet six of those 140 people who have proposed an object. We will briefly hear their story, and why they chose their Object. More detail is available at *socialworkin40objects.com*.

Suzy Croft

Social workers work with people who are often at the most vulnerable time of their lives; they also face the challenge of working with those who are prepared to abuse others, and dealing with the effects of this abuse. Every day social workers make the most complex decisions in areas where answers are seldom black and white, whilst supporting the service user's rights. I am proud to be part of the profession that is social work.

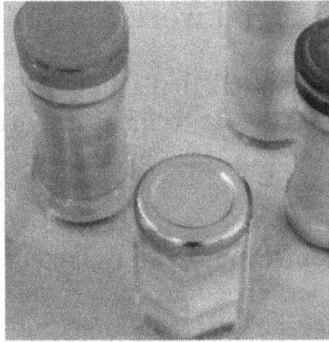

Suzy chose *Memory jar* because it represents some of the most poignant but also the most positive moments of her social work in a hospice. During the hospice's Children's Days, bereaved children create a memory jar of coloured layers. These layers are made by rubbing coloured chalk into salt. The children create a different colour to represent different memories of the person in their life who has died. *Memory jars* are a good way to help bereaved children and this work demonstrates the resilience of children, how they can and do survive despite all that may happen to them. Children can cope with life changing events, serious illness, death and dying, *if* they are given the right support. Social workers provide that support.

Enakele Seun David

I grew up in a small village in Nigeria. Social services are not a new phenomenon in Nigeria – the traditional rulers provide social welfare services through the elders and family heads. The kinship system provides for child and family welfare, mental health, and care for aged people.

David chose *Ileke ibile* (Yoruba for traditional bead) because as a young boy he loved and admired the *ileke Ibile* worn by the village leaders. The leaders meet the social needs of the villagers and deal with problematic behaviours and find solutions.

David sees social workers as 'wearing' the *ileke ibile:* the bead cannot be physically observed, but the social work profession *is* the traditional bead.

Sue Thompson

I became a social worker for a particular reason; to play my part in challenging the ageist attitudes and practices that I'd long observed as widespread in eldercare. I hope I achieve this in my work, by helping those whose right to self-determination is not being respected to fight their own battles.

Sue chose this Traffic sign because it speaks to her of the power to portray particular perspectives of 'reality' as how things are and should be – in this case, that old age is necessarily about decline, rather than growth. Social workers should feel empowered to challenge taken-for-granted negative assumptions about particular groups of people.

Dudzile Sokhela

I've served my people working in different non-profit organisations in South Africa. I was inspired by my late sister and my living mother's altruistic causes in the community I grew up in.

Dudzile chose *Food* because throughout her social work career she has worked with people living in abject poverty – and the direst need is a basic commodity: food. She decided to *own* her country's poverty. "Social work is about owning the community's problems and doing something about them," she writes. She sees social work as activism.

Carol Cohen

Soon after returning to New York in 1974, I joined the Williamsburg-Greenpoint Human Service Center in Brooklyn as Group Work Supervisor and then Program Manager, bringing me into the Coalition of Community Organizations that made my Object - the COCO delegate Button [badge]. I have never forgotten the experience, through 17 more years at Catholic Charities' programs, and my present academic career.

Carol chose Button [badge] because it is an iconic artifact of an exciting and ambitious project, when diverse Brooklyn constituencies living in close proximity faced abandonment by services. In the days before hipsters and gentrification, they all come together to push for a common agenda through Carol's community-based program.

Jill Palmer

I began my working life as a nurse. After a diversion by way of managing a music shop, I coordinated care for people in their own homes in a London borough. I have had a varied social work career: a hospital social worker; a mental health worker; an HIV social worker. Now I work in a prison with disabled prisoners.

Jill chose a *Dalek*. This is a sci-fi monster that embodies destructive evil, exterminating all other living beings. It needed to glide along surfaces, so it couldn't climb stairs! Jill found Dalek to be a perfect symbol for the uphill battle she faces in her work to promote disabled prisoners' access and rights in prisons. For Jill, the Dalek exemplifies the social model of disability, i.e. get the environment right and it minimises the problems. Her work with disabled prisons is made difficult because most prisons aren't adapted for disabled people.

The Dalek also symbolises the frustrations of a job which involves working with hostile colleagues who don't agree with disabled prisoners 'getting special treatment'.

Even in this small sample of six objects it is possible to experience a wide range of 'social works', from individual clinical practice to broad social action.

Each object has its own story rooted in its possessor's personal narrative; yet, by offering the object as a gift to the Collection, the object's 'donor' invites us to weave our own story. Each object evokes its own meanings for each viewer: to me, the Memory jar speaks of both pain and hope and the practical tools social workers can use to make a difference; the *Ileke ibile* prompts me to consider where professional leadership and authority come from and what the place of spirituality is in social work, and it also inspires me to believe in the universal nature of social work values; the Traffic sign epitomises the campaigning, social reforming nature of social work and how it can be overpowered by proceduralised, bureaucratic practices; Food speaks to the nature of social workers' relationships with the people they work with, to intimacy and distance, and the South African food store sadly resonates with the food banks now resurgent in wealthy countries like the UK; the Button (badge) is a tangible remnant from a time when community action was ascendant in western social work practices and puts me in touch with my own early social work experiences; and Dalek throws light on the dystopian elements of social work, that no matter how much 'good' social workers want to do, some clients see them as alien, even destructive.

Social groupwork
and the 40 Objects experiment

From my perspective as a groupworker the gathering of these objects is an interesting process. From the start I had my own notion of what an object looked like, something like this:

This *Chinese bowl* was proposed by Tuck Chee-Phung to symbolise his cultural roots (it has been in his family for generations), and a reminder of the value of feeling 'alien' (he is a Chinese Malay, living and working in Scotland). It gives him a personal connection with others he works with who also feel marginal and perhaps alienated.

As an object, a bowl is a holdable and transportable artefact, but what of these contributions:

Escher's Enigma; Songs; A real-life library; Teflon; Eyes; Bella the dog (long dead); Panopticon; Trees; Dalek

As soon as the experiment began I found my idea of *Object* was challenged, similar to the way a group is changed by the ideas that its members bring. As group leader we can resist or embrace; by embracing we often facilitate a much richer experience for everyone, as well as sharing power. This was my experience with *40 Objects*.

Inspired by the looser notion of *Object* introduced by the group members, I proposed my own metaphysically ambiguous thing: *Mind the gap*. This recording on the London Underground exhorts passengers to be careful of the gap between train and platform; for me, it evoked the gap between the idealism and reality of social work, the social work role of bridging gaps between different sections in society, and the notion that social workers have "one foot in the establishment and the other amongst the poor" (Toynbee Hall). Gaps join as well as separate. Social workers mind this gap, in the sense that we take care of it, and we also worry about it.

Membership of this *40 Objects* experimental group was virtual and open. Many of the contributors responded to my prompting, but others made contact out of the blue, often alerted by social media. Dialogues opened via the commentaries that participants made in relation to each others' stories. It became evident that the background story of the person gifting an object was as illuminating as the information about why they chose the object. When these stories combined, as they often did, it had an especially powerful impact.

For instance, the *Mouthpiece to a french horn* is the sole object that Simon Cauvain was able to rescue from his long-estranged father, who died just weeks after they re-connected. His father's flat had been burgled of his few possessions the day he had died. Simon finds this physical connection has transformed the mouthpiece into a talisman that connects him to a time when *he* was a service user - an infant, at a time when some now-unknown social worker came into his life and acted for his benefit. The mouthpiece is "a lasting personal reminder that service user is *not* a negative term. Service users are fellow human beings who need to be *heard* not just listened to ... the mouthpiece is a metaphorical voice; the opportunity to play one's own tune rather than dance to that of another. It represents that something special that good social workers manage to find," writes Simon.

Simon's story evoked messages of support from other *40 Objects* participants. The fact that they were virtual rather than face-to-face made them no less supportive and powerful.

Many of the proposed objects directly referenced the groupwork element of social work, such as *Coffee cup* and *Cheese fondue*. This is unsurprising as many of those who donated an Object were members of the International Association for Social Work with Groups (IASWG).

The Collections

After six months I took stock of the whole collection (then 127 Objects from 24 countries) and pondered how they might be gathered and displayed. Having focused on the material nature of Objects and the impact of things that are tangible, it is an irony that none of these Objects conformed to this template: by virtue of the nature of a website, they were all *images* of objects! Indeed, some could never be handled in the material world, such as the *Real-life library,* the 1950s *Bella the dog* or my own *Mind the gap.*

I considered the objects as a whole Collection and from my perspective as a researcher developed a typology of five categories of object:

* *metaphorical objects* that illustrate social work by comparing similar characteristics and making parallels;
* *practical objects* that are used in direct social work practice;
* *personal objects* from the donor's own history and relationship with social work;
* *socio-political objects* that illustrate the link between social work and the broader social and political context;
* *historical objects* that have a role in shaping social work and often have a contemporary significance.

Many objects fell into more than one of these categories.

How to exhibit the objects?

The objects are merely images on a website, nevertheless it is worthwhile to ponder how they might be displayed as though they were a collection of material things in a physical Exhibition of Social Work.

In the book that arose from the website (Doel 2017) I gathered the objects into 13 different collections, drawing on the nature of the objects *as objects* to define each collection. For instance, the *Fabric of Social Work* collection comprises a *Foundling hospital token*, a *school bag*, a *cushion*, a *lappieskombers* (South African quilt), a *ball of wool,* a *kete* (Maori bag), a *khurjini* (Georgian knapsack) and a *hammock*. The stories that elaborate each of these objects evoke various social work themes within the same collection, but it was the integrity of each collection as a set of objects that attracted me, gathering the objects together according to the similarity of their material nature or function (Dant 2006).

I wrote the book as though it were a catalogue to an Exhibition, with my own role as curator. Some exhibitions lack a catalogue, but perhaps this is unique in being a catalogue without an Exhibition!

Conclusions

An open approach to seeking Objects has produced great diversity and this has given rise to an inclusive picture of the social work profession. As far as I am aware, objects have not been used as a medium to explore social work nor to explain it to a wider population. It seems reasonable to surmise that exposure to the objects, their donors and the stories that lie behind could increase understanding of social work and, thus, support for it.

The donor's own story is frequently of interest and sometimes of great significance. When the personal story connects the object to both the person *and* the profession, it becomes especially powerful, as we saw with *Mouthpiece*. An object does not necessarily speak for itself, so the donor's explanation is important. Continuing with the Exhibition metaphor, this explanation is the 'plaque' at the side of the exhibit. This given information is only the first step and the observer brings his or her own meaning to an object, just as artefacts in galleries are seen through the lens of our own interpretation.

A collection of objects might benefit the student's practicum by providing direct access to the diversity of social work practice, in the way that abstract phrases like 'a contested profession' do not.

Some people found it perplexing, even impossible, when prompted to nominate an object. This idea of objects that evoke social work is not, then, one that everyone can relate to. There was some evidence that understanding and inspiraton arises once contact has been made with the collection. "Now I see the possibilities."

Objects are already used in direct practice, such as the *Memory jar*.

Bringing tangible objects into groups can help people tell their own story, listen to others' stories, or connect to their past, such as the use of smells in people experiencing severe memory loss. Objects can be used to make a material record of a group's life. There is some evidence from the *40 Objects* experiment that service users can articulate what social work means to them via Objects. *Object work* is worthy of further development as a method of practice, especially in social groupwork.

Further reading

Brown, B. (2004), *A Sense of Things,* University of Chicago Press.

Dant, T. (2006), 'Material civilisation: Things and society', *The British Journal of Sociology,* 57(2), 289-308.

Doel, M. (2017), *Social Work in 42 Objects (and more),* Lichfield UK: Kirwin Maclean Publishing.

Fiol, C. and O'Connor E. (2006), 'Stuff matters: Artifacts, social identity and legitimacy in the US medical profession', in Rafaeli A. and Pratt M. (eds) *Artifacts and Organisations: Beyond Mere Symbolism,* New Jersey: Lawrence Erlbaum Associates, pp 241-259.

Fox, N. and Aldred, P. (2017), *Sociology and the New Materialism,* London: Sage.

Hocking, C. (2000), 'Having and using objects in the western world', *Journal of Occupational Science,* 7(3), 148-157.

Hoybye, M. (2014), 'Social work and artefacts: Social workers' use of objects in client relations', *European Journal of Social Work,* 18(5): 703-717.

IFSW/IAASW (2012) etc.

MacGregor, N. (2010), *A History of The World in 100 Objects,* London: Allen Lane, British Museum/BBC.

Miller, D. and Woodward, S. (2012), *Blue Jeans: The art of the ordinary,* Berkeley: University of California Press

O'Brien, T. (1990), *The Things They Carried,* New York: Penguin.

O'Toole, F. (2013), *A History of Ireland in 100 Objects,* Dublin: Royal Irish Academy.

Pink, S., Moragn, J. and Danity, A. (2014), 'The safe hand: Gels, water, gloves, and the materiality of tactile knowing', *Journal of Material Culture,* 9(4): 425-442.

Reckwitz, A. (2002), 'The status of the "material" in theories of culture:

From "social structure" to "artefacts" ', *Journal for the Theory of Social Behaviour,* 32(2): 195-217.

Rice, T. (2010), ' "The hallmark of a doctor": The stethoscope and the making of medical identity', *Journal of Material Culture,* 5{3): 287-301.

Scholar, H. (2016), 'The Neglected Paraphernalia of Practice? Objects and artefacts in social work identity, practice and research', *Qualitative Social Work, doi 10/1177.1473325016637911*

Turkle, S. (2007), *Evocative Objects: Things we think with,* Cambridge, MIT.

Twigg, J. (2010), 'Welfare embodied: The materiality of hospital dress - a commentary on Topo and Iltanen-Tahkavuori', *Social Science and Medicine,* 70(11): 1690-1692.

Winnicott, D (1953), 'Transitional objects and transitional phenomena: A study of the first not-me possession', *International Journal of Psychanalysis,* 34: 89-97.

Visit *socialworkin4oobjects.com*

The website remains open and continues to collect objects. You can propose your own Object by contacting Mark Doel at: *doel@waitrose.com*

The book, *Social Work in 42 Objects (and more),* can be purchased from the publisher, enquiries@kirwinmaclean.com. All proceeds benefit work with street children in Delhi.

Creative strategies for working with diversity in challenging times

Sarah LaRocque, Melissa Popiel,
William Pelech, David Este,
David B. Nicholas, and Christopher Kilmer

Introduction

Canadian communities are experiencing significant and increasing diversity across a wide range of variables, including: racial and ethnic origin, immigration status, Aboriginal identity, gender identity, religion, language, income, education, employment status, occupation, housing, marital or relationship status, and other characteristics and experiences (Statistics Canada, 2009). Diversity is often defined in terms of demographic variances between individuals or groups (Abernethy, 2002; Doyle & George, 2008; Fellin, 2000; Nagda et al., 1999; Pelled, 1996; Weinrach & Thomas, 1996). However, diversity is also applied to values, attitudes, personality, beliefs, and behaviours (Abernethy, 2002; Pelled, 1996; van Knippenberg & Schippers, 2007) and also with respect to the presenting problem in therapeutic groups (Brabender, Fallon, & Smolar, 2004). Thus, diversity can have both readily detectable and underlying attributes (Haley-Banez et al., 1999; Harrison, Price, & Bell, 1998; Pelled, 1996; van Knippenberg & Schippers, 2007).

As Doyle and George (2008) note, "human beings are, by definition, diverse, as no two individuals are identical in all respects" (p. 106). Ideas concerning diversity and difference, and beliefs about one's own identity and the identities of others, are socially constructed, and rooted in interactions and discourses (Blundo & Greene, 2008; Cheung, 1997; Gergen, 1985). Diversity becomes increasingly apparent and significant when two or more individuals interact, enabling the subtler aspects of identity to be revealed.

As a relational concept, diversity is often associated with conflict.

According to Pelled, Eisenhardt, & Xin (1999), emotional or interpersonal conflict is typically related to perceptions of one's own social "category" or identity and those of others; conflict may be rooted in feelings of anger, mistrust, and fear, and social comparison may result in the development of negative biases and stereotypes. Just as societal responses have not always affirmed and indeed often negated diversity, the expression of diversity in groups may result in suppressive or harmful responses, but alternatively responses can elicit beneficial and generative impacts.

Irrespective of responses, group dynamics, processes, and outcomes indeed are influenced by the diverse identities, attitudes, and perceptions of both group facilitators and group members. Each member enters the group with their own personal and social frame of reference, and these values, beliefs, and prejudices become evident within the group context, either consciously or unconsciously (Brown & Mistry, 2006; Johnson, Torres, Coleman, & Smith, 1995; Marbley, 2004; Shapiro, 1990).

Diversity is present within and between groups, and attention should to be paid to variations among members of all identity groups, acknowledging both similarities and differences (Allessandria, 2002; Anderson, 2007; Roysircar, 2008; Weinrach & Thomas, 1996). As Parrott (2009) states, "groups do not possess a singular unambiguous identity" (p. 620). In addition, individual identification with multiple social categories or social identities ought to be recognized (Fellin, 2000). Van Knippenberg and Schippers (2007) emphasize the importance of recognizing interacting (versus additive) dimensions of diversity.

The concept of diversity is particularly relevant to the social work profession, which has a mandate of seeking social justice and equity for members of, "non-dominant, marginalized or oppressed social groups" (Doyle & George, 2008, p. 97). Even seemingly homogeneous groups commonly include diverse members. For example, substance abuse treatment groups might include members who turned to alcohol for different reasons or who have different perceptions of alcohol abuse and treatment goals (Caplan & Thomas, 2004). Despite this focus and the potential influence of diversity on groups, little research has explored the effects of diversity on therapeutic group processes and dynamics (Haley-Banez & Walden, 1999; Frey, 2000; Saino, 2003) and disagreement exists regarding the effects of diversity (Brown & Mistry, 2006). For instance, some studies suggest that having demographically diverse participants may result in less group integration or cohesion, less frequent communication, less group commitment, and higher rates of group departure (Ancona & Caldwell, 1992; Harrison, Price & Bell, 1998; Chatman & Flynn, 2001; Jehn, Northcraft, & Neale, 1999; O'Reilly, Caldwell, & Barnett, 1989; Shaw & Barrett-Power, 1998; Zenger & Lawrence, 1989). Other studies, however, suggest that diversity enhances problem-solving and general performance in groups, due to the presence of a broad range of alternative perspectives and expertise, which can enhance group creativity and problem-solving processes (Bunderson & Sutcliffe, 2002; Carpenter, 2002; Gruenfeld, Mannix, Williams, & Neale, 1996; Nemeth, 1986; Pitcher & Smith, 2000; Shaw & Barrett-Power, 1998; Watson, Kumar, & Michaelson, 1993).

In order to amplify our understanding of, and embrace diversity in groups, the current study aims to develop and test a model of working with diversity that will enable practitioners to better respond to diversity present in their groups. Specific research questions were: (1) how do practitioners understand diversity in their groups? (2) what strategies would enable practitioners to more beneficially respond to diversity in their groups?; (3) how can these strategies be organized into a practice model?; and (4) how does this model affect group climate and promote therapeutic factors? In this paper, we focus on the initial two questions by exploring group workers' understanding of the concept of diversity in groupwork, how diversity emerges in groups, and strategies used by group workers to respond to instances of diversity in groups.

Methodology

The project reflects an exploratory sequential mixed methods design, encompassing several study phases. In Phase 1, individual group practitioners were interviewed, following a grounded theory design, regarding their experiences with diversity in the various phases of their groups. In Phase 2, focus groups were held with group work practitioners, including those from the first phase, to review study findings to generate a model of working with diversity in groups. In further publications, results from the following phases will be addressed. Accordingly, the third phase of the project (currently underway) involves testing the model in therapeutic groups. In Phase 4, practitioners will be brought together in focus groups to explore their experiences of applying model. This article explores findings from Phase 1 of the project, with a focus on group workers' experiences related to diversity in their groups.

Data collection

In the initial phase of the study, in-depth, semi-structured interviews were conducted with the 24 group workers who agreed to participate in this part of the project. Within the literature, there is a strong consensus that the semi-structured interview format provides the interviewer the flexibility to gain a thorough understanding of the experiences of those individuals who are being interviewed (Patton, 2014; Marshall & Rossman, 2014).

All members of the research team contributed to the development of the initial interview guide. As the interviews progressed, changes were made to the guide based on our initial analysis of previously completed interviews. The interviews focused primarily on the following areas: (1) participants' understandings and definitions associated with the concept of diversity; (2) the emergence and manifestations of diversity in groups; and (3) strategies used to engage and respond to the various forms of diversity that surfaced during group sessions. All of the interviews were completed by trained research assistants. The interviews ranged from 45 to 90 minutes in length. With the exception of one, all interviews were audio-recorded, and subsequently transcribed verbatim (including notes from the one non-recorded interview).

Data analysis

Given the nature of the study's research design, an inductive data analysis was used. In defining this type of approach, Thomas (2003) states, "the primary purpose is to allow research findings to emerge from the frequent, dominant, or significant themes inherent in the raw data without restraints imposed by structured methodologies." Consistent with grounded theory, the data analysis process was guided by the constant comparative method (Glaser and Strauss, 1967), which involved breaking down the data into discrete incidents or units, and coding, and classifying them into categories.

We integrated the coding process guideline put forth by Corbin and Strauss (2015) to assist in analyzing the data. These included the following:

1. *Open coding,* which involves the process of breaking down, examining, comparing, conceptualizing, and categorizing data (p. 229);
2. *Axial coding,* which is a set of procedures whereby data are put back together in new ways after open coding by making connections between categories (p. 220);
3. *Selective coding,* which is the process of selecting the core category, systematically relating it to other categories, validating those relationships, and embarking on further data collection and analysis in instances in which categories required further refinement and development (p. 87).

Each interview was reviewed and initially coded by at least two team members. During our team meetings, the interviews that were coded to that point were reviewed and revised by the entire team. This process was repeated throughout the data analysis process, and data saturation was achieved, as demonstrated by referential adequacy, theoretical fit, and substantial peer debriefing, contributing to a rigorous data analysis process. As a result, a series of key themes emerged from the data.

The analytical process was enhanced with the use ATLAS.ti 7, a software program that supports qualitative and mixed methods research. Use of ATLAS.ti in Phase 1 helped the research team organize, analyze, and discover insights in qualitative data. Confidentiality of the data was ensured by removal of identifying information, and the study was reviewed and approved by the University of Calgary Conjoint Faculties Research Ethics Board (CFREB).

Sample

A total of 24 individuals participated in the first phase of the study; their demographic information is outlined in Table 1. Group workers represented groups from a wide array of focus areas of engagement and support, including: living with disability, personal development, intimate partner violence, addictions, psychoeducation groups, support, and social skills. Groups varied in duration and number of sessions, ranging from 4 weeks to a year in length; they further ranged in membership from closed to open, and drop-in membership. Group settings varied, including: not-for-profit agencies (n=11), government agencies (n=4), hospital settings (n=4), private practices (n=2), and a post-secondary institution (n=1).

Results

Seven themes emerged from the phase 1 interviews: (1) multi-faceted definition of diversity, (2) how diversity emerges in groups, (3) the relational experience of diversity in groups, (4) power dynamics within diversity, (5) macro level influences, (6) professional uses of self, and (7) strategies for dealing with diversity. Each is explored below.

(1) Definition of diversity

Conceptualizations of diversity varied amongst the participants, although many began their discussion of what diversity means by discussing externally attributed (social) forms of diversity. Theoretical saturation was reached with socially ascribed definitions. They most often cited gender, age, health status, socio-economic status, sexual orientation, race, ethnicity, power, privilege, and status as core elements within a definition of diversity. Several also described the group members' personal identities and lived experiences within their definition of diversity: "There's diversity in their experience" (Interviewee P10). Examples of this type of diversity included the group members' and group facilitators variations in terms of lived experiences relative to the content and/or purpose of the group, affective regulation and responses, values, beliefs, biases, assumptions, and patterned responses: "so the diversity within diversity, there's usually individual considerations that have to be recognized" (Interviewee P11). Diversities within each person and their context were reported as

Table 1
Participant characteristics

Variable	Frequency (%)	
Gender [a]		
Female	18	(78.2)
Male	5	(21.7)
Age, years [a]		
25-34	4	(17)
35-54	13	(56)
55+	6	(26)
Group Work Experience, years [a]		
< 5	5	(21.7)
5-15	13	(56.5)
15+	5	(21.7)
Education [b]		
Bachelors/college	4	(21.7)
Masters	17	(73.9)
Doctorate	1	(4.3)
Discipline [c]		
Social Work	10	(43.4)
Other	3	(13.0)
Relationship status [b]		
Single	1	(4.3)
Divorced/widow/widower	5	(21/7)
Married/Common law	16	(69.5)
Sexual Orientation [b]		
Heterosexual	19	(86.3)
LGBTQ	3	(13.6)
Race [c]		
Caucasian	16	(69.5)
Asian	4	(40.4)
Experiencing a disability [a]		
Yes	4	(17.3)
No	19	(82.6)
Cultural/Ethnic Origin [b]		
Hispanic/Latina	2	(9.1)
European	9	(40.9)
Asian/middle eastern	6	(27.2)
Canadian	5	(22.7)

a Missing data for 1 participant; b Missing data for 2 participants; c Missing data for 11 participants; d Missing data for 4 participants multiple and shifting over the life course. Additionally, group members discussed how they self-determine the relevance of a socially ascribed diversity; conscientiously internalizing the identifying feature as part of their personal identity versus rejecting, or discounting the salience of, the social identity. Thus, social views on an individual may differ from individual conceptualizations.

A more complex definition of diversity emerged as the group facilitators considered diversity within their groups. They described diversity as relational and shifting based on group composition, process, stages of development, and time. Relationally, diversity was reported to arise in the context group of group process, and can become inclusive or exclusive. Of note however, this form of diversity was recognized by some, but not all participants.

(2) Emergence of diversity in groups

The respondents described diversity emerging in groups over time as a function of many variables. They identified various ways that diversities may surface within a group, the degree to which the emergence is recognized, and the responses of group members and facilitators. Diversity reportedly emerged from within the relational space of group, shifting and morphing throughout the life course of group. The group process was described to constructed and re-constructed through interactions, including habits and patterns, established as the group forms and moves through its various phases. Within this space of forming and shifting relationships, the emergence of diversity evolved relationally.

(3) The relational experience of diversity in groups

Three factors emerged as contributing to the emergence of diversity throughout the life of a group. These factors are (1) individually internalized forms of diversity, (2) socially ascribed forms of diversity, and (3) the relationships amongst all members of the group. Each of the factors will be explained in turn.

Individually internalized forms of diversity represent a space where conscious, individual agency is used to determine which forms of diversity are personally relevant and provide meaning to the concept of personal identity. This process is a conscious one where individuals self-select the image they wish to identify and reflect to others. These forms of diversity may be subject to shifts over time. As well, which forms of diversity are most salient to the individual may shift depending on the social context. Cultural influences may be relevant when considering which influences are of primary meaning to an individual, as adherence to the beliefs of the broader cultural group may vary from individual to individual.

Socially ascribed forms of diversity represent the labels and constructs associated with or placed upon individuals for the purposes of discursive or social identity, and/or categorization: for example, gender, socio-economic status, race, and marital status. Individual group members may be more or less aware of these identities but each member comes to group with an internalized concept of self, based on externally ascribed categories. An example of the interplay between socially ascribed and individual concepts of diversity can be seen in the following example:

> *I don't think of myself as a minority. I don't know why Canadians label me a minority?' And that was a very interesting point that she made that none of us would have been aware of. And so I think if you put it out, it's just one way to begin to understand better other people's definitions and views and relations of the power dynamics in the room, in the organization, in the community. (Interviewee P1)*

Although these concepts of self are often relatively permanent, individuals and groups may experience shifts over time.

Within the context of group, individuals come together for a particular purpose; hence both group and individual goals are present. Within this space is where socially ascribed and individually internalized forms of being/identity interact with the variant diversities of other members of the group. As group members come to know one another, interact, form relationships, and bring different aspects of themselves into group, the result can be termed the emergence of diversity. This emergence depends upon the intentions of individuals to participate in the group process in a given session and over the course of the group. This pattern of emergence may have a better (or more developed) fit within a closed group context where the commitment of members to participate is clear. For open groups, diversity will emerge but when and in what ways may be different than in closed groups.

(4) Power dynamics within diversity

Power emerged as a critical factor influencing both when and how diversity arises within the group context. Participants noted however that power may be experienced and felt before it is consciously acknowledged. They frequently discussed issues related to power, including its presence and influence of power dynamics within the group as impacting directly or indirectly within the group. Many participants described challenges associated with the use and misuse of power within groups, between group members, and also between group workers and members. The following sections describe dichotomies noted by the participants, relating to how power was recognized and acknowledged as a part of the group process or left unacknowledged, with resultant impacts on group members.

Acknowledging the influence of power dynamics within group

Some participants spoke directly about power, acknowledging its presence in group. These group workers anticipated that attempts to influence group dynamics through power assertion were an expected part of the process. Anticipation and/or awareness of power dynamics, though, reportedly does not equate to having clear answers on how to proceed. Within this subgroup of those who acknowledged power, many continued to struggle with how to address power-related tensions when they arose.

Unacknowledged power dynamics within group

For those who did not directly acknowledge manifestations of power within group, both their recognition and understanding (or perhaps, their lack of recognition and/or variant understanding) of power dynamics were impacted, which in turn resulted in a lack of group facilitator action to address power inequities. Many were uncertain about how to resolve power issues, which itself led to escalating power inequities within groups. The phrase, "elephant in the room" was used by multiple participants to speak to how power influences may be left unaddressed, resulting in a problem that persisted and grew over the course of a given group. These individuals also reported difficulty knowing how to respond to power and control challenges from group members.

In terms of how power manifested in negative ways, multiple participants referred to diversity as a problem. For example, one participant hinted at this idea by saying:

I don't know if the diversity is the reason for someone keeping themselves outside the group or if it's maybe it's their previous experiences of being outside of the margins that's doing that ... an outsider doesn't want to be joined with the group as opposed to the group preventing somebody from joining the group ... (Interviewee P19)

This, diversity thus became an issue possessed by an individual, as opposed to arising relationally within group. Another participant said "...the concern is that when it's around an issue of diversity that there's an 'us versus them' that can happen that I'm never very comfortable with". (Interviewee P17)

Another negative manifestation of power was demonstrated as impeded group cohesion, as demonstrated by a participant who noted:

...as a society we tend to think that one way is right...a better or worse, a right or wrong and that separates us from people. And what we really want is connection. (Interviewee P10)

This implies that the ability to forge personal relationships is influenced by individual expressions of diversity, namely differences in thought and beliefs, and then respectfully coming together in acknowledgement of and acceptance of differences.

When uncertain about how to respond to challenges with power dynamics, some group workers reported experiencing feelings of disempowerment. These negative expressions of power dynamics at times had significant impacts on others in the group, including attrition from group. One respondent stated: "Usually they just don't show up. They don't want to be there. They don't try to get themselves kicked out" (Interviewee P11). The loss of members from the group, as a vicarious impact of power imbalance, was described as having lasting consequences for both group members and workers. Unaddressed negative power dynamics within groups thus appears to have ripple effects throughout the life of the group. Recognizing the need to identify and find ways to address these difficult dynamics is central in ultimately creating an environment that allows for participants to grow through the group process, allowing them to work towards therapeutic goals. Figure 1 presents a means for conceptualizing diversity as a relational construct emerging in group from the interactions amongst the group members and group worker, the group format and processes, and macro level influences.

Figure 1
The Emergence and Manifestation of Diversity in Groups

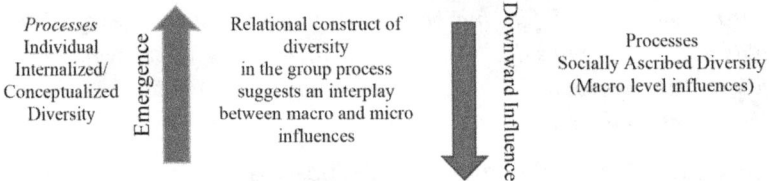

(5) Macro-level factors

In addition to factors impacting the emergence of diversity that directly relate to the relational experience of the members of group, participants also made reference to broader social factors that indirectly influence how diversity arises in groups. For example, one participant said the following:

> *My experience is that most men are hungry for a different understanding of masculinity and different ways of being a man. But most of them are resigned to the fact that other people can't change. Oh we're not going to change society, you just have to go along with what the conversation is about women because that's the way it is and this is how people always talk about women at our workplace. It's those kinds of sort of resignations to the issues that we see coming up. (Interviewee P002)*

Such macro or perhaps discursive level factors emerged in groups, based on socio-systemic influences. This element reportedly included cultural, political, social, or structural impacts and can influence the group process in positive and/or negative ways. The cultural, political, and structural aspects of the organization sponsoring a group was noted to potentially also exert influence on that group, as this participant's statement reflects: "the organizations own policies is not very anti-oppressive" (Interviewee P11).

While these broader or macro factors are expressed on large groups of people simultaneously, their influence can also be felt by groups on a smaller scale. A challenge with macro factors is that when identified, workers often expressed a sense of diminished power in their ability to create change due to the broad scope of the problem to be addressed, particularly if a contentious issue or position was counter to organizational or discursive positions: "Agencies have to be committed to this or it doesn't work" (Interviewee P16). Another participant noted the lack of resources available to address diversity:

> *I was also thinking about educating the organization, that the Canadian way is not to necessarily to have a lot of food, and with budget cuts and everything, I remember telling my manager, 'listen, I need money for group if I'm going to run it because no one will come without food.' And, wow, we don't have the money. And so that's not something that was thought about in the organization generally speaking. (Interviewee P10)*

(6) Professional uses of self

The data revealed two sub-themes with respect to professional uses of self. First, although a number of the study participants described learning anti-oppressive practices in university courses, particularly the social work interviewees, this training did not appear to translate into direct practice in groups. The following statement reflects the uncertainty described participants when conflict around differences arose in groups: "Concern is that when it's around an issue of diversity and there's an 'us versus them' that can happen, I'm never very comfortable with it" (Interviewee P17). A consistent theme reported by the majority of group facilitators was a lack of training in inclusive group work, and a dearth of knowledge or available strategies for role modeling acknowledgement, communication, self-disclosure, and/or empathy around issues of diversity. Nonetheless, some of the group workers described engaging in critical self-reflection to explore the impact of their personal socio-cultural identities on group dynamics: "I'm a woman ... then I'm a (cultural group) woman. If they have some bias against Muslims or (cultural group) women, they just probably won't come back" (Interviewee P18).

The second sub-theme reflected two distinct approaches in professional use of self in response to the emergence of diversity in groups, as well as the level of comfort, or discomfort experienced by the group facilitators. Several of the participants did not recognize or understand the power dynamics that arose with diversity, as this participant reported: "in other groups prior to this I might just not have thought about power, and not have thought about critical theory as it is applied to a group" (Interviewee P15). Other participants described being uncertain about how to respond to diversity when perceived conflict occurred due to lack of training: "If the anxiety reaches too high, you're afraid and you'll avoid, even if the idea is to let people talk about their differences (Interviewee P11). Respondents who were uncomfortable with how to understand power in groups more often reported negative outcomes when diversity emerged.

In a second approach, the group facilitators described acknowledging and accepting the power imbalances that arose with diversity in their groups. These group facilitators described an awareness relative to their own experiences, and a comfort and openness in discussing negative experiences: "I can share my own experience and knowledge of diversity in my own culture and personal experience as an individual coming from an ethnic background" (Interviewee P12). Other facilitators described using professional uses of self in the group to role model disclosure around diversity, as this participant reported: "Often if I share my experience about something, it gives other people permission to share theirs too" (Interviewee P5). Table 2 presents the strategies that emerged as methods to increase the level of comfort and safety for group facilitators to support members' exploration of differences, engage in conflict resolution, and use diversity to increase the group's capacity for problem solving.

Table 2
Ways to engage in critical self-reflection to promote professional uses of self as a strategy for responding to diversity in groups.

Critical self reflection	In group facilitator interventions. Role model:
Awareness of one's own experiences around diversity influences openness to diversity in groups	Identifying individual social location
	Respecting differences
Reflective practice in group to recognize when diversity is creating discomfort	Intentional disclosure of own diversity to support the group processes
Acknowledge organizational climate on diversity	Being comfortable working with diversity
Build and anti-oppressive practice	Normalizing fear of differences
Identify social location	Norming acceptance of differences without needing to challenge
	Macro to micro understanding of diversity

(7) Strategies for responding to diversity in groups

When asked about some of the ways that group facilitators can respond to diversity in groups, the study participants reflected on a number of strategies and approaches that they have used, or considered using, in response to diversity emerging at different phases in a group. Table 3 outlines these strategies at each stage of group development. These strategies emerged as phased approaches that are intended to increase inclusiveness at the pre-planning phase, as well as approaches for recognizing, acknowledging, and responding to the emergence of diversities at the beginning, middle, and ending phases of groups. During the pre-group planning phase, a commonly identified strategy was to prepare the group members in advance around group norms and the group facilitator's approach to emerging diversity. One respondent described pre-planning for diversity as a purposeful component of the pre-group interview and preparation phase:

> *The pre-screening is asking group members what diversity means to them and then you can gauge where people are at. Identify some of the challenges that might arise or you might foresee. (Interviewee P2)*

Another participant noted that an early group work task was to start "the group so people feel comfortable with their differences and everybody recognizes that there are going to be differences" (Interviewee P3).

In the middle phases of group, some participants identified strategies to respond to diversity as it emerged. Examples included acknowledging differences: "...just go ahead and acknowledge and open it up for discussion" (Interviewee P24), drawing on the strengths of difference in coping/abilities of members: "I think in the working phase of the group diversity is typically viewed as a strength and a positive and that's what makes the group really work." (Interviewee P13), and challenging language that creates barriers: "...challenging them to look at things from a different perspective" (Interviewee, P22).

In the ending phases of group, many participants described perceived benefits of diversity in groups to include building compassion: "...the more we know about other people, the more compassionate we can be (Interviewee P11), respecting differences: "people leave group with a sense of acceptance...for everybody to be different (Interviewee P22), and impacting communities by teaching group members about inclusivity: "Builds inclusion within communities outside of group" (Interviewee P20). Table 3 outlines other strategies the participants described at each stage of group development.

Table 3

Strategies for Responding to Diversity in Groups

Stage of group development	Strategies
• Pre-group Phase • Beginning Phase • Middle Phase • Ending Phase	• Critically consider inclusion/exclusion criteria • In interviews, discuss diversity as it relates to the group purpose • Include inclusive practice language in the group member norms • Understand organizational policy and culture with regards to diversity • Plan for meaningful interaction amongst diverse group members • Reach out to relevant communities to learn about diversities therein • Engage in critical reflection • Facilitate open dialogue on language, meaning, and impact of diversity on group processes and relationships • Be willing to bring socio-political issues into the conversation • Address problematizing diversity when it occurs • Challenge negative perceptions of diversity • Role model respecting differences • Anchor member needs to the group goals • Normalize differences and using diversity to enrich discussions • Reduce discomfort by listening • Inviting diverse members to participate may require other members to relinquish privilege and power • Focus on personal self and the lived experiences of group members • Use diversity to support differences in problem solving • Negotiate time frames when acknowledging/discussing diversity • Validate members for taking risks in talking about differences • Challenge group members on oppressive language and behaviours • Hold discussions about differences and how they manifest in the group • Recognize that participants may have differing understandings or needs in term of ending • Engage in relevant rituals for members as a form of goodbye • Reflect on how the group-as-a-whole responded to macro socio-political issues that emerged in the group and possible social justice activities that could be engaged in after group has ended

Discussion

As a way of highlighting the findings of this inquiry, we will begin our discussion of the findings and their implications by revisiting a vignette we presented at the 2017 IASWG Symposium. This vignette is based upon an actual group experience described by one of our research participants. The setting is a psycho-educational group for female adolescents designed to enhance group members' self-esteem through interpersonal learning, exploring negative beliefs, messages and stereotypes, and acquiring skills. It is composed of Caucasian and First Nations (Indigenous) members; with one group worker and six female members ranging in age from 13 to 15. The worker is a Caucasian female. The group meets once a week for 1.5 hours. First Nations students (Tanya and Shania) (pseudonyms used) sit to the immediate left of the worker, followed by four Caucasian members (Brittany, Katie, Emma & Morgan). There is substantial tension in the community between Caucasian and First Nations families, with overt incidents of expressions of racism in school and other locations in the community. Below is an example of one group session in which diversity is manifest.

This is the third class session. The class today focuses on respectful communication. Each session begins with a brief check-in wherein group members share incidents over the past week in which they noticed internalized negative self-talk and practiced affirming self-talk. The worker is aware of the tensions in the community. In an earlier meeting, the worker helped the group develop norms around respectful communication and valuing diversity in the group. She also noticed that two of the Caucasian girls (Brittany and Katie) were giggling and having brief side conversations during the last meeting, especially when a First Nations girl (Tanya) was speaking. As a result, in this session, the worker decided to introduce a talking feather to the group to be used during the group check-in.

> *At the beginning of the group, the worker welcomes the class members back and introduces the talking feather, which honors a First Nations tradition of using a revered spiritual symbol which is passed in a clockwise direction in the group. The worker states that only the person holding the talking feather may speak.*
>
> *The worker then passes the feather to Shania, who then begins speaking about her experiences over the past week. As she is speaking, the worker notices that Britany rolls her eyes and begins whispering with Katie. The*

group worker decides to address the issue in the group by having Brittany and Katie leave the group for the day

In this example, diversity emerges personally but is exemplified relationally. Of concern, the "problem" and the apparent power imbalance with potentially racist components, was removed from the group and in doing so, an opportunity for addressing diversity was lost. A key finding of this inquiry has been the reconceptualization of diversity as an emergent and relational construct. Forms of diversity emerge from a complex interplay of individual, interpersonal, and community factors. The emergence of diversity is also mediated by group composition, processes, and development. It is also influenced by the power dynamics in the group as well as the organizational and community context in which the group is situated.

We propose a redefinition of diversity as a relational concept which shifts our understanding from one in which diversity is something possessed by an "other" to a condition that exists in relationships. That is, diversity emerges and exists in the relational space between group members. Rather than limiting our definition of diversity to individual or socially ascribed characteristics, diversity can also be defined as an attribute of interpersonal or social relationships (Green & Stiers, 2002). In this way, diversity (defined according to age, ethnicity, race, gender, sexual orientation, disability, and other cultural dimensions) is a socially constructed concept, relative to the social context (Greene, 2004), and "possessing little meaning in and of themselves. The social contexts in which these are perceived, experienced, understood and defined is what renders them salient" (Greene, 2004, pp. 58-59). As such, diversity is not as significant when defined according to individual characteristics in isolation. Thus, diversity becomes apparent and significant when two or more individuals interact, enabling the more subtle aspects of identity to be revealed.

The task of working with diversity includes not only how to engage with those who are perceived to be diverse but also how to promote productive relationships between group members when diversity emerges in the group. The work begins with the worker critically reflecting upon their own experiences with respect to diversity and social location. Understanding that diversity is omnipresent in groups, in the pre-group phase, the worker reflects upon how group composition may influence the emergence of diversity in the group. In the beginning phase, the worker demonstrates their respect for diversity by normalizing it and using diversity to enrich discussions, as well as challenging negative perceptions of diversity. During the middle phase, the worker supports group members to share their personal self and lived experiences relating to diversity as it emerges in the group. The worker also validates members who take risks in acknowledging the presence of diversity in the group, and invites group members who hold power and privilege to allow others to participate in the discussion and inform problem-solving as well as conversely supporting interactional space for others with seemingly less ascribed power to assert their power in group. In the ending phase, the worker continues to appreciate diversity through their recognition that members may have diverse ways of ending their participation in the group. Finally, the worker also encourages group members to reflect on how the group discussions and responses to macro socio-political issues and other growth from the group can be transferred to possible engagement in social justice advancement after the group has ended.

There are a number of important implications of this inquiry which serve to generate a more inclusive and relational understanding of diversity. First, for both practitioners and group members, a relational understanding of diversity challenges us to continuously redefine ourselves by examining our beliefs, values, and perspectives rather than unconsciously accepting them as "received truths," "normal" or "superior". Adopting such a stance creates opportunities to learn from one another as we recognize that diversity is present in our relationships. Second, a more inclusive understanding eliminates many harmful conflicts that arise from the assumption that diversity is something that is only possessed by another. When diversity is perceived as characteristics possessed by others, individuals often define their own identities against positive or negative perceptions of other individuals and groups. By shifting the perception of diversity from an attribute possessed by "the other" to a condition existing in our relationships, diversity becomes more amenable to exploration and negotiation. Third, a relational understanding of diversity enables greater realization that it is not the outward characteristics of individual members that are important to the effectiveness of a group, but rather the different perspectives, worldviews, and experiences that they bring. Fourth, shifting the notion of diversity to the relational realm may foster greater opportunity for a discussion of power in these relationships. For example, a diverse idea proposed in a task group is or is not adopted by the group, may be influenced as much as by the relative status of the individual in the group who proposed the idea as by the idea's relative merits. Viewing diversity as relational and imbued by power dynamics that are inherent in relationships, naturally allow for consideration of the emergence and application of power in this context. This naturally invites the group, with the support of the facilitator, to critically reflect on power imbalance and social justice/injustice in relationships and other contexts within society.

Finally, while many scholars have noted the importance of highlighting commonalities amongst group members early in group development in order to promote group cohesion and identification and then differences later in the group, there have been some theorists that have offered a more protracted and longitudinal perspective. For instance, Brown and Mistry (2005) and Anderson (2007) demonstrated a convergence of ideas relating to diversity, where they noted that practitioners using a multicultural perspective can continually focus on the meaning of differences. Anderson (2007) suggested that this goal can be achieved by ensuring that all members have an authentic opportunity to voice their perspective and experience within the group context. Anderson's notions are particularly helpful in terms of understanding the construct of common ground from a diversity lens. This is evident when he states that it is not the content of the group that forms the foundation for how members will help each other, but rather it is the contract or agreement between members and the dialogue of differences that form the foundation for how members will help each other.

Limitations

Charmaz (2006) outlines four criteria for evaluating research which adopts a grounded theory methodology including credibility, originality, resonance, and usefulness. Credibility is determined by such factors as the depth of familiarity with the topic, variation, number and depth of observations and categories, and the strength of the linkages between the data and the findings. In this inquiry, we sampled 24 experienced group workers from a range of disciplines and practice settings. While the sample is limited in its representativeness, it did allow for saturation to occur in the data and represents relatively diverse substantive group foci and constituents. Notwithstanding this attempt for diversity, outcomes may have been in part a product of our use of theoretical sampling to inform our choices in research participants. However, these findings will be the focus of further discussion and testing during the later phases of this multi-year inquiry. For these above reasons, our findings continue to be speculative and tentative.

Originality is assessed by the relative freshness of the emergent categories, the emergence of new conceptual understandings from the data, the significance of the findings, and the contribution that they make to theory and practice. We have been careful to avoid the imposition of predetermined theoretical frameworks and categories upon the data. However, where the inductive process yielded conceptualizations which are reflected in the literature, we have included these conceptualizations in the presentation of our findings. At a minimum, we believe that our findings potentially extend and enhance our current ways of looking at diversity in group work. Resonance speaks to the extent to which categories generated by the research fully capture the experiences of group workers and make sense to group workers. At this point, we can assert that these findings fully capture the experiences of 24 group workers and resonate with our peer debriefing processes. The findings were noted to make sense to those group workers who have participated in our recent workshops, in that the findings were seen to offer a deeper understanding of diversity and how they can work more effectively when diversity arises in groups. For this reason, the tentative findings may be potentially useful to group workers; however, a further examination of the relative usefulness of these findings will come with the future phases of this study.

Conclusion

This grounded theory guided inquiry has generated findings which broaden our understanding of diversity in social work groups. In this inquiry, we have moved beyond a seemingly simplistic, under-developed and authoritative conceptualization of diversity to a more relational, dynamic, and tentative reconceptualization of diversity. Through repositioning diversity in the relational space between group members, group facilitators can focus on building a structure for more productive and respectful relationships among group members. If addressed productively and sensitively, it appears that diversity in all of its forms can become a strength and resource to the group and its participants therein, with potential societal implications relative to the pursuit of social justice. From this reconceptualization of diversity emergent from this study, new strategies have been identified, which in turn may enable group workers and members to more fully harness the presence and promise of diversity within their groups.

References

Abernethy, A. D. (2002). The power of metaphors for exploring cultural differences in groups. *Group, 26*(3), 219-231. doi: 10.1023/A:1021061110951

Alessandria, K. P. (2002). Acknowledging White ethnic groups in multicultural counseling. *Family Journal, 10*(1), 57-60. doi: 10.1177/1066480702101009

Ancona, D., & Caldwell, D. (1992). Demography and design: Predictors of new product team performance. *Organization Science, 3*(3), 321-341. doi: 10.1287/orsc.3.3.321

Anderson, D. (2007). Multicultural group work: A force for developing and healing. *The Journal for Specialists in Group Work, 32*(3), 224-244. doi: 10.1080/01933920701431537

Blundo, R., & Greene, R. R. (2008). Social construction. In R. R. Greene (Ed.), *Human Behavior and Social Work Practice* (pp. 237-264). New Jersey: Transaction Publishers.

Brabender, V., Fallon, A., & Smolar, A. (2004). *Essentials of Group Therapy.* Hoboken, NJ: Wiley.

Brown, A., & Mistry, T. (2006). Group work and 'mixed membership' groups: Issues of race and gender. *Social Work with Groups, 28*(3/4), 133-148. doi: 10.1300/J009v28n03_10

Bunderson, J.S., & Sutcliffe, K. (2002). Comparing alternative conceptualizations of functional diversity in management teams: Process and performance effects. *Academy of Management Journal, 45*(5), 875-893. doi: 10.2307/3069319

Caplan, T., & Thomas, H. (2004). "If we are all in the same canoe, why are we using different paddles?": The effective use of common themes in diverse group situation. *Social Work With Groups, 27*(1), 53-73. doi: 10.1300/J009v27n01_05

Carpenter, M. (2002). The implications of strategy and social context for the relationship between top management team heterogeneity and firm performance. *Strategic Management Journal, 23*(3), 275-284. doi: 10.1002/ smj.226

Charmaz, K. (2006). *Constructing grounded theory*. London: Sage.

Chatman, J. A, & Flynn, F. J. (2001). The influence of demographic heterogeneity on the emergence and consequences of cooperative norms in work teams. *Academy of Management Journal 44*(5), 956-974. doi: 10.2307/3069440

Cheung, M. (1997). Social construction theory and the Satir model: Toward a synthesis. *The American Journal of Family Therapy, 25*(4), 331-343. doi: 10.1080/01926189708251077

Corbin, J., & Strauss, A. (2015). Basics of qualitative research: Techniques and procedures for developing grounded theory (4th ed.). Thousand Oaks, CA: SAGE Publications.

Doyle, R., & George, U. (2008). Achieving and measuring diversity: An organizational change approach. *Social Work Education, 27*(1), 97-110. doi: 10.1080/02615470601141235

Fellin, P. (2000). Revisiting multiculturalism in social work. *Journal of Social Work Education, 36*(2), 261-278. doi: 10.1080/10437797.2000.10779007

Frey, L. R. (2000). Diversifying our understanding of diversity and communication in groups: Dialoguing with Clark, Anand, and Roberson (2000). *Group Dynamics: Theory, Research, and Practice, 4*(3), 222-229. doi: 10.1037/1089-2699.4.3.222

Gergen, K. J. (1985). The social constructionist movement in modern psychology. *American Psychologist, 40*(3), 266-275. doi: 10.1037/0003-066X.40.3.266

Glaser, B. & Strauss, A. (1967). *The discovery of grounded theory: Strategies for qualitative research*. New York, NY: Aldine De Gruyter.

Green, Z., & Stiers, M. J. (2002). Multiculturalism and group therapy in the United States: A social constructionist perspective. *Group, 26*(3), 233-246. doi: 10.1023/A:1021013227789.

Greene, B. (2004). African American lesbians and other culturally diverse people in psychodynamic psychotherapies: Useful paradigms or oxymoron? *Journal of Lesbian Studies, 8*(1/2), 57-77

Gruenfeld, D. H, Mannix, E. A., Williams, K. Y., & Neale, M. A. (1996). Group composition and decision making: How member familiarity and information distribution affect process and performance. *Organizational Behavior and Human Decision Processes, 67*, 1-15. doi: 10.1006/obhd.1996.0061

Haley-Banez, L., Brown, S., Molina, B., D'Andrea, M., Arrendondo, P., Merchant, N., & Wathen, S. (1999). Association for specialists in group work principles for diversity-competent group workers. *The Journal for Specialists in Group Work, 24*(1), 7-14. doi: 10.1080/01933929908411415

Haley-Banez, L., & Walden, S. L. (1999). Diversity in group work: Using optimal theory to understand group process and dynamics. *The Journal for*

Specialists in Group Work, 24(4), 405-422. doi: 10.1080/01933929908411446

Harrison, D. A., Price, K. H., & Bell, M. P. (1998). Beyond relational demography: Time and effects of surface- and deep-level diversity on work group cohesion. *Academy of Management Journal, 41*(1), 96-107. doi: 10.2307/256901

Jehn, K. A., Northcraft, G. B., & Neale, M. A. (1999). Why differences make a difference; A field study of diversity, conflict, and performance in workgroups. *Administrative Science Quarterly, 44*(4), 741-763. doi: 10.2307/2667054

Johnson, I. H., Torres, J. S., Coleman, V. D., & Smith, M. C. (1995). Issues and strategies in leading culturally diverse counseling groups. *Journal for Specialists in Group Work, 20*(3), 143-150. doi: 10.1080/01933929508411338

Marbley, A. F. (2004). His eye is on the sparrow: A counselor of color's perception of facilitating groups with predominantly White members. *The Journal for Specialists in Group Work, 29*(3), 247-258. doi: 10.1080/01933920490477002

Marshall, C., & Rossman, G. (2014). *Designing qualitative research.* Thousand Oak, CA: Sage

Nagda, B. A., Spearmon, M. L., Holley, L. C., Harding, S., Balasson, M. L., Motse-Swanson, D., & De Mello, S. (1999). Intergroup dialogues: An innovative approach to teaching about diversity and justice in social work programs. *Journal of Social Work Education, 35*(3), 433-449. doi: 10.1080/10437797.1999.10778980

Nemeth, C. (1986). Differential contributions of majority and minority influence. *Psychological Review, 93*, 23-32. doi: 10.1037/0033-295X.93.1.23

O'Reilly, C., Caldwell, D., & Barnett, W. (1989). Work group demography, social integration and turnover. *Administrative Science Quarterly, 34*, 21-37. doi: 10.2307/2392984

Parrott, L. (2009). Constructive marginality: Conflicts and dilemmas in cultural competence and anti-oppressive practice. *Social Work Education, 28*(6), 617-630. doi: 10.1080/02615470903027322

Patton, M. (2014). *Qualitative research and evaluation methods: Integrating theory and practice.* Thousand Oaks, CA: Sage

Pelled, L. H. (1996). Demographic diversity, conflict, and work group outcomes: An intervening process theory. *Organization Science, 7*(6), 615-631. doi: 10.1287/orsc.7.6.615

Pelled, L. H., Eisenhardt, K. M., & Xin, K. R. (1999). Exploring the black box: An analysis of work group diversity, conflict, and performance. *Administrative Science Quarterly, 44*(1), 1-28. doi: 10.2307/2667029

Pitcher, P., & Smith, A. (2000). Top management team heterogeneity: Personality, power and proxies. *Organization Science, 12*, 1-18. doi: 10.1287/orsc.12.1.1.10120

Roysircar, G. (2008). A response to "Social privilege, social justice, and group counseling: An inquiry": Social privilege: Counselors' competence with systemically determined inequalities. *The Journal for Specialists in Group Work, 33*(4), 377-384. doi: 10.1080/01933920802424456

Saino, M. (2003). A new language for groups: Multilingual and multiethnic group work. *Social Work With Groups, 26*(1), 69-82. doi: 10.1300/J009v26n01_05

Shapiro, B. Z. (1990) The social work group as social microcosm: "Frames of Reference" revisited. *Social Work with Groups, 13*(2), 5-21. doi: 10.1300/J009v13n02_02

Shaw, J. B., & Barrett-Power, E. (1998). The effects of diversity on small work group processes and performance. *Human Relations, 51*(10), 1307-1325. doi: 10.1177/001872679805101005

Statistics Canada (2009). Selected Demographic, Cultural, Educational, Labour Force and Income Characteristics, Mother Tongue, Age Groups and Sex for the Population of Canada, Provinces, Territories, Census Metropolitan Areas and Census Agglomerations, 2006 Census. Retrieved September 19, 2010, from http://www.statcan.gc.ca/subject-sujet/result-resultat.action?pid=30000&id=-30000&lang=eng&type=CENSUSTBL&pageNum=1&more=0

Thomas, D. (2003). Qualitative data analysis: Using a general inductive approach. Retrieved July 25, 2017 from http://www.heathauckland.ac.nz/hrms/resouras/qualdataanalysis.html van Knippenberg, D., & Schippers, M. C. (2007). Work group diversity. *The Annual Review of Psychology, 58*, 515-541. doi: 10.1146/annurev.psych.58.110405.085546

Watson, W., Kumar, K., & Michaelsen, L. (1993). Cultural diversity's impact on interaction process and performance: Comparing homogeneous and diverse task groups. *Academy of Management Journal, 36*, 590-602. doi: 10.2307/256593

Weinrach, S. G., & Thomas, K. R. (1996). The counseling profession's commitment to diversity-sensitive counseling: A critical reassessment. *Journal of Counseling and Development, 74*, 472-477. doi: 10.1002/j.1556-6676.1996.tb01895.x

Zenger, T., & Lawrence, B. (1989). Organizational demography: The differential effects of age and tenure distributions on technical communications. Academy of Management Journal, 32, 353-376. doi: 10.2307/256366

Making group theories real:

A brief cultural exchange activity that translates theory into experience

Donald G Jordan and Daphne Henderson

Introduction

As is likely true with any professionals-in-training, there exists a pedagogical gap for the field of social work between what is being taught theoretically and didactically in the classroom, and what is being encountered and practiced in the flesh between real human beings. One specific challenge for social work educators is that, as the profession's value of group work has moved in and out of style for decades, the research for both pedagogical and practical theory falls behind that of more micro-level approaches (Gutman and Shennar-Golan 2012). Social work students entering practice environments of all kinds are increasingly faced with scenarios requiring significant group process and understanding and skill, whether or not the setting is considered a "group work" setting (Gutman and Shennar-Golan 2012). A consistent push for group theory and practice approaches has maintained the charge toward the development of individual skills and social justice through collective empowerment and group education (Toseland and Rivas, 2017; Abels, 2013), but the need for a robust pedagogy to match this important charge remains.

In addition, while the social work profession has always given great value to diversity and cultural competence, effectively including these concepts in light of oppression, marginalization and intersectionality as social work educators and practitioners has been another precarious discussion (Jani, Ortiz, Pierce, and Sowbel, 2011; Rosenthal, 2016). Didactic efforts in the classroom on culture, diversity, oppression, injustice and intersectionality often do not translate into empathic skills in students (Hoover, Giambatista, Sorenson, & Bommer, 2010). The experiential learning activity to be discussed here introduces students to concepts of group work and diversity in meaningful, pedagogical ways. The purpose of this paper is to explore how students experience group dynamics and diversity during a brief cultural exchange activity at a small public university in the rural, southern United States.

Group work, diversity, and context

Located in Northwest Tennessee, the undergraduate Social Work Program is one of 22 degrees offered at a public university whose average annual enrollment ranges from 6,000 to 7,000 students. The university is nestled in the center of a rural, agricultural community with a population of approximately 11,000 citizens (Tennessee Demographics, n.d.), where individuals identifying as white make up 78% of the population (United States Census Bureau, n.d.). The university's racial makeup for undergraduate students is almost identical, with 77 percent identifying as white (UTM Office of Institutional Research, n.d.). This overwhelming lack of diversity has a definite and complex impact on the classroom setting as, prior to entering college, a vast majority of these students have never been exposed to individuals who are different from themselves in terms of race, religion, belief systems, and more.

Within this context the Social Work Program has continued to grow and change, moving beyond its original title of the "Social Welfare Program" in the 1970s to the current "Social Work Program" nomenclature (About the Program, n.d.). It has also joined the changing landscape of U.S. national social work educators and practitioners defining and redefining the profession over and again, including changes in doing, viewing, and teaching both group work and diversity (Maier, 1967; Popple, 1985; Jani, 2011; Abels, 2013; Sweifach, 2014; Rosenthal, 2016).

Accreditation by the Council on Social Work Education (CSWE) requires that students graduating in the U.S. be able to competently engage with diversity and difference in social work practice across multiple settings (CSWE, 2015). In working to both meet these standards and prepare students for their interactions with the diversity of the world outside of this small town (Jani, et al., 2011), the curriculum is shaped to address these issues throughout students' interactions within the program.

Social Work 220 Understanding Diverse and Oppressed Populations is a pre-professional course required for all social work majors at the introductory stage of possible admittance to the Social Work Program. The purpose of this course is to help students identify the dynamics and consequences of discrimination, economic deprivation, individual and systemic injustice, and multiple forms of oppression on vulnerable populations. Through assigned readings, classroom discussion, and various activities, students are provided with the opportunity to identify and explore the personal and professional values, beliefs, identities, and norms of culturally diverse groups.

One major activity in this course is *BaFá BaFá* (Shirts, 1974) which provides students the opportunity to experience a new culture firsthand, and the development of group dynamics as diverse cultures engage each other. Students are assigned to one of two new cultures and required to learn and then "live out" the associated roles, rules, languages and norms of that culture. Students experience the very elements needed for diverse groups to form and function in a relatively short time. Abstract concepts and theories about diversity and group theory become experiential rather than didactic learning activities, shifting this lesson from the whiteboard to the students themselves, resulting in better outcomes for students' actual skill and value development (Hoover, et al., 2010). They begin to consider: What are the necessary conditions for individuals to come together to form a complete unit? How long does it take for a sense of belonging to develop? What causes inclusion and exclusion in these newly formed groups? Without experiencing the many abstractions and developmental theories of group work in diverse contexts, students would likely not translate the lesson into actual skills with which social workers must be equipped (Zastrow, 2015; Jani, et al., 2010; Hoover, et al., 2010).

BaFá BaFá

Exposure to new languages, values, rules, and expectations has caused psychological stress (Lantrip, Mazzetti, Grasso, Gill, Miller, Haner, Rude, & Awad, 2015), self-doubt and fear (Edwards-Joseph &

Baker, 2012) identity conflict, disorientation, interpersonal conflict, and feelings of powerlessness (Pitts, 2010). All of these emotions and challenges are often referred to collectively in this context as *culture shock*. Students enter a previously established culture as an outsider, often without any significant thought given to their own cultures' specificity, and suddenly find themselves required to learn new ways of interacting and engaging to survive (Flanja, 2009). The purpose of *BaFá BaFá* (Shirts, 1974) is to provide students this cross-culture group simulation, offering opportunities to obtain experiences, awareness, insight, and dialogue about the impact of cultural differences. Ultimately the experience leaves students examining their own personal biases and unseen cultural characteristics by experiencing those of a new, simulated culture.

BaFá BaFá in summary involves separating students into either the *Alpha* or the *Beta* culture, each with its own respective set of values, norms, roles, and rules. They are then moved to two separate rooms and introduced to their new cultures, followed by a brief time to learn and practice their new culture's rules and behaviors. A few members at a time from each culture then visit the other culture to observe in an effort to make sense of the other group so they can return to their own culture and report back their observations and impressions. Once every member has scouted out the other culture and both Alphas and Betas have completed a discussion on the nature of the other culture, all the students are brought back together for a shared time of debriefing. Typically lasting between one and two hours from beginning to end, students experience several elements of group development in rapid succession as multiple abstract concepts of group process and diversity are manifested.

From students to explorers

Students enter the activity as one single group whose shared identity is simply that of student. But once divided and instructed of their new identities as members of either Alpha or Beta, individuals speedily begin a quest to determine a new identity which will guarantee belonging as is to be expected whenever new groups are formed by outside forces (Tuckman, 1965; Bonebright, 2010). Students initially wrestle with facilitators and each other, described in Tuckman's (1965) storming phase, deciding how they will engage or obstruct the process of the group. As they are given and then practice their culture's shared norms, roles, and rules, most begin to build a sense of identity and belonging by finding other students who seem to have shared characteristics and opinions about the situation. This itself is another key element social workers observe as group work begins (Greitemeyer, 2012). These characteristics usually range from the overly-enthusiastic student to the overly-underwhelmed student, as the members begin to experience the reality of roles group members take on and the impact this has in traditional group work (Toseland and Rivas, 2017). Students assimilate with their new cultures and find a sense of belonging by identifying other students who seem to respond in similar ways to the experience. Most students ultimately form a sense of group identity centered around lighthearted stumbling through the new and somewhat strange rules, roles, and norms of their assigned culture together.

So many of the experiences students face at this stage of the process are common elements and dynamics in classic group work literature currently available (Ormiston, 2016). Beyond this sense of belonging, observer reports of the "other" cultures ultimately add to a group's sense of cohesion and identity. It becomes necessary as they begin to define their own identities by contrasting themselves against and in more favorable ways to those of the "other" culture, common in groups seeking a common cause and identity (Cavazza, Pagliaro, and Guidetti, 2014).

The Alpha and Beta cultures

The primary characteristics of the Alpha culture are social interaction and patriarchy, governed by specific rules for interactions and communication among its members (Shirts, 1974). The patriarchal culture is led by the eldest male in the group, the *Alpha Elder*, in the group who is then provided a special seat in the middle of all members with an explicit, visible barrier separating them (masking tape on the ground, a ring of chairs, etc.). The men must ensure the women's safety, and the women may not be spoken to without gaining permission from the Alpha Elder. The women must constantly discuss the positive characteristics of the men in their lives in the native Alpha language of English.

The Alphas spend time playing a non-competitive, social card game purely for social enjoyment, and if the Alpha Elder is playing the game, he is always the winner. Standing in small groups playing the game, friendship and affection are dramatic as members stand closely to one another, often hugging and looking for reasons to touch each other (hand holding, back patting, etc.). Any visitors from other cultures who violate any of these rules or norms are banished by one of the male members.

The Alpha culture's patriarchal structure and norms are reminiscent of heavily-gendered dynamics of masculinity and femininity often present and occasionally explicit in rural areas (Keller, 2014), including those from which a large majority of this student group comes. Initially giggling or protesting this patriarchal structure, students ultimately follow the rules and adapt to the norms. It is common for individuals entering new cultures to have never considered the inherent characteristics and of their own cultures (Flanja, 2009), so while many students may not consider their own individual backgrounds or realities as mirroring much of the Alpha culture, they are able to experience frustration with these basic constructs in a way that does not initially seem to be realistic at all.

The Beta culture is very different as its primary characteristics are competitiveness and individualism (Shirts, 1974). The Betas are a trading culture, and individuals are guided by the value of personal gain which results in greater personal power. They also play a card game but with the ultimate goal of accumulation of power within the culture. The Betas' game is based on trading for points so that effective trading results in the accumulation of more points. The Beta's leader is the most powerful person in the culture at the time, determined by who has accumulated the most points through card trading. The individual with the most points is given the culture's coveted title of *Most Effective Trader,* and remains the leader until someone else accumulates more points and earns the official title.

Another distinct characteristic of the Betas is their unique and limited language consisting only of each member's name, the colors and numbers of their trading cards, and a handful of specific gestures required for card trading agreements (Shirts, 1974). Culture member names are created by combining a person's initials and adding an additional vowel to each one. For example, if a Beta student's name is *Jane Smith*, she would use the initials for her first and last name and add any vowel to each (see *Figure 1*). If she chose the vowel *A,* then her name becomes *JaSá* in the Beta language. If she chose the vowel *O,* her Beta name would be *JoSó.*

Each trading card includes one of six colors with a number between one and seven, and translating these six colors and seven numbers utilizes the trader's initials and follows the very specific rules of the Beta language (see *Figure 1*). Applying these rules, if the student now named *JaSá* because she chose the vowel *A* wants to ask another trader for their *blue one* card to accrue points, she would say *Ba Ja.* If she needs a *green two,* ask *Ga Ja Sá.* If *Ty Roberts* needs an *orange seven* and had chosen the vowel *U,* he would say *Ou Ti Rí Ti Rí Ti Rí Ti* while giving a specific gesture to explain he is requesting an *orange seven* card rather than needing to trade one.

Figure 1. The Beta Language (Shirts, 1974)

NAMES || Your initials + Any 1 vowel (a, e, i, o, u)

Example 1	Example 2	Example 3
Jane Smith could be any of these:	Ty Roberts could be any of these:	Bisma Malik could be any of these:
JaSá	TaRá	BaMá
JeSé	TeRé	BeMé
JiSí	TiRí	BiMí
JoSó	ToRó	BoMó
JuSú	TuRú	BuMú

COLORS || First letter of the color + Any 1 vowel

Blue could be any of these:	**Orange** could be any of these:	**White** could be any of these:
Ba, Be, Bi, Bo, or Bu	Oa, Oe, Oi, Oo, or Ou	Wa, We, Wi, Wo, or Wu
Green could be any of these:	**Red** could be any of these:	**Yellow** could be any of these:
Ga, Ge, Gi, Go, or Gu	Ra, Re, Ri, Ro, or Ru	Ya, Ye, Yi, Yo, or Yu

NUMBERS 1–7 || Your initials + Any 1 vowel X Repeated to equal that number

For Jane Smith 1 could be any of these:	If Ty Roberts chose the vowel E, then 3 would be:	If Bisma Malik chose the vowel O, then 5 would be:
Ja, Je, Ji, Jo, or Ju	Te Ré Te	Bo Mó Bo Mó Bo
2 could be any of these:	If Ty chose the vowel I, then 4 would be:	6 for Bisma, still with O, would be:
Ja Sá, Je Sé, Ji Sí, Jo Só or Ju Sú	Ti Rí Ti Rí	Bo Mó Bo Mó Bo Mó
If Jane chose the vowel A, then 3 would be:	5 for Ty, still with I, would be:	If Bisma chose the vowel U, then 7 would be:
Ja Sá Ja	Ti Rí Ti Rí Ti	Bo Mó Bo Mó Bo Mó Bo

Obviously, new members of the Beta culture find this language challenging and frustrating. This specific dilemma is representative of the lived experience of many people entering contexts and cultures where the language and structure behind it is completely unfamiliar to the "newcomer," yet must still be quickly learned to ensure all other needs and supports can be secured (Warriner, 2007).

In sharp contrast to the Alpha culture, Betas operate within a power structure organized around accumulation rather than personal demographics such as gender or age, which in many ways is a more familiar paradigm for most of the United States-born students who are familiar with capitalism and associate power, money, and competition as the means to self-preservation. As students work to establish a sense of identity that can help them belong and succeed in the Beta culture (Cavazza, et al., 2014), they also mirror general group dynamics of Tuckman's (1965) stages of storming and norming. Should a student work to succeed at the activity and thereby take on the role of leader, or should she work to create the appearance of ambivalence about the activity, to protect her current identity as an outsider rather than participate in this new group and risk failing to learn the motions or acquiring trades? Students are faced with experiences reminiscent of minorities first encountering majority cultures, as well as the beginning stages in group work experienced by individual group members with rich and diverse histories and identities now being forced to determine what to keep and what to disregard as they either seek to assimilate into the group or remain an outsider within it (Flanja, 2009; Cavazza, et al., 2014).

The first student to successfully make several trades is often suddenly viewed as a possible threat to the security of the rest of the Betas. Originally, belonging to the Beta culture by way of random assignment and therefore sharing the sense of being *new, fumbling* members of the culture, resulted in a sense of shared identity and inclusion in the group (Greitemeyer, 2012). But once a Beta member has elevated in status by successful trading, the group and its members experience again new storming characteristics including anxiety and instability (Lantrip, et al., 2015; Cavazza, et al., 2014), forcing each member to reevaluate his or her status and subsequently determine what new identity they must take on to now insure inclusion.

These sudden, identity-defining (and redefining) moments become pivotal as students must choose to take on the Beta value of competitiveness and individualism by competing with the most effective trader, or instead excluding themselves from the culture because the "new and fumbling" descriptors that initially shaped a shared identity no longer offer belonging for the student having difficulty learning the language and making the trades. Research and history itself have commonly documented what students are now unknowingly experiencing; a change in a group's membership or circumstance often forces the group to travel again through the storming and norming phases of development to remain functional. Students must again work to find a shared identity after any changes, thereby re-establishing rules for exclusion and inclusion equipping them to finally return to the performing stage and trading of cards for individual advancement (Bonebright, 2010; Greitemeyer, 2012; Ormiston, 2016).

If a student continues to rise to power through successful card trading and point accumulation, they are likely seen by their peers as threatening the equilibrium of group power (Greitemeyer, 2012). These power dynamics begin to shape trading, partnerships, alliances and enemies just as typical group or community motivations often operate and play out (Cavazza, et al., 2014; Pitts, 2010). Students also experience another element of culture shock as they begin to fear exclusion if they cannot perform, leading to a questioning of a personal sense of self-efficacy (Flanja, 2009).

Although students in both groups at this stage are already experiencing multiple concepts associated with group work and diversity, it is clearly in two very different contexts, which students will learn for the first time as they begin sending smaller groups to scout out the nature of the other strange culture.

Figure 2. Summary & Comparison of Cultural Characteristics (Shirts, 1974)

ALPHA & BETA COMPARISON ‖ Foundational Values and Cultural Characteristics	
ALPHA CULTURE	**BETA CULTURE**
Focus on social interaction with specific rules	Focus on individual gain and acquiring power
Permission needed to enter into a conversation	Trading society
Patriarchal	Fast-paced and outcome-oriented
Approval needed to speak to females	All play competitive card game with specific rules
Women must talk about accomplishments of the men	All seek the title of *Most Effective Trader*
All play a non-competitive card game for enjoyment	Sole purpose is trading cards to advance toward title
Enjoy physical affection	One's value determined by points earned from trading
Look for reasons to touch and hug one another	Speak a unique language with complicated rules that
Speak the English language	sounds different from each member

Observing the Strange New World of the "Other"

After each new culture briefly practices living out these new lives through their respective card games and norms, a few members at a time from each culture are guided to visit and observe the other culture in nearby rooms. These small scouting groups are charged by the facilitators to observe some descriptive characteristics of the other culture which they will then

share with others upon returning to their own (Shirts, 1974). As each member of the Alpha culture visits the Beta culture and vice versa, everyone must adhere to the guidelines of their respective cultures, and may not engage in explaining their own or the other culture's games, rules, or norms in any way. At this point in the activity, each culture has only been informed about the existence of their own culture, so it is not until they go to visit "the other culture" that they begin to see they are now quite different from one another.

To offer an example with perhaps an optimal number, if 40 students are participating, both the Alpha and Beta cultures would each be assigned 20 students. After learning and briefly practicing their new cultural identities, each culture sends students in groups of five to observe the other culture for roughly four to five minutes, and then return to their own cultures with a report. The Alphas continue to speak English while carrying out the culture's key elements of male praise, casual card play, female protection, and strict submission to the wishes of the Alpha Elder. The Betas continue speaking only in their native language while carrying out the culture's key element of card trading as a means of accumulating points and power. Now that both cultures, different from each other in foundational ways, are fully functioning and have learned their rules, the next phase of the activity begins.

Students now bravely observing the strange new world of the other culture, they are rapidly experiencing an acute sense of emotional and cognitive processes common to cross-cultural interaction and outgroup observation of in-group behaviors (Abrams, Palmer, Rutland, Cameron, and Van de Vyver, 2014). While students in their own lives have real cultural and demographic differences with those they are learning to interact and communicate with at university, it is often difficult for a student to take note of the framework and values of her own culture and perspective of history, and the reality of how this shapes her interpretations of someone she encounters who is bringing a very different culture and perspective (Flanja, 2009; DiAngelo, 2011; Abrams, et al., 2014).

While students are observing aspects of the other culture's interactions, they seek to make sense of the language, the values, the power dynamics, the gestures, and the rules of the card game. They initially assume and thereby attempt to compare what seems familiar from their own culture, as is a common direction taken by someone new to a group already established (Abrams, et al., 2014), but they quickly become aware of stark differences and begin interpreting them in contrast to their own new culture. Alpha members who have been taught to enjoy themselves, give praise to men, and give unquestioned authority to the oldest male would be quite confused as they observe perhaps a younger woman in the Beta culture yelling at older men in rapid, repetitive, and seemingly nonsensical syllables and gestures, and who is apparently revered and celebrated as the most powerful.

Individuals from the Alpha culture attempt making sense of the Beta's card game rules and the meaning of their language during those 4 or 5 minutes, but they are not allowed to speak unless they attempt to learn and speak in the language of the Beta culture. Betas in turn cannot offer explanations in English to a visiting observer from the Alpha culture as they only speak their Beta language. And when Betas visit the Alpha culture, they are not allowed to speak or ask for clarity in English when observing the Alpha culture unless they only use their Beta language, and Alphas are not allowed to explain anything about their culture to their visitors, as theoretically the Betas would not understand the English language.

Student observers from both cultures experience the awkwardness of being an outsider who suddenly does not belong and stands out (Abrams, et al., 2014; Flanja, 2009), seeking to understand and make sense of unfamiliar communication, power structures, and apparent but unclear expectations and values. If the observers attempt interacting with members of this strange new culture, the result is often the experience of being laughed at without knowing why, frustration in an inability to identify oneself and shape a narrative for oneself (Edwards-Joseph and Baker, 2012), anger at being misunderstood or unable to engage effectively. This often results in an overwhelming sense of powerlessness as they realize whatever wisdom, knowledge, status, and values were attributed to them in their initial culture, they can no longer draw on those resources as they experience increasing isolation and ultimately despair (Lantrip, et al., 2015; Flanja, 2009; Cavazza, et al., 2014; Abrams, et al., 2014).

This phase of the activity allows students to experience the specificity of their own cultures in a way not usually possible. Because their culture for the activity has just been explained in detail and practiced, they are keenly aware of the values, activities, norms, expected roles, and hidden social contracts. In addition, any discomfort, oppression, judgment, exclusion, etc. are being "acted out" in these ultimately fictional cultures, so hypothetically they do not speak to the students' personal, real-life identity, history, and culture, but still allow the student a vicarious experience in a less emotionally-weighted setting (Lee and Priester, 2015). In contrast, this kind of thoughtful and self-aware experiencing of one's differences in real-time often results in individuals shutting down, being overcome with guilt, or acting out defensively or combatively with the "other" who they suspect is attacking them (DiAngelo, 2011).

Members of each scouting team return to their cultures, and the process is continued until each student in both cultures has had the opportunity to observe the strange other culture. Students are now again in rooms with only members of their own cultures, and the facilitators for each group begin to solicit feedback from their students on the impressions and thoughts they had regarding the other observed culture. Documenting their comments on large sheets of paper taped to the wall, facilitators take care to write the precise wording used by students as they share their thoughts to ensure as rich and thick a description as possible can be captured (Monk, Winslade, Crocket, & Epston, 1997). This process continues until each group has separately exhausted their thoughts and all have been documented on these large sheets so the comments are legible to the students.

Students' comments and thoughts about the other culture begin with a common theme of "strange" or "weird" in describing what they saw, as is often the first response when one with little cultural awareness or competence experiences people with diverse thoughts, actions, and behaviors (Vauclair, et al., 2014). After a short amount of time students in each culture begin solidifying their own sense of belonging to their assigned group by creating a derogatory picture of the other culture,-strengthening their own sense of connectedness and belonging by asserting they are all not as bad or unreasonable as the other group (Greitemeyer, 2012). During this effort, descriptors begin deteriorating toward negative, value-laden interpretations of the other culture as is often experienced by outsiders who are negatively perceived by the majority in-group (Abrams, et al., 2014). Alphas often report the Betas as "mean", "loud," "mad if you don't understand what they're yelling, but it's all blah blah blah and waving these random cards in your face," etc. Betas in return often report that Alphas "don't do anything," "worship some random dude," "kicked me out for no reason at all when I just tried to say something," "are lazy," "are way too touchy-feely," etc. These kinds of character determinations and descriptions are common in group work as well as when one group or culture attempts to describe or define the other, but students are not yet aware they are operating in these very typical but often oppressive and diminishing ways. Without a deeper understanding as to the foundation on which a culture's identity is built, observers make interpretations about individuals in that culture based blindly and comparatively on the values and identity of the interpreter's culture (Vauclair, et al., 2014). Since identity for the Alpha culture is built on a foundation of patriarchy and socialization, the loud and rapid trading practices of male and female Beta members translate to Alphas as mean, loud, and angry. In reverse, since the identity of the Beta culture is built on a foundation of individualism, competition, and accumulation, the lives and behaviors of Alphas translate to Betas as lazy, inactive, oppressive to women, and aggressive to outsiders.

Once these written lists are finalized separately by both cultures, all students and facilitators from both Beta and Alpha make their way back to the activity's initial meeting space, as one group of students again, to debrief the experience.

The debriefing

Now that both cultures are back together and have shed the language and values of their fictitious cultures, a representative who had been in the Alpha culture is chosen to report on their groups observations about the Beta culture as a facilitator tapes the Alpha's written descriptors of the Betas on the wall where both groups can see. The Alpha representative then explains the perceptions of the Betas which is generally met initially with laughter, jokes between friends who had been separated, and playful banter among students. After the entire list of observations is reported out, a facilitator then offers an accurate and brief description on the basic, foundational structure and behavior of the Beta culture. Again met with playful banter, a new layer is added as students gain sudden insights and begin meaning-making of their experiences with a completely new perspective. Before much conversation the Betas now select a representative, and complete the process from their perspective about the Alpha culture.

Once completed, the discussion moves toward a slightly more serious space as facilitators assist students in applying their experiences of concepts surrounding diversity including ethnocentrism, assumptions, faulty observations and interpretations, stereotypes, and judgements to name a few.

Students begin to recognize specific elements of the social work program that will continue to be encountered as they progress through the curriculum. They first experience here what they will learn to be the complex dynamics found across stages of group development from norming and storming to define roles and establish power bases. They will later come to identify how individuals' feelings and perceptions influence power dynamics which shape group identity and rules for inclusion. Ultimately as student skills are refined, they will skillfully and competently employ all of this knowledge to facilitate tap into the exponential power found in good group work.

Conclusion

Cultural competency and group work are both vital components of social work education as well as practice. Effective social work with groups will continue to be needed in every practice setting where social workers find themselves. Traditional "group work" or therapy cannot limit the students' ideas of where group work is happening. Work with diverse groups of any size and any purpose demand a keen awareness of group processes and dynamics, as well as sharpened skills and honed professional knowledge to ensure group members in the care of any social worker are able to offer and receive mutual aid from one another toward their personal and collective goals. Competency in facilitating groups empowers social workers across a wide spectrum of practice areas such as human resource training (Zastrow, 2015; Bonebright, 2010); and organizational structure, funding, leadership, and development; academic and research-oriented endeavors from the field to the classroom (Gurrie, 2015), therapeutic milieus (Shor, Kalivatz, Amir, Aldor, & Lipot, 2015); work with immigrants and refugees as well as policy-makers and policy stakeholders (Warriner, 2007; Vauclair, et al., 2014), play and group games (Thompson & White, 2010), and even summer camps of all kinds (Garr, 2006).

The social work faculty at this university have found *BaFá BaFá* an excellent introduction for students to consider why diversity and group work must be valued and studied, and require serious introspection into each student's own foundational values and perspectives. As students seek to learn skills and adopt values to empower them as they launch into their careers with individuals and groups across multiple and diverse populations, the social work classroom bears a heavy burden to assist students while they sit in their circled classroom chairs to find and own for themselves the soul of the profession seriously. Ultimately, this is what is required to ensure a commitment to culturally competent and excellent social work practice. *BaFá BaFá* has provided this program the opportunity to do just that.

References

Abels, P. (2013). History of the standards for social work practice with groups: A partial view. *Social Work with Groups (36)*, 259–269. DOI: 10.1080/01609513.2012.763009

About the Program (n.d.). Retrieved from http://www.utm.edu/departments/socwork/about.php

Abrams, D., Palmer, S. B., Rutland, A., Cameron, L., & Van de Vyver, J. (2014). Evaluations of and reasoning about normative and deviant ingroup and outgroup members: Development of the black sheep effect. *Developmental Psychology, 50*(1), 258–270.

Bonebright, D. A. (2010). 40 years of storming: A historical review of Tuckman's model of small group development. *Human Resource Development International, 13*, 111–120.

Cavazza, N., Pagliaro, S., & Guidetti, M. (2014). Antecedents of concern for personal reputation: The role of group entitativity and fear of social exclusion. *Basic and Applied Social Psychology, 36*, 365–376.

Council on Social Work Education (2015). *Educational policy and accreditation standards.* Alexandria, VA: Author. Retrieved from http://www.cswe.org/File.aspx?id=81660 DiAngelo, R. (2011). White fragility. *International Journal of Critical Pedagogy, 3*(3), 54–70.

Edwards-Joseph, A., & Baker, S. B. (2012). Themes Caribbean overseas students perceive influence their levels of culture shock. *College Student Journal, 46*(4), 716–729.

Flanja, D. (2009). Culture shock in intercultural communication. *Studia*

Universitatis Babes-Bolyai.Studia Europaea, 54(4), 107–124.

Fowler, S. M. (1994). Two decades of using simulation games for cross-cultural training. *Simulation & Gaming,* 464–476.

Garr, M. (2006). Understanding group processes. *The Camping Magazine, 79*(2), 46–48.

Greitemeyer, T. (2012). Boosting one's social identity: Effects of social exclusion on ethnocentrism. *Basic and Applied Social Psychology, 34,* 410–416.

Gurrie, C. (2015). Group work: A millenial myth-improving group work in the basic course and beyond. *International Journal of Social Science and Humanity, 5*(11), 962–965.

Gutman, C. & Shennar-Golan, V. (2012). Instilling the soul of group work in social work education. *Social Work with Groups (35)2,* 138–149. doi:1 0.1080/01609513.2011.631103

Hoover, J. D., Giambatista, R. C., Sorenson, R. L., Bommer, W. H. (2010). Assessing the effectiveness of whole person learning pedagogy in skill acquisition. *Academy of Management Learning & Education, 9*(2), 192–203.

Jani, J. S., Ortiz, L., Pierce, D. & Lynda, Sowbel, L. (2011). Access to intersectionality, content to competence: Deconstructing social work education diversity standards. *Journal of Social Work Education, (47)*2, 283–301. doi:10.5175/JSWE.2011.200900118

Keller, J. C. (2014). "I wanna have my own damn dairy farm!": Women farmers, legibility, and femininities in rural Wisconsin, U. S. *Journal of Rural Social Sciences, 29*(1), 75–102.

Lantrip, C., Mazzetti, F., Grasso, J., Gill, S., Miller, J., Haner, M., Rude, S. & Awad, G. (2015). Ethnic identity and acculturative stress as mediators of depression in students of Asian descent. *Journal of College Counseling, 18*(2), 144–159. doi:10.1002/jocc.12011

Lee, O. E., & Priester M. A., (2015). Increasing awareness of diversity through community engagement and films. Journal of Social Work Education, 51, 35–46.

Maier, H. (1967). Application of psychological and sociological theory to teaching social work with the group. *Journal of Education for Social Work, 3*(1), 29–40. Retrieved from http://www.jstor.org/stable/23038170.

Monk, G., Winslade, J., Crocket, K., & Epston, D. (Eds.). (1997). *Narrative therapy in practice: The archaeology of hope.* San Fransisco, CA: Jossey-Bass.

Ormiston, M. E. (2016). Explaining the link between objective and perceived differences in groups: The role of the belonging and distinctiveness motives. *Journal of Applied Psychology, 101*(2), 222–236.

Pitts, M. J. (2010). *Culture shock.* In R. L. Jackson (Ed.), *Encyclopedia of identity.* Thousand Oaks, CA: Sage Publications.

Popple, P. (1985). The social work profession: A reconceptualization. *Social Service Review, 59*(4), 560–577.

Rosenthal, L. (2016). Incorporating intersectionality into psychology: An opportunity to promote social justice and equity. *American Psychologist, 71*(6), 474–485.

Shirts, R. G. (1974). *BaFá BaFá: A cross culture simulation.* Del Mar, CA: Simulation Training Systems.

Shor, R., Kalivatz, Z., Amir, Y., Aldor, R. & Lipot, M. (2015). Therapeutic factors in a group for parents with mental illness. *Community Mental Health Journal, 51*, 79–84.

Sweifach, J. (2014). Group work education today: A content analysis of MSW group work course syllabi. *Social Work With Groups, 37*(1), 8–22. doi :10.1080/01609513.2013.816920

Tennessee Demographics, (n.d.). *Tennessee Demographics Online.* Retrieved July 24, 2017, from https://www.tennessee-demographics.com/ martin-demographics.

Thompson, P. & White, S. (2010). Play and positive group dynamics. *Restorative Practices, 19*(3), 53–57.

Toseland, R. W. & Rivas, R. F. (2017). *An introduction to group work practice* (7th ed.). Boston, MA: Allyn & Bacon.

Tuckman, B. W. (1965). Developmental sequence in small groups. *Psychological Bulletin, 63*(6),   384–399.

United States Census Bureau (n.d.). *United States Census Bureau Online.* Retrieved July 24, 2017, from https://www.census.gov/search-results. html.

UTM Office of Institutional Research (n.d.). *UTM Office of Institutional Research Online.* Retrieved July 24, 2017, from https://www.utm.edu/ departments/irp/_pdfs/2016-2017.

Vauclair, C., Wilson, M., and Fisher, R. (2014). Cultural conceptions of morality: Examining laypeople's associations of moral character. *Journal of Moral Education, 43*(1), 54–74.

Warriner, D. S. (2007). Language learning and the politics of belonging: Sudanese women refugees becoming and being "American". *Anthropology & Education Quarterly, 38*(4), 343–359.

Zastrow, C. H. (2015). *Social work with groups: A comprehensive worktext,* (9th ed.). Belmont, CA: Brooks/Cole.

All education is group work:
Group work in education in challenging times
Hilda Baar-Kooij

Introduction

In recent years the educational system in the Netherlands has increasingly become more responsible for dealing with social problems such as safety, inclusion, obesity, alcohol abuse, or dealing with different cultures (Onderwijsraad – Education Council – 2008). Lessons have been developed to address the varying needs and that include a focus on social skills, citizenship and media use. These lessons are generally taught with the help of text books, and the outcomes of these lessons are measured through tests. These lessons are added to the standard educational demands and many teachers appear to feel that these extra responsibilities take time at the expense of valuable learning time. Teachers are particularly concerned about this since they have to account for the outcomes of their academic education, and these outcomes are compared on a local, national and international level.

The theme of the 39th Annual Symposium of the International Association for Social Work with Groups was: *"Group Work in Challenging Times: Creative Strategies for Facing Change".* In consideration of the modern challenges facing young people today, I agree with the symposium planners that group work can contribute to making changes. Since the organisation is called the IASWG, the International Association for Social Work with Groups, the symposium focus was on group work skills and the knowledge required for social workers and social work education and all those working with groups. However, I wonder whether the focus of Group Work should be on *Social Work* or on *Work with Groups* since I missed teachers in primary and secondary education in the presentations and as participants. Although not trained as social workers, teachers work with groups of young children in challenging times and also need creative strategies for facing change. This omission of two major educational sectors is contrary to the belief of Kurt Lewin (1943:115) who stated that *"all education is group work"*. The emphasis on *all* in this quote is mine, since I seriously doubt that practitioners in education, other than in group work education, are aware of what goes on in groups and the importance of group work. And likewise, I doubt that professional group workers are aware of this lack of knowledge in teachers.

Teachers work with groups all day, but does that make them group workers? Most often they think they are. It is not unusual for teachers to claim that they know all about groups, that they involve their pupils in making group rules, solving problems and finding solutions (Silverlock, 2000). In many classrooms, statements on the walls start with "we" as in "we do not exclude others" or "we walk quietly in the hallways". Having over 30 years of experience in Dutch primary education, I have to agree with Miedema (2002) and Luitjes & de Zeeuw-Jans (2011) that: having a knowledge about groups, group dynamics and group processes, is an important condition for good education, however it is not regarded as an equally important subject in teacher training courses in the Netherlands.

Teachers in general are used to being in control and knowing all the answers. Listening and waiting for pupils to argue their way towards their own solutions, from a teacher's perspective, is costing valuable learning time since the focus at present is on the academic learning and on the best didactics for increasing the outcomes of their education (Onderwijsraad, 2008; Ministerie van Onderwijs, Cultuur en Wetenschap, 2011). Schools however also have a social obligation (SLO, 2006). My interest in social group work inspired me to carry out an Action Research study, using group work skills and knowledge in a primary school classroom.

Would a primary school class in Netherlands count as a group?

Before being able to answer this question, the concept of group needs to be defined. There are many different definitions of group such as:

"We mean by a group a number of persons who communicate with one another often over a span of time, and who are few enough so that each person is able to communicate with all the others, not a second-hand, through other people, but face-to-face" (Homans, 1951:1).

"A group is a collection of individuals who have relations to one another that make them interdependent to some significant degree. As so defined the term group refers to a class of social entities having in common the property of interdependence among their constituent members" (Cartwright and Zander, 1968:46).

"A group may be defined as a collection of interacting people with some reciprocal influence over one another" (Schmuck & Schmuck, 2001:29). "We speak of a group when there is a common interest or a common assignment that requires cooperation" (van Engelen, 2014:14).

"A group is a class or a year in primary education" (Van Dale Groot Woordenboek van de Nederlandse Taal, 2015).

Social group work and education seem to have different views on what defines a group. The first two definitions derive from social group work literature, but as a teacher in Dutch primary education, I have to work with the last two definitions of group. This educational view on groups suggests a pragmatic, organisational use of groups. Children are divided into groups by age, ability or instruction for reasons of efficiency (Braster, 2011). Group work in the classroom consists of working in a small group, for example on an assignment for geography or a presentation for a history project and thus can be defined as: "A form of active learning whereby students carry out a group assignment together" (TU Delft, 2017). Education would not be education if group work assignments were not a "learning component." However, at least in primary education, it is the teachers who assign the roles and who make sure that all pupils fulfil all possible roles, regardless of their talents or preferences. That is not the same as facilitating the learning process of the group knowing that a group is more than the sum of its parts.

Dutch primary education

At this point some explanation about the Dutch educational system is needed. Since the Education Act of 1985, a year or form in primary education is called a group. Primary education in the Netherlands knows eight groups: group 1 (4 year olds) till group 8 (12 year olds). As of 2014 in the Netherlands we have Adequate Education, the Dutch answer to the world-wide call towards more inclusive education. Adequate Education is about presenting all children an adequate educational offer (Ministerie van Onderwijs, Cultuur en Wetenschap, 2011). The central question is: What does this child need to reach the set targets (Pameijer & Beukering, 2008). Children are diagnosed and labelled and their needs are written down in individual learning or behaviour plans. External specialists advise teachers on how to deal with the needs of their pupils.

An average group in mainstream primary education in the Netherlands consists of 23 – 32 pupils (Rijksoverheid, 2015). It is not uncommon that in one group there are at least one or more children with a hearing impairment, speech impairment, physical impairment, Dutch as a second language, learning difficulties, behaviour problems, dyslexia, PDD-nos, ADHD, highly gifted and so on. In other words, these groups can be very diverse.

External experts on speech impairments, autism, behaviour etc. advise teachers on the needs of these pupils. It is not unusual that, for example, the advice of the behaviour specialist for pupil A conflicts with the needs of pupil B with a hearing impairment, resulting in giving teachers the feeling that the 'best horseman' is always on his feet, since it is the teacher who has to find ways of translating this contradicting advice while working with the entire class.

Teachers are responsible for enabling all their pupils, with their individual needs, to reach their individual targets. Although the education is aimed at individual outcomes, it is organised in groups. With the focus on the individual needs, these groups can be defined as collections of individuals, with inevitable consequences for the social learning of the pupils. I not only experience this in every day practice, but it also becomes evident in the reports of the Inspectorate in which they write that for example 17% of the pupils in Dutch primary education stated that they had been the victim of bullying in the last year (Inspectie van het Onderwijs, 2014:20). Also in the school year 2012-2013 the inspectorate received almost 2300 complaints about sexual harassment, sexual intimidation, physical and psychological violence, discrimination or radicalisation within an educational context. More than half of these reports were about psychological violence such as bullying, threatening, ignoring, cyber bullying, extortion or stalking (ibid:21).

Social media and safe use of the internet

As mentioned above, society and hence education are facing more than one challenge nowadays. In this study, I have focused on social media and in particular on the WhatsApp.

In response to a series of suicides of young children who had been the victim of cyber bullying, the Dutch government introduced the Social Safety Act in 2015. This Act states that schools have to prevent all forms of bullying and can be held legally responsible unless they can show sufficient proof of actions taken such as:

* Offering social skills lessons
* Having an anti-bullying protocol
* Having a school confidant person for children to talk to about their problems in school or at home
* Monitoring the feelings of safety and wellbeing of their pupils twice a year

The educational inspectorate (Inspectie van het Onderwijs) monitors if schools live up to these rules (PO raad, 2015).

In the Netherlands, 86% of the children in the last two years of primary education (10 – 12 year old) have a smart phone or a tablet and use WhatsApp and / or Facebook (Broek, 2014) although the legal age for using these media in the Netherlands is 13. The children bring their problems, which originated in WhatsApp or on Facebook, with them into the classroom. In my professional circumstance in the period of 2014 - 2016 for example, these problems varied from hacking Facebook pages, being the victim of sexting, humiliation, stalking or gossiping on Facebook or in WhatsApp.

In the fall of 2016 I was asked to help solve a cyber-bullying problem in Year 7 of a school in my region. The problem had originated in the

WhatsApp group. Now related to the theme of this paper, one could wonder whether a WhatsApp group is a group.

According to the WhatsApp Support Team, a WhatsApp group can be defined as:

> "a group of up to 256 people who can create an unlimited number of groups, in which only administrators can add or remove group members, and who communicate through chats", (https://faq.whatsapp.com/en/general/21073373).

The problems in this class began after a mother of one boy created a group app for the class. Her son and his friends assumed the role of administrators and felt they could "punish" peers for their behaviour through chats, or by removing peers that did not belong to their "inner circle". This resulted in conflicts in class between pupils who were friends but denied access to the WhatsApp group.

The problems had reached a level that made teaching difficult and sometimes almost even impossible. The school/teacher had acted according to the new legislations and after eight weeks of interventions, an evaluation was conducted. The school/teacher had employed an individualized approach, aimed at the victim(s) and alleged perpetrators. In addition, the class received a netiquette[2] protocol that all pupils had to sign. According to the evaluation, these actions had been very successful since all pupils had signed the protocol. Despite this, the problems continued. A bullying problem, in real life or in the cyber world, is never an issue only between the bully and victim. All members in the group play a role, which already becomes evident in the term 'social media' since it incorporates the word 'social'. To emphasize this point, it is worth mentioning that the word social means *"living in groups, not separately"* (Oxford English Dictionary, 1975).

With social media a new phenomenon entered the classroom and teachers had to start educating children in skills and knowledge that were, and in many cases still are, new to them as well. The children in this Year 7 were born in 2005 and 2006. Facebook was 'born' in 2004 and WhatsApp in 2009. The children have grown up with Facebook and WhatsApp whereas their teachers and parents have to learn how to use new technology and how to communicate on line. It seems obvious that, in dealing with this new phenomenon, a different approach to learning is needed when compared to learning to read or write. Although 'media wisdom' has become a new subject in primary education, teachers teach this subject with the help of programs and text books.

Methodology: Practical action research and experiential learning

Carr & Kemmis (1986) explain how education is a practice sustained in society by the institution of schooling. There is always a tension between education and schooling and practitioners in education should be aware of the fact that schooling, at some point, might undermine the values of educational practice (ibid). In the particular example mentioned, such a tension became evident. Based on the latest "protocol" deriving from the 2015 Social Safety Act, the teachers had tried to school their pupils in a netiquette protocol. The effects of this schooling appeared to have been successful since the pupils were able to explain how "in general" one should behave on social media. This theoretical knowledge however, had not resulted in a change of behaviour in the WhatsApp group, which is why I was asked to intervene.

The educational challenge and focus of this study was how to make pupils in this Year 7 of primary school in the Netherlands responsible for their own problems originated in WhatsApp, using experiential learning strategies as opposed to teaching them how to act. Being an educator and practitioner in group work, it felt obvious to me that I had to choose a methodology rooted in both disciplines. Kurt Lewin (1890 – 1947) is not only credited for creating the term 'Action Research' (Smith, 2001), but also for the term 'Group dynamics' (Doel & Kelly, 2014) and for his influential ideas on Experiential Learning. Although at first sight the Action Research cycle (figure 1) and the Experiential Learning cycle (figure 2) show many similarities since in both cycles the learner/practitioner is going through a sequence of actions, they are not the same. Action Research by definition is deliberate and planned and thus involves strategic action (McMahon, 2006).

In this study I was able to use the insights I had gained from 'practical action research' (Carr & Kemmis, 1986), in which I, as an outside facilitator, formed a collaborative relationship with the teacher of the class involved, to help him develop a strategic plan for change, monitor the problems and the effects of the changes, and help him to reflect on the value of the achieved changes and the consequences of these changes as opposed to offering expertise and advice. Secondly, for the process of the class in raising awareness of what exactly was going on, the experiential learning cycle was used.

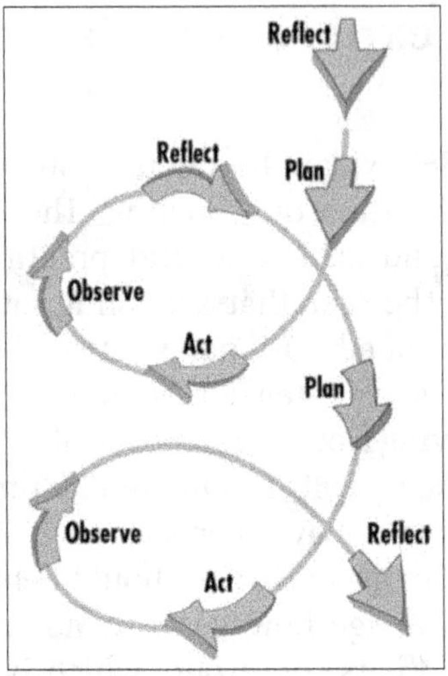

Figure 1: Action Research cycle Lewin

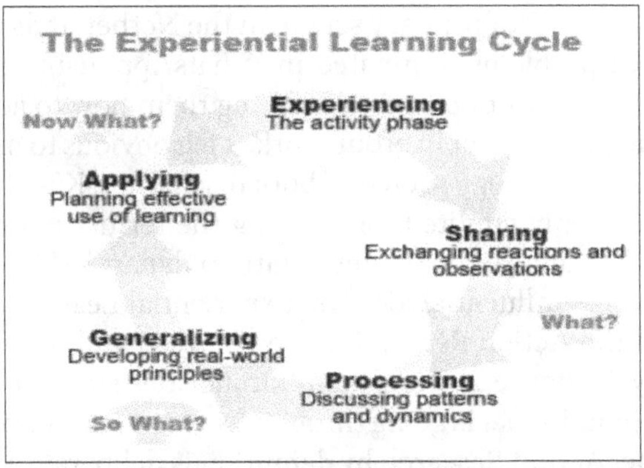

Figure 2: Experiential Learning Cycle rooted in Eyler, Giles, Dewey and Kolb (retrieved from: http://www.servicelearning.umn.edu/info/reflection.htm). in Eyler, Giles, Dewey and Kolb (retrieved from: http://www.servicelearning. umn.edu/info/reflection.htm)

In this particular case study, I not only worked with the teacher, but also with the class. Carr & Kemmis (1986) describe my role as facilitator as 'Socratic' in that I provide a sounding-board, first of all for teachers to learn how they can assist their class in the process of collaborative self-reflection through a deliberate and planned strategic action. Secondly for the pupils to become aware of their reasons for their own actions, to learn about the process of self-reflection and to try out their new insights. Therefore I combined the teacher's Action Research cycle with the pupils' Experiential Learning cycle (figure 3). In this way the first Action in the teacher's AR cycle would be the first Experience in the pupils' EL cycle which involves: handing the problem back to the group and letting them identify the problem(s) themselves.

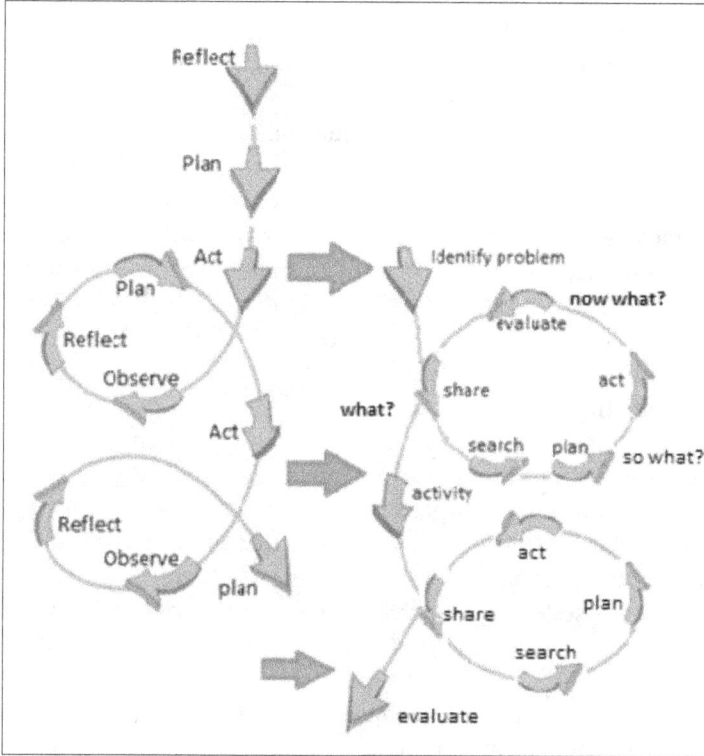

Figure 3: my combined cycle of Action Research and Experiential Learning

Process findings and analysis

In this section the research process and findings will be shared. As already mentioned, the teacher's Action Research process was combined with the Experiential Learning cycle of the pupils. In this collaborative approach, one afternoon a week I facilitated the group while the teacher filmed. This meant that I was in the more vulnerable position whilst at the same time I could model facilitating group discussion, promoting active and respectful listening, creating a safe space for sharing, how to deal with emotions and expression of feelings, how to coach in conflict situations, and how to use activities for experiencing or understanding problems. The teacher was assigned the role of observer. His assignment was to film interaction (who is looking for 'permission to speak'; what non-verbal communication is taking place; what messages are communicated). Once the problem was handed back to the pupils, a lively discussion started in class. Letting the group discuss (as opposed to raising their hand and waiting for a turn) was difficult for the teacher to observe without interfering. In the first video, the teacher focused on individual pupils (playing with their pencil, not paying attention; talking to their neighbour,) and on my role. The way we reflected on what had happened in class was adapted from Video Interaction Counselling (Brons, 2008). First the teacher would show me selections of the video and query some decisions I made. For example he asked: Why don't you intervene? Why didn't you correct this pupil? Why did you allow and even repeated that statement yourself without judging it? Why did you want that pupil to make a contribution? Following this I would select fragments, and share my observations: Do you see this pupil? He is eager to say something but when he has an opportunity to share, he 'forgot' what it is he wanted to say. Now let us go back a few seconds..........do you see this other boys' non-verbals? How is the relationship between these two boys and what are their roles in the group? What are they trying to communicate?

Action research cycle teacher

Teachers are encouraged to improve their practices in a deliberate and planned way, which is what this teacher had been doing prior to this study. He had stated the problem and had planned what he wanted to achieve.

Problem*: "The atmosphere in the classroom isn't comfortable for all pupils. Once in the classroom it seems to be okay, but outside and after school many things occur which influence the atmosphere in the classroom and take time at the expense of learning time. Most of these 'things' have originated in the class' WhatsApp group. Parents come to school with their concerns and expect that the school comes up with solutions or they announce that their solution is that their child is not allowed to have contact with certain other children and that school has to make sure this doesn't happen".*

Goal: *"I want to create a safe learning and living environment in which all children give room to each other to be who they are and in which all feel safe to express themselves. I want to make children aware of how they react to each other and what the consequences of their behaviour are to others in the group".*

Outcomes: *"All pupils have signed the protocol. They know how they should act, but it is not what they are doing".*
Possible causes:

Pupils don't feel responsible
* *It is difficult to involve pupils*
* *Social media / society in general*

In this collaborative approach, I first asked the teacher to reflect on the process asking: Whose problem is it? Who should try to solve it? Who has been trying to solve it?

The first step in the Action Research cycle was: handing back the problem to the group.

Experiential learning cycle pupils

In the first group discussion we made a list of all the things that caused irritations, problems and conflicts. Apart from the problem of who could and could not be administrators, varying concerns were also raised such as: sending messages of only one word or one letter, sending 50 emoticons after each other, repeating "like" more than 30 times, sending photos, private quarrels in the group app, ignoring requests, misinterpreting what was written, and so on. Although the group agreed on what was written on the list, there was no willingness to change their behaviour. The general conclusion was that others had to change their behaviour to ultimately solve the overall problems.

For the next session I told the group that this time we would not verbally communicate but instead chat on the digital board. The suggestion was accepted with great enthusiasm at first, but it did not take long before irritation and frustration arose. I started the conversation with the words: "He has gone". After half an hour and pages full of text, no one could answer the questions: Who has gone? Why has he gone? How does that make me feel? They had all been writing their own assumptions related to their own thoughts instead of reacting on what was written. When asked if this resembled their WhatsApp conversations, the group stated "yes" clarifying that they reacted without taking much notice of what others had written, and "no" because in this chat no one used abusive language. *"In this text we all react nice to each other because you are in the group. In our WhatsApp group we are never so nice to each other"* (pupil statement).

Before diving into the "abusive language", we first analysed a part of the text we had written in this chat. Below is an excerpt of this: What has happened and why does not anyone know who has gone, why and how does that make me feel? (names have been changed for privacy reasons).

Hilda: He has gone
Mohammed: Who?
Justine: I think someone left the WhatsApp group
April: Yes but that has to have a reason
Sergio: You have to scroll back
Sandra: Yes perhaps he/she didn't like the group
Stephan: I think we have to ask the administrator to put him back into the group

In the chat, Justine starts with her own assumption. She explains that because we are working on the WhatsApp problem, she assumed that my opening sentence was related to the WhatsApp group. April reacts on Justine, but the reaction of Sergio doesn't make sense at all since there is nothing to scroll back to. He explains that he wrote this remark because: *"mostly you have missed 40 new messages when you haven't looked for 5 minutes so I thought that this could be the case now too"*. Stephan assumed the chat was about a particular boy in the group with a history of 'leaving the group' when things don't go his way.

To raise awareness of the limitations of chats and the fact that, in communication, we rely on more than just words, five students were asked to leave the classroom with five different scenarios of which the last sentence was: "he has gone". Back in the classroom, they were only allowed to say that one sentence, in line with the scenario they had studied. What do we know now compared to the same statement in the chat? Why do we know it?

Although the text was the same, in all cases the group at least knew how the person stating this one sentence was feeling about the fact that "he had gone' because they had extra information through tone of voice, body language and facial expression. Based on this information, it was also easier to interpret who had gone (boyfriend, burglar, bully). The group realised that this information was missing in written text. Perhaps feelings can be expressed with the help of emoticons, but other information does not automatically derive from written words and/or emoticons and additional text may be needed if one wants to avoid assumptions.

This information is not new and could have been explained to the group, substantiated with scientific evidence that most of our communication is non-verbal. However, now the group has discovered it for themselves, opening the possibility of finding ways to avoid falling into previous assumptions.

The next activity was to understand that words can be interpreted in different ways. In this activity, the group split up in groups of four. Two children (A and B) sit opposite of each other with a barrier between them. The other two children (C and D) sit in the middle and can see both A and B and their table. A and B both get the same amount of blocks and small items. A builds something and provides instructions to B, to build the same. C and D are not allowed to say anything, but have to observe.

This activity was a real eye opener for the group. The assignment was easy, and the words used were simple and known. But nevertheless, the results were disappointing. How come? *"Because we know the words and we think that we know what the other means. And then we continue with our own interpretation of these words to end up with something completely different"* (summary of pupils' statements).

Now how does that relate to the groups 'WhatsApp problem? The group used what they had learned in this activity and at this point one of the pupils suggested to "write down some rules". The list started with:

• No one word or one letter messages; the whole text in one message
• Read what the other has written before reacting
• If it is not clear to you, first ask before making your own assumptions

In the next session we pulled up a "real" WhatsApp chat on the digital board and analysed it since the group had stated that they used more abusive language and were less friendly to each other in the WhatsApp group when compared to our classroom chat.

Analysing this chat resulted in a discussion about what it means to be part of a: WhatsApp GROUP? What should be communicated in the group and what is private? What triggers irritation and abusive language? New items were added to the list:

• The group app is for sharing information that concerns all, or at least most members of the group
• No announcements that no one is interested in should be shared
• Individual appointments, arguments or problems should be communicated in private

A last but not unimportant problem still needed to be addressed: who should be administrator of the group. The boy whose mother created the group app, was still of the opinion that he (and his friends) were entitled to be the administrators. The group however believed that the administrators had to be chosen by the group. The group deliberated and voted. Four children were elected as administrators with the restriction that none of them had an individual veto and every problem had to go through the group first.

The boy in question had no other option but to agree with the group's decision. Meanwhile he created a new WhatsApp group in which he only invited his friends and still had the power to decide who could be in and who should be out. This became the topic of the next session. The boy himself was pleased with his own solution. This way he could obey the new group rules while at the same time remain in charge of his own new group. However, his best friend and member of the second group stated that he was not happy with this situation but did not know what to do because he agreed with the group rules but on the other hand, he did not want to go against his best friend. This resulted in the themes for the next sessions: loyalty and perspective.

Perspective: in this activity all the pupils had to find their way through a labyrinth. They had to help each other, but were not allowed to talk. In this activity they experienced why it is easy to see the right way when you are standing at the side but extremely difficult when you are in the labyrinth. This activity opened the discussion about why the boy in question had different ideas than the group. It is all a matter of perspective. Now how does that relate to loyalty? Again, a difficult concept that needed defining.

With the help of the video that was made of the labyrinth activity we addressed the concept of loyalty. The goal of the activity was that the entire group had to go through the labyrinth. At some point a boy responsible for finding the right way at that moment, received directions from his friends but the rest of the group signalled that he had to go in another direction. He listened to his friends and went the wrong way, costing the group points. Viewing this on video made it possible to discuss whether you should always be loyal to your friends, even if you know they send you in the wrong direction or get you in trouble. Where does your own responsibility come in? What does the word "loyalty" mean? When should you be loyal to your friends and when is it important to take your own responsibility?

Action research cycle teacher

When viewing the first video, the teacher stated that he was surprised and impressed by the way the pupils approached the problem. He also confessed that, at first, he doubted my "teacher skills" because I did not intervene when the group was discussing in an unstructured way, voices were raised and emotions got high. *"I had no idea where you were going and felt frustrated that you took so long to discuss single words or statements"*. After the last session we summarized the skills and knowledge that were gained:

- Less can be more (less control can lead to more own responsibility)
- Some skills and knowledge cannot be 'instructed', but need to be learned by doing
- Knowledge about informal leadership in the group; about group dynamics
- Active listening as opposed to hearing what pupils answer
- Asking 'open' questions (clarifying and summarizing)
- Assessment of social skills 'in action' as opposed to questionnaires and tests

Outcomes

After 7 weeks the group managed to solve their WhatsApp problem. That does not mean that there were no more problems at all. As one of the pupils stated: *"Of course we still have fights and conflicts. That is normal. But now we have learned where they come from and how to solve them"*. In other words, the group had learned to talk *with* each other and not *to* each other, that there is more than one perspective, the importance of common definitions and the risks of assumptions. The teacher stated:

> *"Sometimes a colleague tells me that my group is having an argument on the playground or in the corridors. I prepare myself for dealing with it, but by the time the group comes back into the classroom, they mostly have solved it themselves or ask if they can have some time to talk about it".*

Seven weeks after this study, the teacher stated in a follow-up meeting that what he had most taken away from this study was the ability to see the class as a group; to be able to appreciate the dynamics instead of looking at individual pupils and their behaviour. He definitely wants to use this new learned knowledge and skills in next year's' group.

Conclusion

For experienced group workers this all might sound like "preaching to the crowd". For the teacher on the other hand, the process of raising awareness of what goes on in WhatsApp chats and making the group responsible instead of teaching them how to behave on-line, was new. At first sight, the end result of this study was not so different to what the teacher had in mind: a written netiquette contract. Content-wise it was almost the same as the netiquette contract the teacher had offered. The difference however, was that now the contract was made up by the children, based on their own experiences, group discussions, and decisions that resulted from a democratic process. The group reached the outcomes themselves through experiential learning and felt responsible for living up to their own rules.

Teachers teach their pupils in ways they have learned in teacher training: by steering towards the right answers that are in the back of the book. Indeed, there is only one correct answer for questions like: what is the capital of France or how do you spell taxi? However, when it comes to dealing with problems, as in this case with the WhatsApp group, there is no *one* correct answer. My personal experience is that group workers themselves, like the pupils, do not know the right answers. What group workers do differently is facilitating learning by helping the children to find their own answers that work for them.

We never dealt with the original question of excluding children from the group or bullying peers in WhatsApp, simply because we did not have to.

Implications & recommendations

When looking at the implications of this study for practice and teacher training I argue that, at least when educating children on appropriate use of social media, group work methods should be made available to all teachers. In this instance, these group work methods include handing the problem back to the group, facilitating group discussion, using activities to raise awareness and defining difficult concepts such as perspective, and respecting differences of opinion. If education wants to be successful in reaching the attainment targets for citizenship and social skills (in real life as well as on-line) beyond just theoretical knowledge, then at least teachers have to learn (again) that, indeed, education is group work. Group work and education share the same roots. In the last decades however, education and group work both went their separate ways. Where group work specialised in collaborative learning, education specialised in teaching techniques or didactics.

As a teacher, I grew up in the 1980's with the ideas of Dewey, Rogers, Freire, Illich and Lewin, names that are familiar in group work history as well. The definition of pedagogy I learned was *"the science of raising"* (Van Dale Groot Woordenboek van de Nederlandse Taal). At present, the definition of pedagogy is more in line with the Anglo Saxon definition: *"the science of teaching"* (Oxford English Dictionary) since teachers in the Netherlands know in detail what "this child needs to reach the academic targets set by the Ministry of Education". However, society is making social demands on those same teachers. Group workers know that this is not a contradiction. The goal of the IASWG is to advance social work with groups. Therefore I suggest that they include 'groups in (primary) education' in their endeavour and expand their invitations for the next symposium to the educational field as well.

Finally I want to propose a new definition of pedagogy that brings the roots of education and group work back together: *the science of facilitating learning.*

Acknowledgement

I owe many thanks to the children of Year 7 and their teacher who participated in this study. Without them this study would not have been possible. The group showed that, if given the responsibility, children in the last years of primary education are capable of finding solutions for problems. They also gave evidence to the fact that some knowledge cannot be handed over, but needs to be learned by actual experience. I want to thank the teacher for his trust in handing over his group to me one afternoon a week.

Notes

1   Netiquette = a combination of the words network and etiquette; rules of etiquette that apply when communicating over computer networks, especially over the Internet; an informal code of behaviour on the internet. (http://www.encyclo.nl/lokaal/10511)

References

'Antipestwet' treedt in werking. (n.d.). Retrieved June 27, 2017, from PO-raad website, https://www.poraad.nl/nieuws-en-achtergronden/antipestwet-treedt-in-werking

Braster, S. (2011). *Passie en pragmatisme. De onderwijsinspectie en de opkomst en ondergang van het klassikaal onderwijs.* (Passion and pragmatism. The Education Inspectorate and the rise and fall of whole group teaching). Utrecht: Inspectie van het Onderwijs.

Broek, T. van den (2014, December 11). Kinderen hebben vanaf hun 11e een smartphone. [Web log post]. Retrieved from http://www.adformatie.nl/blog/kinderen-hebben-vanaf-hun-11e-een-smartphone

Brons, C. (2008) *Video Interactie Begeleiding op School* (Video Interaction Counselling in Schools). Groningen: Christine Brons bv.

Carr, W & Kemmis, S. (1986). *Becoming Critical. Education, Knowledge and Action Research.* London and New York: RoutledgeFalmer Taylor & Francis Group.

Dewey, J. (1915). *The School and Society.* Mineola / New York: Dover Publication Inc.

Doel, M. & Kelly, T.B. (2014). *A – Z of groups and groupwork.* Palgrave Macmillan.

Engelen, R. van. (2014). *Grip op de groep.* (Grip on the group). Amersfoort: ThiemeMeulenhoff.

Experiential Learning Cycle rooted in Eyler, Giles, Dewey and Kolb (retrieved June 2017 from: http://www.servicelearning.umn.edu/info/reflection.htm).

Homans, G. (1951). *The Human Group.* London: Routledge and Kegan Paul.

Hoe zijn de groepen in het basisonderwijs samengesteld. (n.d.) Retrieved August 22, 2016, from Rijksoverheid website, https://www.rijksoverheid.nl/onderwerpen/basisonderwijs/vraag-en-antwoord/hoe-zijn-de-groepen-in-het-basisonderwijs-bo-samengesteld.

Inspectie van het Onderwijs. (2014). *Jaarverslag 2013. Inspectie van het Onderwijs.* Utrecht: Inspectie van het Onderwijs.

Lewin, K. (1943). Psychology and the process of group living. *The Journal of Social Psychology, S.P.S.S.I. Bulletin, 17,* pp.113-131.

Luitjes, M. and Zeeuw-Jans, I. de. (2011). *Ontwikkelingen in de groep. Groepsdynamica bij kinderen en jongeren.* (Developments in the group. Group dynamics among children and youngsters). Bussem: Couthinho.

McMahon, T. (1999). Is reflective practice synonymous with action research? *Educational Action Research, 7:1,* 163 – 169. Doi: 10.1080/09650799900200080

Miedema, P. (2002). Moeilijke klas. Moeilijke kinderen? (Difficult class. Difficult children?). In J. van Balkom, Th. Dollevoet & F. Faber (Eds.) *De moeilijke klas* (pp. 49-55). Antwerpen-Apeldoorn: Garant.

Ministerie van Onderwijs, Cultuur en Wetenschap. (2011a). *Nota Werken in het onderwijs 2012.* (Working in Education 2012). Den Haag: Rijksoverheid.

Onderwijsraad (2008). *Onderwijs en maatschappelijke verwachtingen – Advies.* (Education and expectations of society – Advice). Den Haag: Onderwijsraad.

Pameijer, N. and Beukering, T. van., (2008). *Handelingsgericht werken: een handreiking voor de interne begeleider .* (Working Action orientated: a manual for the senco). Leuven: Acco.

Samenwerkend leren / Groepswerk. (n.d.) Retrieved June 17, 2017, from TU Delft website, http://www.icto.tudelft.nl/onderwijsthemas/samenwerkend-lerengroepswerk/

Schmuck, R.A. & Schmuck, P.A. (2001). *Group Processes in the Classroom, Eighth Edition.* Boston-New York-San Fransico-St.Louise: McGrawHill.

Silverlock, M. (2000). Learning beyond the classroom: Groupwork in schools. In Oded Manor (Eds.), *Ripples Groupwork in different settings* (pp.123-135). London: Whiting & Birch.

Smith, M.K. (2001). Kurt Lewin: groups, experiential learning and action research. www.infed.org/mobi/kurt-lewin-groups-experiential-learning-and-action-research

Stichting Leerplan Ontwikkeling (2006). Core objectives Primary Education. Available at: http://www.slo.nl/primair/kerndoelen/Kerndoelen_English_version.doc. (Accessed: 12-05-2013).

Using group chat. (n.d.) Retrieved June 14, 2017, from WhatsApp website, https://faq.whatsapp.com/en/general/21073373

The VAWA/U Visa Self Prep Course:

Socio-political and organizational influences on an interdisciplinary legal and social work group model for immigrant survivors of intimate partner violence

Martha L. Garcia and Diana Halperin

Introduction

When developing group programs that seek to support clients and their communities with transformation and transcendence of personal and social challenges, social workers must be aware of and respond to multiple spheres of influence on the client, the worker, and the agency that provides the program. Agency context within larger socio-political environments produce powerful conditions around the work and provide both possibilities and limitations that group workers encounter in the creation and implementation of groups. The purpose of this paper is to consider elements of socio-political and organizational contexts that influenced and continue to have impact on the development, implementation, and adaptation of the VAWA/U Visa Self-Prep Course (VAWA SPC), a group model designed to prepare immigrant women survivors of intimate partner violence (IPV) to be actively engaged in their legal immigration cases. The course is a multi-week, interdisciplinary (legal/social work) group that provides legal information, support, and tools to complete the legal requirements in pursuit of particular immigration remedies. The model has been shown to be flexible and adaptable to different agency contexts. However, current socio-political milieu, restricted policies, and anti-immigrant sentiment create an environment that challenges the ability to utilize the model for its intended purposes. Implications for practice are discussed.

Immigrant survivors of interpersonal violence: Social context and need

Social workers are increasingly exposed to diverse immigrant populations, as the demographics in our country rapidly change (Census Bureau, 2016). It is likely that as social workers we will encounter immigrant women who have been victims of gender violence and crime, particularly intimate partner violence (IPV), requiring us to identify their particular needs and work with the minimal resources available to them. For those who are accustomed to working with immigrant women, the model discussed was designed to respond to joint legal and socio-emotional needs, providing an additional option.

Unique vulnerability to abuse and exploitation of immigrant women

Women represent over 51% of the immigrant population and are vulnerable in both public and private areas of their lives that overlap and reinforce each other. These vulnerabilities may be exacerbated by cultural values and norms that serve to silence and isolate immigrant women. In the intimate sphere, immigrant women may be subject to IPV, particularly women who depend on their husbands or partners for their immigration status and/or financial support. IPV is the current term used to describe a combination of coercive and abusive behaviors from one intimate partner to the other which renders the survivor powerless and in many ways defenseless. The level of abuse immigrant women are exposed to may range from threats of deportation, losing their children, or actual death (New York City Department of Health and Mental Hygiene, 2004). Statistics suggest that immigrant women are more in danger of being killed by their intimate partners than other women (Messing, Amanor-Boadu, Cavanaugh, Glass & Campbell,

2013; Counts D., Brown J., & Campbell, J.C., 1999). In New York City, in a ten-year span (1990-1999) more than half of the women killed by their intimate partners were immigrants (Frye, Hosein, Waltermaurer, Blasney & Wilt, 2005).

Immigrant women may be more dependent on their partners because they are more at risk in the workplace. They typically work in informal labor markets where rights are difficult to assert (American Immigration Council, 2012). This makes them vulnerable to rape, sexual harassment, and other gender based exploitation. They may be unaware of their rights or afraid to enforce them as they may be threatened with deportation, being fired, or not paid.

Immigrant women may be married to lawful permanent residents (LPR) or US citizens who use their privilege to threaten and abuse them (Newman, 2009). Abusive spouses can use immigration status as a means of control over their partners by filing immigration petitions on behalf of their wives and non-citizen children then delaying, revoking or failing to follow through on the requirements. This power imbalance leaves the women at the abuser's mercy (American Immigration Council, 2012). Women who are unmarried or who are married to an unauthorized partner face a different kind of challenge. They are silenced by the fear of deportation for herself, her children, or partner.

Legal remedies for immigrant women: VAWA.

To address the need of immigrant survivors of IPV to obtain legal immigration status in the United States, a number of immigration "remedies" evolved. A pivotal legislation of assistance to immigrant women, the Violence Against Women Act of 1994 (VAWA), is a U.S. federal law (U. S. Congress, 1993) approved by a bipartisan Congress to address the inadequacies of state jurisdictions to respond to violence experienced by women (Laney, 2010; Kish Sklar & Lustig, 2001). Organizing efforts by feminists as well as demonstrated increases in gender violence led to the reauthorization of the Act in 2000, 2005, and 2013 (U.S. Department of Justice, 2013). Advocates and immigrant women ensured that each of the reauthorizations included regulations to protect immigrant survivors of violence. VAWA 1994 provided immigration relief from abusive spouses through "self-petitioning." VAWA 2000 created immigration relief to victims of crime and sexual assault through the U-Visa. In 2004, T-Visas offered relief to survivors of trafficking.

Over the last few decades, several options have opened for immigrant women to stabilize and legalize their immigration status:

- *Battered Spouse Waiver* (BSW) - The BSW, made available by the Immigration Act of 1990, was the first legal resource and set a precedent for assisting immigrant women. The BSW allows women married to US citizens who have filed documents with immigration and can prove they are victims of IPV to petition for their green cards directly without the assistance or knowledge of the abusive husband.
- *"VAWA Self Petition"* - Like the BSW, the VAWA self-petition is available to immigrant women married to US citizens or Legal Permanent Residents. It allows IPV survivors to file for LPR status independent of their husbands and under certain circumstances for women who have separated from or divorced the abusive husband. The approval of a VAWA Self Petition opens eligibility to work authorization, deferred action (stops deportation process) and green card.
- *U Visa* - The U Visa was created to protect noncitizen victims of certain crimes who "assist or are willing to assist in the investigation or prosecution of a criminal offense" (U. S Congress, 2000). The U Visa provides an avenue for deferred action and work authorization to unmarried women or those married to undocumented men. The victim is required to cooperate with law enforcement (and can create a situation of women having to choose between the abuser and herself). Only 10,000 U Visas are granted each year (American Immigration Council, 2012; Laney, 2010).
- With new possibilities for self-advocacy among undocumented survivors, advocates looked for ways to disseminate information about the various remedies as well as involve the survivors in the development of their applications. The VAWA self-prep course model was developed as a way to respond to the community's need for legal access, education, skills building, and support for their immigration cases.

Creation of interdisciplinary group model

The VAWA self-prep course was created in 2002-3 to address the legal immigration needs of immigrant women survivors of IPV. The initial model was a creative response to women seeking legal assistance from the City University of New York (CUNY) School of Law Immigrant Rights and the Battered Women's Rights Clinics. With a commitment to empowering grassroots women's organizations, the faculty elected to work with an agency serving Central American and South American women. Working in close collaboration with the agency's director, faculty from the CUNY clinics, the social work supervisor, and students implemented the first version of the model. Law and social work students under the supervision of the faculty delivered all consecutive courses.

Although not designed as a support group, a learning environment is created in which women can be empowered through education while demystifying the legal process. Each session is structured to build on the next to meet specific legal and social work objectives. The interdisciplinary nature of the model allows for multiple goals to be accomplished simultaneously. A requirement of the immigration remedy dictates a written recounting of the abuse or crime against the survivor. The VAWA SPC may be the first time survivors speak of their violence. Working from a trauma-informed perspective, social workers recognize that "telling the story" of being criminally victimized by one's abuser is potentially re-traumatizing for most IPV survivors. Many immigrant women have endured extensive histories of trauma that may include their immigration as well as abuse experiences. As undocumented persons in the U.S., they are often marginalized, exploited and mistreated with few services and resources available for support. Cultural barriers and belief systems raise doubts and fears regarding sharing deeply personal information. These variables come together in ways that interfere with remaining engaged in the legal work, potentially preventing survivors from successfully completing the program. Therefore, a safe and healing environment must be created.

From the legal perspective, the women learn how to describe what they endured in a credible, well-documented fashion. For lawyers, developing a well-supported application is mandatory, and clients who are not overwhelmed by recounting their stories make better collaborators. Group support helps participants understand that they share common experiences while at the same time validates their individual histories. The survivors become better able to create coherent personal narratives of the crime and to account for inconsistencies in the incidents of abuse. Women develop skills in self-advocacy, learning to gather the necessary documents that provide evidence and substantiate their stories. From the social work perspective, the group work serves to minimize the pain, memory, and retelling and accentuates the transformative capacities of the process.

Group work in a legal setting faces many challenges. Many low income clients find it daunting to prioritize legal cases over the competing needs of family, work, childcare, and the demands of bureaucratic systems that invade many corners of their lives. People do not rush to see attorneys because of positive events in their lives; public interest attorneys are consulted during moments of urgency, crisis, or a serious breakdown in an important system. The prevalence of histories of trauma in so many people's lives further complicates the level of participation. The legal experience can trigger or retraumatize clients, and the possibility of being triggered may cause clients understandably to avoid engaging in the legal work. All of these factors make consistent group work participation difficult to achieve. The VAWA SPC model works to minimize this challenge. The potential for legal status is a powerful lure to clients and helps them to maintain a level of commitment to the process. At the same time their socio-emotional needs are recognized in a safe, supportive space that validates their experiences. Participants develop relationships with others like themselves, and they are able to draw on resilience and skills that help them remain engaged.

Theoretical framework: Popular education

The principles of feminist popular education and group work (Miller & VeneKlasen, 2012) guided the VAWA SPC project. This methodology was adapted from the original ideas of Paulo Freire's Popular Education (Freire, 1970) to address the particular forms of oppression toward women. Popular education conceives of learning and knowledge as potentially catalyzing processes for critical thinking and action. Feminists adapted Freire's consciousness-raising methodology, creating opportunities for women to share their personal experiences and for realizing their collective reality. This collective awareness led to analysis of forces shaping women's oppression, in particular violence in the streets, the workplace, and the family and home. The concept "the personal is political" emerged from this understanding, leading to a powerful feminist movement (Miller & VeneKlasen, 2012).

The first author and co-creator of VAWA SPC had been exposed to ways women's organizations used popular education to educate and empower Latin American women and presumed that this approach might be appropriate to working with immigrant women. Popular education's premise is that people are the experts of their own world and that knowledge can be built from their lived experiences. The facilitators of the VAWA SPC impart legal information and knowledge about IPV that is then integrated by the participants through reflection and comparison to their own circumstances. The participants guide every activity, lecture, and discussion as they transform the knowledge into a reclaiming of their voices and power.

Traumatic memories and experiences of violence are stored in the body (van der Kolk, 2017); it is not enough to talk about what happened or to learn the law. Though not psychotherapeutic groups, during self-prep sessions a great deal of emotion surfaces. Women are supported with processing, and if possible integrating, the very personal and emotional material evoked for the legal work through the use of complementary/traditional healing ways such as breath work, visualization, relaxation, and other modalities. Creation of an emotional and physical safe space has the additional benefit of encouraging solidarity and support amongst the women.

The creators replicated the original model seven times with four different community organizations. Six replications directly assisted immigrant women with preparing their legal immigration cases. An additional version was offered to social workers and lawyers on the model. As a result of the project, the majority of the participants have been successfully able to regularize their legal statuses and begin the transformational healing process from abuse. Each replication of the model provided lessons learned about cultural, organizational, and socio-political issues that were then integrated into the subsequent versions.

New adaptation of the model:
The U Visa Prep Group

The need of the immigrant survivor community for assistance with immigration remedies continues to grow, and as more law enforcement agencies became familiar with the certifying process, additional opportunities existed to offer U Visa remedies for more clients. Given the ability for the self-prep course to meet multiple legal and socio-emotional needs of immigrant women survivors of IPV, the question arose as to the model's flexibility outside the support of the University. Would the model sustain transition to a law firm with alternative resources and priorities?

In 2015, a public interest legal services agency providing free civil legal services to low-income clients and who had observed one of the CUNY self-prep courses elected to replicate the model. The agency sought to serve a large group of clients eligible for the U Visa. Because the numbers of clients needing immigration assistance was greater than the legal services agency's capacity to serve them, many eligible clients had to be placed on long wait lists or be referred out to other agencies to receive timely assistance. Delays in filing applications added years to applicants' wait time because of limited annual government quotas. The model would enable more legal services agency clients to receive timely assistance.

Other elements from the CUNY model translated to the new agency context; to fulfill its mission, the legal services agency worked to assist individuals and their communities through an anti-poverty, social, and racial justice lens. They welcomed an opportunity to work with immigrant survivors not only through direct service but also through group education and support around their IPV experiences. The agency employed both immigration attorneys and social workers experienced in working with immigrant survivors of IPV, making it possible to continue to utilize the interdisciplinary collaboration with the clients.

Socio-political and organizational contexts

Serving clients via a group model addressed the agency's goals in other ways that were of particular interest. As a recipient of federal funds, the legal services agency struggled to develop methods of working progressively with low-income populations. In 1996 under the conservative Congress lead by Newt Gingrich, in an effort to disable federally funded services available to the poor, specific restrictions were legislated that forbade the agency in engaging in any form of community organizing with its clients. The same restrictions prohibited the agency from working with clients who were not U.S. citizens or LPR green card holders. Certain exceptions were later granted in the service of crime victims (Legal Services Corporation website, n.d.).

Through the adapted model, the legal services agency became able to partner with clients in innovative ways and fulfill its objectives of working more holistically with community members. Although community organizing activities were restricted, community education was allowed. As survivors of IPV, the undocumented clients were also able to meet the qualifications by being considered crime victims. Utilizing the group model enabled the legal services agency to expand its social, economic, and racial justice initiatives as well as develop new ways of "community lawyering," an approach in which lawyers share tools and work in partnership with the community to help solve the community's problems (Sargent Shriver National Center on Poverty Law website, n.d.). This sentiment reflected the original model's intent and spirit. Because the interdisciplinary model couples social work with the legal work, it would allow the agency to work with community members in a much more integrated, egalitarian way.

During the planning of the replicated model, the new agency did not have the benefit of first-hand knowledge from the model originators. Nevertheless, this absence enabled the legal services agency to discover and interpret the model in ways that reflected the agency's particular structure and goals. The new setting, with its external socio-political constraints and specific internal mission and resources, dictated changes in three particular ways:

1. The model's methods and goals would now be determined by a single agency, reflecting internal priorities as opposed to collaborative goals between external partnerships, types of agencies, and collaborations. The agency could draw from its existing pool of clients to participate in the model and serve both the legal and socio-emotional needs internally. The agency's resources would determine the project's timeframe and energy parameters.
2. The emphasis of the work focused on direct service of participants

in contrast to parallel goals of educating law and social work students and macro community development. As a service agency that answered both to achievement of clients' legal objectives as well as to limits mandated by external funding requirements, the work needed to be highly task-driven and result-oriented.

3. The social worker tasked with developing the project in the new setting (re)conceived and implemented the model through a lens of social group work theory.

Social group work theory in agency context

In developing the group within the legal services agency context, the social worker/second writer was familiar and experienced with social group work concepts that facilitated accomplishment of the task (prepare for attorney collaboration and develop materials for the U Visa application) while addressing the socio-emotional needs of the clients (building a supportive environment that validated and deepened their understanding of their experiences). To develop the revised model, the social worker relied on multiple social group work concepts including: Kurland's pre-planning model (1978), paying particular attention to agency context issues, and stages of group development and purpose (Northen & Kurland, 2001; Kurland & Salmon, 1998, 2006). The group was conceived with a dual purpose: task (meeting the legal goals) and process (meeting participants' social-emotional needs). Purposeful use of activity/non-deliberative practice were incorporated throughout for building group cohesion, teaching skills, facilitating expression, and containing difficult emotional material (Wright. 2000; Kaplan. 2001) Creating community from the group experience (Halperin, 2001) and mutual aid were cultivated among the group's participants (Steinberg, 2004). Because of limits in the agency resources, the group was compressed and intensified and needed to accomplish more work product in a significantly shorter timeframe. This narrowed focus required the social worker to pay specific attention to the balance of process and task. And, for this participant community in the focused, intimate environment, social group work concepts needed continual reframing to address participants' traumatic stress reactions.

An important social group work planning component, the screening process for the U Visa prep group was purposely designed to dialogue with the women about expectations of group process, assess interest in participation and safety concerns, determine group readiness, and learn availability to commit to the group. Seeking to acknowledge the racial and political power imbalance between the survivors and the agency, consideration was given as to how clients might perceive the invitation to participate in the group. Clients who might feel pressured or compelled to become involved in the group or lose the opportunity for legal help were assured that they could choose to opt out at any time and for any reason and still receive legal assistance on an individual basis.

Clients were extensively screened for multiple reasons. The agency recognized that it was offering clients an outcome of very high stakes - the expectation of obtaining legal status in the US. Prior to inviting clients to engage in the long, emotionally difficult process of preparing the application, the legal services agency wanted to ensure the best conditions for the clients' success while acknowledging that there were no guarantees. The screening was used as means to share information up front so that clients could make informed decisions about the expectations of participation.

The legal services agency completed four cycles of the U Visa group. All clients remaining engaged during the group, and they are in process of waiting to hear responses to their U Visa applications. Clients consistently reported that they originally came for the legal assistance but remained committed to the group because they felt acknowledged and reflected by each other. The agency had planned its next cycle of the U Visa group when the socio-political climate forced a reconsideration of the entire project.

Change in socio-political context and impact on the group model

The impact of the 2016 Presidential election in the United States on the lives of its immigrants cannot be overestimated. The Obama administration deported high numbers of immigrants but did not reverse established rights for immigrants (Young, 2017). While none of the approximately 11 million undocumented persons was ever entirely safe from detention and deportation, many immigrants could live fairly confidently that they would not be explicitly targeted. This has changed under the Trump administration. Persistent anti-immigration rhetoric and policies incite real fears among undocumented persons.

The Trump administration issued Executive Orders specifically targeting immigrants from Islamic countries ("The Muslim Ban") as well as those from Latin America. Lack of documentation becomes equated with criminality, and the administration cultivates terror as an aggressive means of implementing what have been called racist, xenophobic, and Islamophobic policies against the immigrant community (Hureta, 2017). ICE (Immigration and Customs Enforcement) agents carry out the apprehension of thousands of immigrants for detention and deportation as part of the criminalization of the immigrant community. Reports exist of ICE agents impersonating police officers to gain entry then raid apartments and places of work (Rein, Hauslohner & Somashekhar, 2017; Cornish, 2017). The level of crisis, anxiety, and fear in the immigrant community has risen exponentially. Anecdotal reports from social workers and immigration advocates describe clients afraid to leave their homes to go to work or take children to school. Rumors pass through immigrant communities about actual and alleged ICE sightings. Families, including IPV survivors, become preoccupied with the possibility that undocumented parents would be separated by detention or deportation from U.S. born children.

Countless examples circulate that confirmed that the relative stability of immigrant life was being systematically dismantled. Immigrants who previously benefited from some element of protection have been detained. Once possible avenues of protection from their abusers for immigrant survivors of IPV, criminal and family courts now serve as target areas for ICE patrols (Honan, 2017). When the public sphere becomes a danger, people retreat to the private. With courts representing a greater risk for IPV survivors to report their abuse, and ICE agents indistinguishable from the police tasked with protecting survivors, women stay home and stay quiet. They endure violence rather than risk detention and separation from children (Lockhart, 2017). The number of undocumented clients who seek legal immigration remedies has plummeted.

Impact of the political environment on the U Visa Prep Group:

All of these factors have had a direct impact on the capacity of the legal services agency to carry out the U Visa Prep groups. Clients regularly report fears and their significantly changed lives. Daily conversations in legal services and immigrants right organizations query about what grants clients the most protection: to file applications or not to file? Expose clients to government scrutiny, submit them to background checks and fingerprinting, or tell clients it was not worth the risk? Clients already traumatized by immigration experiences and intimate partner violence are forced back into survival mode.

Seeking to balance information coming from clients and immigration advocates, the U Visa group project has been placed on hiatus since it does not address the community's current level of crisis: what survivor will sustain commitment to an eight-week group when imminent concerns focus on possible separation from her children? The agency has shifted to provide "Know Your Rights" and family safety planning information and services to clients individually and in community meetings. The legal services agency collaborates with the pro bono services of large private law firms who recognize the need to challenge current immigration policies by contributing their services to support the immigrant community. In these pro bono clinics, attorneys quickly develop and send off individual applications with the hope of protecting clients with provisional status.

Implications for practice and conclusion

The socio-political climate continues to change rapidly, sometimes daily. As of the date of this writing, information circulates that the District Attorney's office in the borough where the agency practices is now limiting the kinds of criminal cases that they will certify for immigration purposes (personal communication with immigration advocate, 8/2017). This policy will cut short for many survivors the only avenue available for immigration remedy. Such policies warrant new advocacy and strategies to support the immigrant survivor community.

Social work with groups benefits from a sensitivity to and understanding not only of the individual needs of our clients but also the impact of socio-political environment on the client, the worker, and the organizational capacity to address those needs. It is important to ask how socio-political environments change over time and affect the particular relevance and resonance of group purpose at a given moment. Modifications in purpose and structure may be required to reflect current realities and urgent changes in group participants' lives.

The VAWA/U Visa SPC has worked in multiple contexts to raise the consciousness and awareness of the participants, address legal immigration work, and support participants through potentially retriggering recounting of traumatic experiences. The format ensures the legal case is served and the socio-emotional needs for support, giving voice, and creating solidarity are accomplished. In each version of the project immigrant survivors experience benefits from the group. Each organizational context demands that the group worker consider inherent tensions of the micro/macro divide. It is impossible to separate direct practice with immigrant women and the context that directly affects their lives from what is possible in the group. The task of the group worker looking to today's current and future political realities is to assess and adapt the group model to serving the needs of the immigrant survivor community.

In the most recent iteration of the model, it was necessary to stop the group to determine safety considerations and changes in clients' needs. The legal purpose changes but the social-emotional goals of empowerment, knowledge and support have not. These types of groups may still be useful to immigrant women, to assist them with stresses and uncertainties of the moment and to inform them of their legal rights. We have challenged ourselves to continue to adapt the model to respond to the current anti-immigrant environment and its impact on women, and we invite you to consider the same.

References

American Immigration Council. Immigration Policy Center. (2012). Violence Against Women Act (VAWA) Provides Protections for Immigrant Women and Victims of Crime. Retrieved from https://www.americanimmigrationcouncil.org/research/violence-against-women-act-vawa-provides-protections-immigrant-women-and-victims-crime

Baker, B. & Rytina, N. (2013). Estimates of the Unauthorized Immigrant Population Residing in the United States: January 2012. Population Estimates. Retrieved from https://www.dhs.gov/sites/default/files/publications/Unauthorized%20Immigrant%20Population%20Estimates%20in%20the%20US%20January%202012_0.pdf

Census Bureau. 2016. Current Population Survey. Current Population Survey. Retrieved from www.census.gov/cps/

Cornish, A. (2017). NPR: Without Warrants, Immigration Agents Often Pose As Police Officers. Retrieved from http://www.npr.org/2017/02/21/516488396/without-warrants-immigration-agents-often-pose-as-police-officers

Counts D., Brown, J. & Campbell, J. C. (Eds.) (1999). *To have and to hit: Cultural perspectives on the beating of wives.* (2nd ed.) Champaign, IL: University of Illinois Press.

Erez, E., Adelman, M. & Gregory, C. (2009). Intersections of immigration and domestic violence, *Feminist Criminology*, 4, 32-56.

Freire, P. (2000). *Pedagogy of the Oppressed.* (30th Anniversary Ed). New York, NY: Bloomsbury.

Frye V., Hosein, V., Waltermaurer, E., Blaney, S. & Wilt, S. (2005). Femicide in New York City, *Homicide Studies*, 9, 204-228.

Halperin, D. (2001). The play's the thing: how social group work and theatre transformed a group into a community. *Social Work with Groups*, Vol. 24 (2), 27-46.

Homeland Security. US Department of Justice. (2017). Immigration Data & Statistics, Retrieved from https://www.dhs.gov/immigration-statistics

Honan, K, (2017). ICE Arrests 3 at Queens Court as Judge Says They Sought Trafficking. *DNAinfo*. Retrieved from https://www.dnainfo.com/new-york/20170617/kew-gardens/queens-criminal-courthouse-ice-agents-legal-aid

Huerta, A. (2017). The 'War on immigrants': Racist policies in the Trump era, *Huffington Post.* Retrieved from http://www.huffingtonpost.com/entry/the-war-on-immigrants-racist-policies-in-the-trump_us_5980bf68e4b0d187a596909b

Kaplan, C. (2001). The purposeful use of performance in groups: a new look at the balance of task and process. *Social Work with Groups*, 24 (2), 47-67.

Kurland, R, (1978). Planning: the neglected component of group development. *Social Work with Groups*, 1(2), 173-178.

Kurland, R., & Salmon, R. (1998). *Teaching a methods course in social work with groups.* Alexandria, VA: Council on Social Work Education.

Kurland, R. & Salmon R. (2006). Purpose: a misunderstood and misused keystone of group work practice, *Social Work with Groups*, 29 (2/3), 105-120.

Laney. G.P. (2010). Violence Against Women Act: History and Federal Funding. Cornell University ILR School, Retrieved from http://digitalcommons.ilr.cornell.edu/cgi/viewcontent.cgi?article=1716&context=key_workplace

Legal Services Corporation website. (n.d.). Retrieved September 9, 2017 from https://www.lsc.gov/about-statutory-restrictions-lsc-funded-programs

Lockhart, P. R., (2017). Immigrants fear a choice between domestic violence and deportation. *Mother Jones*. Retrieved from http://www.motherjones.com/politics/2017/03/ice-dhs-immigration-domestic-violence-protections/

Messing. J.T., Amanor-Boadu, Y., Cavanaugh, C.E. & Glass, N.E. (2013). Culturally Competent Intimate Partner Violence Risk Assessment: Adapting the Danger Assessment for Immigrant Women. *Social Work Research*, 37 (3), 263–275, retrieved from https://doi.org/10.1093/swr/svt019

Miller, V. & VeneKlasen, L. (2012). Feminist Popular Education & Movement-Building. Draft Discussion Paper. JASS Just Associates. Retrieved from https://justassociates.org/sites/justassociates.org/files/feminist-popular-education-movement-building-miller-veneklasen.pdf

New York City Department of Health and Mental Hygiene. Femicide in New York City: 1995-2002. October 2004. Retrieved from http://www.ci.nyc.ny.us/html/doh/html/public/press04/pr145-1022.html

Newman, A., (2011). Bridging the justice gap: Building community by responding to individual need. *Clinical Law Review,* 17 (2), 615-680.

Northen, H. & Kurland, R. (2001), *Social Work with Groups,* (3rd ed*.).* New York, NY: Columbia University Press.

Rein, L, Hauslohner, A. & Somashekhar, S. (2017). Federal agents conduct immigration enforcement raids in at least six states, *The Washington Post.* Retrieved from https://www.washingtonpost.com/national/federal-agents-conduct-sweeping-immigration-enforcement-raids-in-at-least-6-states/2017/02/10/4b9f443a-efc8-11e6-b4ff-ac2cf509efe5_story.html?utm_term=.523171a3ea19

Sargent Shriver National Center on Poverty Law (n.d.). Community Lawyering. Retrieved August September 9, 2017, http://povertylaw.org/clearinghouse/collections/community

Steinberg, D.M. (2004). *The mutual-aid approach to working with groups: Helping people help one another,* (2nd ed.). Binghamton, NY: Haworth Press.

van der Kolk, B. (2017, March 9). Bessel van der Kolk: How trauma lodges in the body (K. Tippet, interviewer) [Transcript]. Retrieved from https://onbeing.org/programs/bessel-van-der-kolk-how-trauma-lodges-in-the-body-mar2017/

U.S. Congress. (1993). Title IV, sec. 40001-40703 of the Violent Crime Control and Law Enforcement Act, H.R. 3355. Retrieved from https://www.congress.gov/bill/103rd-congress/house-bill/3355/text

U.S. Congress. (2000). H.R.357 - Violence Against Women Act of 1999.

Retrieved from https://www.congress.gov/bill/106th-congress/house-bill/357

Wright, W. (2000). The use of purpose in on-going activity groups: A framework for maximizing the therapeutic impact. *Social Work with Groups*, 22(2/3), 31–54.

Young, E., 2017. The hard truth about Obama's deportation priorities, *The Huffington Post*. Retrieved from http://www.huffingtonpost.com/entry/hard-truths-about-obamas-deportation-priorities_us_58b3c9e7e4b0658fc20f979e

Zong, J., & Batalova, J. (2017). Frequently Requested Statistics on Immigrants and Immigration in the Uniterd States. Migration Policy Institute. Retrieved from http://www.migrationpolicy.org/article/frequently-requested-statistics-immigrants-and-immigration-united-states#Demographic

"Putting it out on the table:"

Exploring the impact of difference in group work through the experience of a male group worker in an all-female member group

Kyle T. Ganson

Introduction

Groups are formed around individuals coming together based on commonalities with the intention of fulfilling a group purpose. These commonalities, for example members who all suffer from depression or have experienced a death loss, are often manifest to all members and workers, and the discussion of these commonalities are a major component of the group's interactions. While exploring the commonalities between members promotes cohesion and fosters mutual aid, differences between members may remain latent and unexplored.

Group composition, a fundamental component to the formation of a group, "refers to the number and characteristics of both members and workers who will participate in the group" (Malekoff, 2014, pg. 78). These characteristics include, but are not limited to, sex, gender, ethnicity, race, religion, and socioeconomic status, all of which will equally unify and divide group members. In considering these characteristics, Northen (1988) stated that workers want the group member base to be "homogeneous in enough ways to ensure their stability" and "heterogeneous enough in ways to ensure their vitality" (as cited in Malekoff, 2014, p. 78). A group that is too homogenous may become stagnant and a group that is too heterogeneous may lack cohesion. This balance between homogeneity and heterogeneity is sought when forming a group, however differences between members can have great importance in the group process. Steinberg (2014) states that differences between group members allows the group to remain stimulating and ever-changing.

Group discussions on the commonalities between members will be inherent in each session. A primary function of the group worker is to facilitate discussions that link member commonalities, thus promoting connection, collaborative problem solving, mutual support, and the overall process of mutual aid (Steinberg, 2014). It is equally as important for the group worker to facilitate discussions around member's differences. Often, member differences are equivalent to taboos that keep them isolated in their social environment. Taboos are sensitive and often stigmatized topics that are uncomfortable to talk about and avoided in greater society (Rubin, 2011). The group is a micro-society (Steinberg, 2014), with its own culture (Shulman, 2003), where the discussion of differences will aid in the process of reducing these stigmatized taboos members experience in their lives outside of the group. It is the group worker who is responsible for addressing the group culture, as well as the taboos, in order to help the culture of the group shift and change throughout the process of group development (Shulman, 2003). Additionally, it is vital for the group worker to reflect on his own personal and professional fears and understandings of taboos in order to then help the group address these same issues (Shulman, 2003).

When discussing differences, members and group workers must strive to leave their biases and judgements out of the group and learn to understand differences in people they may be unfamiliar with (Fluhr, 2004). Group workers must be self-aware and understand they may avoid discussing a certain difference due to their own countertransference. However, it is ultimately the worker's responsibility to raise the topic for discussion (Rubin, 2011). After the discussion of differences within the group, workers should return to the group purpose to reinforce why members are part of the group and the unified goal all members share.

Even lesser explored in groups is the differences between members and workers. Inevitably, group workers have influence on the group process, and each group member individually. The interactional model supports this notion, stating that "both client and practitioner are affecting and being affected by each other almost moment by moment" (Shulman, 2009, p. 5). Similarly, mutuality, defined as "the therapist's participation in the process and the extent to which it is acknowledged that influence moves in both directions – from group leader to group members and vice versa" (Dean, 1998, p. 34), encourages the process of "acknowledging" the connection between the workers and members as an intervention. By acknowledging the differences between group workers and members, workers are aiding the process of decentralizing authority and supporting the creation of a member-led group (Steinberg, 2014). It also shows group members that the worker is invested, present, and has a shared desire for the group to succeed.

Group work practice example

With the theoretical framework of the interactional model and mutuality, I noticed the obvious gender difference between myself, as a male group worker, and the all-female member group I was working with. Our gender difference was a latent issue in the group, and while the group's purpose was not focused on addressing this issue, it was important that our gender difference was acknowledged and discussed. If not addressed, our gender difference may have impacted group safety, group development, and stalled the fulfillment of the group purpose.

Individuals define their gender equally due to biology, culture, and social influences (Lippa, 2005). Because gender is in part socially constructed, the group members bring their own "explicit and implicit gender experiences, biases, anxieties, and beliefs into their relationships" (Bunnell, 2016, p. 2). The gender differences within the group began to become more apparent to both myself, the members, and my colleagues both in the group and in the milieu of the program. For example, members would share that they would prefer to talk about personal topics with a female clinician or staff would joke that I was the token male in the program or families of members would be surprised to see a male worker in the room during family groups. All of these moments led to the realization that it was vital that I began a discussion for group members to share about their experience being in an all-female group with a male group worker. Additionally, I came to an awareness of how our descriptive difference, my male gender and the socialized, structural, and unjust power differentials men have over women in various aspects of life, may have been impacting the group members (Northen & Kurland, 2001). This awareness and consideration to the cultural understanding of differences, gender in this case, from both the worker and member's perspectives, is essential for group work (Northen & Kurland, 2001) and I felt it was imperative the topic be put on the table for discussion.

The setting of the group was a residential treatment program for women with eating disorders, including anorexia nervosa, bulimia nervosa, and binge-eating disorder, where I was the only male clinician on staff. The group was a mix between a support group and a therapy group, thus the purpose was to connect members with each other and to create an environment of open discussion that fostered support as the members worked towards recovery and their therapeutic goals.

Topics often included addressing symptoms related to their eating, body image distress, depressive symptoms, substance use, family difficulties, and interpersonal relationships, among others. At times, the nature of these topics, including interpersonal relationships and body image distress, often led to a moment where members would apologize to me for being in the room when talking about "female" topics or questioned whether I was able to fully understand their feminine body image concerns. These moments furthered my realization that putting the topic of our gender difference on the table for discussion was needed for the group.

The responses summarized below were gathered from two distinct cohorts of clients, all self-identified as female, during discussions about our gender differences. Most of the group members reported previously having negative experiences with men in their lives. This included sexual assault and/or abusive and unhealthy familial and romantic relationships. Group members ranged from 16 years old to 40 years old, were from varying levels of socioeconomic status, and resided both locally to the treatment program and from across the United States. During the discussions, I was the only group worker facilitating the group. The responses are separated into dominant themes that arose and all names have been changed to pseudonyms for confidentiality purposes.

Themes & responses

Learning/corrective experience

Several group members reported having a male group worker helped them relearn how to interact with men without feeling judged or judging them. Multiple group members thought it was helpful to have a male at the facility to have a positive experience with a trusting male, as oppose to the previous males in their lives who were assaultive, abusive, and inconsistent. One group member, Lauren, reported she grew up with only her mother and sister. She shared that she felt more familiar with women, however realized through her experience working with me, that men are not as intimidating as she initially thought. She also reported realizing that she can have deeper and more meaningful relationship with men.

Desire for more males

Overwhelmingly, the group members agreed there should be more male staff members to mimic the world outside of treatment. They shared that this would help them feel more comfortable with men in their daily lives. Jennifer reported feeling more comfortable with males due to the composition of her friend group. She also reported that she wished there was a male mental health worker to help and be present in the milieu.

Non-judgmental stance

Many of the group members agreed that I had a more non-judgmental stance compared to the female clinical staff members. They reported an understanding that the female therapists don't judge them, however they inherently compared themselves to the other females, which led to feeling that they are "lesser than." Group members reported feeling that they don't need to, and can't, compare themselves to me as a male. Similarly, Elizabeth reported that she doesn't feel she can be as honest with the female therapists. She reported she can't talk about her substance use because she believes that they judge her.

My experience

Lauren asked what it was like for me to be with all women and work in an all-female environment. I shared that I felt comfortable with the environment and the gender differences, and I was excited about the many ways I could help them. Kiley and Kristine asked whether it was "weird" for me being the only male. I shared that it didn't feel weird due to my desire to work with them. I shared that I had an interest in working with people experiencing eating disorders and gender is only one aspect of the work.

Miscellaneous

Kiley and Kristine didn't even think of the difference between our genders until I prompted the discussion. Alanna reported that the all-female environment felt empowering to her. Alanna also reported she was more worried about age differences than gender. A few of the members agreed and wondered whether they felt more comfortable and could relate more to me based on my apparent age, though group members did not know my actual age. Many of the group members believed that several of the issues they struggle with, including body image, are universal and men experience them also, so they felt it was normal to talk about these issues with me.

Discussion

Group workers must be aware of the impact differences may have on group dynamics and individual group members (Toseland, Jones, & Gellis, 2004). Putting the differences "out on the table" for discussion in a group is significantly important, as it allows a necessary, and often rich, discussion to occur. Based on the responses from group members in this group work practice example, it is evident that members had a positive, and at times corrective, experience due to our gender differences. Importantly, the discussions about our gender differences were particularly fruitful. These conversations led to larger dialogues about romantic and family relationships, friendship, boundaries, assertiveness, harm avoidance, social anxiety, and sex and intimacy. Additionally, many members were thankful for the discussions and I often sensed relief, through verbal affirmation and body language, that the topic was presented and the "elephant in the room" was discussed.

Analyzing this group work practice example from a theoretical perspective, putting the differences out on the table for discussion decentralized authority in the group and moved power and ownership of the group to the members. As the worker, I had an influence on the group and the group members, thus aligning with both the interactional model, as well as mutuality, both emphasizing the ways members and workers influence one another. Bringing the differences up for discussion focuses the group's attention on the present moment and the process of the group, which can help members develop insight into themselves and others (Thomas & Caplan, 1999). While both group cohorts had established safety within the group, the discussions about our differences further developed the relationships between members and myself, both in group and in the milieu, and propelled the group into a strong state of intimacy (Garland, Jones, & Kolodny, 1973). Following these discussions, risk taking and self-disclosure were readily seen by group members, as well as an overall increase in mutual aid and a decrease in conflict and avoidance.

In the discussions of our gender differences, my role as the worker was to float between taking more responsibility and authority in the group by raising the topic and maintaining safety, and stepping down from this role and joining the members in their discussion and exploration of the topic. This was exhibited in member's interest, and the discussion of, my experience as the only male in the group. It was imperative that I was self-aware of my own influence on the group members and the group process and purposefully self-disclose my experience. My self-disclosure also modeled effective self-reflecting and self-referencing (Steinberg, 2014).

Implications for practice

The responses from these discussions, I hope, will inspire further exploration on the impact of worker/member differences and commonalities in groups, as well as encourage males to not only enter the field of social work, but work with female clients. Group workers should use their response to the group process to assess whether there are differences that remain latent in the group and decide whether the group would benefit from bringing this latent content forward. If the group would benefit from this discussion, and relationships and safety have been created (Kurland, 2002), it is recommended that group workers address the differences by skillfully and subtly putting the topic "out on the table" for the group to discuss. Group workers can use introductory statements such as, "I've noticed *example difference* in this group. What are your thoughts about this?" or "How does it feel that there is *example difference* within this group?" These statements present the differences in a non-judgement manner, as well as present them without the assumption that group members will have a specific emotion, thought, or opinion about them. They simply allow group members to notice the differences and discuss them however they feel is necessary. However, having the discussion about differences should be avoided if it is strictly out of obligation or because of the workers own discomfort (Kurland, 2002).

Inherently, differences will be present, as no group is completely homogenous. Exploring differences will help the group become more cohesive and learn about each other. The group worker should be aware of roles and dynamics between the group members to maintain safety within the group and be sure that differences are discussed on a group-based level and not a member-based level. Since the group worker is part of the group, self-disclosure may be necessary. Worker self-disclosure should be carefully considered as not to share unnecessary or inappropriate information. Each group worker must assess what they self-disclose based on the group composition, population, setting, agency protocol, and stage of group development, among other personal factors (Northen & Kurland, 2001).

Limitations & conclusion

There are limitations to this paper. It should be noted that this group work practice example occurred in a residential treatment setting where group members resided together. Thus, members spent a significant amount of time together outside of the formal group setting. Additionally, as the group worker, I was also a clinician at the program and had regular interactions with members, including individual sessions with my caseload, time in the milieu, and during periodic meal and snack times. This increased their trust and safety with me and likely fostered member's ability to be open and honest when discussing our gender difference. However, there is a chance that the group members withheld information or were not honest with the group during these discussions. Thus, the validity of these responses cannot be measured nor is it the intention of this paper to do so. While it remains important to address differences in groups across settings, outcomes will likely vary due to levels of safety, threats to confidentiality, and member profiles within the group.

Should I have had the opportunity to go through this process all over again, there are multiple aspects I would change. First, I would have addressed our gender differences sooner in the group process. I would have built it into the beginning phases of the group to assess how the members felt and thought about the differences. This would have assisted me in understanding the level of safety in the group and whether or not a remedy needed to occur. Second, I would have had a female co-facilitator in the groups when these discussions were taking place in hopes of neutralizing myself as the only clinician and male with power, both within the program and culturally, in the room. Finally, I would have allowed the topic of gender difference to be a regular and naturally occurring topic that didn't need to be "put on the table" intentionally. This likely would have allowed for a more open, honest, and fluid conversations between members and myself. It also likely would have normalized the taboo.

In sum, discussing differences in groups is an important component of effective group work. Addressing the differences is likely to increase cohesion, foster mutual aid, and decentralize authority, as well as further group development and the fulfillment of the group purpose. Group workers should be mindful of the differences in their groups and be confident to "put them on out on the table" for discussion.

References

Bunnell, D. (2016). Gender socialization, countertransference and the treatment of men with eating disorders. *Clinical Social Work Journal, 44*(1), 99-104.

Dean, R.G. (1998). A narrative approach to groups. *Clinical Social Work Journal, 26*(1), 23-37.

Fluhr, T. (2008). Transcending differences: Using concrete subject-matter in heterogeneous groups. *Social Work with Groups, 27*(2-3), 35-54.

Garland, J., Jones, H., & Kolodny, R. (1973). A model for stages of development in social work groups. In S. Bernstein (Ed.), *Explorations in group work* (pp. 17-71). Boston: Milford House.

Kurland, R. (2002). Racial difference and human commonality: The worker-client relationship. *Social Work with Groups, 25*(2-3), 113-118.

Lippa (2005). *Gender, nature, and nurture* (2nd ed.). New Jersey: Lawrence Erlbaum Associates.

Malekoff, A. (2004). *Group work with adolescents: Principles and practice* (2nd ed.). New York, NY: The Guilford Press.

Northen, H. (1988). *Social work with groups.* New York: Columbia University

Press.

Northen, H. & Kurland, R. (2001). *Social work with groups* (3rd ed.). New York, NY: Columbia University Press.

Rubin, S. (2011). Tackling taboo topics: Case studies in group work. *Social Work with Groups, 34*(3-4), 257-269.

Shulman, L. (2011). *The skills of helping individuals, families, groups, and communities.* (7th ed.). Belmont, CA: Brooks/Cole, Cengage Learning.

Shulman, L. (2003). Learning to talk about taboo subjects: A lifelong professional challenge. *Social Work with Groups, 25*(1-2), 139–150.

Steinberg, D.M. (2014). *A mutual-aid model for social work with groups.* (3rd ed.). New York, NY: Routledge.

Thomas, H. & Caplan, T. (1999). Spinning the group process wheel: Effective facilitation techniques for motivating involuntary client groups

Toseland, R. W., Jones, L. V., & Gellis, Z. D. (2004). Group dynamics. In Garvin, C. D., Gutiérrez, L. M., & Galinsky M. J. (Eds.) *Handbook of social work with groups* (13-31). New York, NY: The Guilford Press.

Who cares for the caregivers of the elderly?

Strength-based groups and diversity considerations

Thelma Silver and Linda McArdle

Introduction

This paper examines the needs of elders who want to age in their own home ('in place'), the stressors on both the caregivers and care recipients, and the need for social support through strengths-based group intervention. The factors that impact on caregiver stress are examined in regards to the available research. Moreover, the research on best practices for caregiver group support is also examined with specific focus on the needs of diverse populations and a multifamily psychoeducational group intervention is suggested.

Case scenario

Lisa is a 55-year-old African-American divorced female, who is the caregiver of her aging mother, Rae, who is 73 years old and has heart disease. Lisa never had a good relationship with her mother during her child and adult life. She became the caregiver after her father passed away, although Lisa herself is coping with diabetes and high blood pressure. Lisa's other siblings live out of state. She loves her mother, but is experiencing burnout and stress from caring for her mother who wants to remain in her own home.

Both in the United States and globally, the elder population is increasing at unprecedented rates (Barusch, 2015; United Nations, 2010; US Census Bureau, 2010). The per cent of the population who are 65 years of age or older in the United States is expected to increase from 10.6% of the population in 1975 to 18.2% by 2025. The elderly population is increasing almost twice as fast as the rest of the population in the United States due to many reasons, one of which is the demographic of the Baby Boomer population, those individuals born between 1946 and 1964. This elder population, both globally and in the United States is becoming more diverse in many ways, including ethnically, economically, and in terms of their physical and emotional well-being.

Some seniors are active and want to contribute to their communities and families, while others have serious health care needs that require attention (Barusch; United Nations, 2010; US Census Bureau, 2010). Thus, seniors may provide assistance, support, and care to others as caregivers, but some seniors require the services and help of others as care recipients, as in the case scenario where Lisa has become a caregiver for her mother, Rae.

In regards to their housing situation, 95% of Americans 75 years and older say they want to stay in their homes indefinitely; they want to age 'in place'. However, over one third live with some sort of disability, thus often needing some type of assistance (California Health Care Foundation, 2012). Most times this requires the intervention of the family to provide either instrumental or material support, such as transportation, banking and help with self-care, or emotional support to cope with various changes in the lives of the senior members; thus, family members become caregivers of their elderly family members.

As seniors begin to have concerns about their healthcare needs or other needs for which they require assistance, they may begin to have many worries or stressors in their lives (Ashford, LeCroy & Lortie, 2016). Some of these concerns relate to: access to information about their health; freedom to request help from others in making healthcare decisions; considerations about the location and manner of where they want to live; communicating their wishes prior to the onset of a terminal illness, including naming an agent to speak for them. Elders may also have concerns about burdening their friends and families, and become more withdrawn and isolated.

Social isolation is another serious issue for people over the age of 65 and their families who want to keep them involved (Hooyman & Kiyak, 2002). When people retire from their jobs around the age of

65, especially for males, they lose one of their major connections with other people. Loneliness has a negative effect on physical and mental health. Feelings of loneliness increase the risk for cognitive decline and dementia. Feelings of loneliness can also lead to unhealthy behaviors: poor diet, lack of physical activity, smoking, and lack of interest in contact with peers. One of the major risk factors for social isolation for elders is the loss of a spouse or partner which can cause depression, which could be a risk for Rae in the case example above.

Social isolation also leads to higher rates of elder abuse (Wolf, 2000). According to the National Council on Aging (n.d.), one in 10 people over the age of 60 years experiences abuse at some time in their life.

As stated above, most elders want to age in place, like Rae does in the opening example. In fact, 70% of elders live in their community; a majority are being helped by informal family caregivers, with most of these caregivers being spouses or adult children (Lopez-Hartmann et al, 2012). As seniors begin to have more needs that have to be met by others, family caregivers often take on these tasks which can exact a toll on the caregivers, as we see in the example of Lisa.

Caregiving of the older person can impact on the family caregivers financially, as they may need to decrease their work duties or leave their work situations (Lopez-Hartmann et al., 2012); for example, a social worker had to leave her position to care for her own parent full time as the parent had terminal illness and did not have any other resources to help her. Caregiving can also impact on the individual's physical health through sleeplessness, fatigue and somatic complaints. The caregiver's mental health can be impacted through depression, anxiety, worry and social isolation (Lopez-Hartmann et al., 2012.

Stress and coping theory

One of the theories that addresses caregiver stress is Lazarus & Folkman's (1984) stress and coping theory. This theory was applied to caregivers by Haley, Levine, Brown, & Bartolucci (1987) whose research demonstrated that stress can be mediated by coping methods and support. Stress and coping models have identified various variables that impact on the caregivers' coping ability and methods: demographic factors such as age, gender, relationship to the recipient; care recipient's needs, functioning ability and behavior; caregivers' appraisal of stress, caregivers' social support and coping styles; caregivers' psychological and physical state (Haley et al. 1987). These factors which have to be considered when designing interventions, as we will address below.

Lin & Wu (2014) have noted that caregivers use different sets of coping strategies. One class can be labeled emotion-focused coping, where the caregiver focuses on decreasing the stress or negative feelings associated with the problem. Examples of this are talking with friends or relatives, reading, engaging in meditation or prayer, and engaging in exercise. Another class of strategy is grouped as problem-focused, where caregivers direct efforts to alleviate the problem causing the distress, such as obtaining assistive devices, and personal or nursing care for the care recipient. This category includes caregiver support services.

These same researchers found that it was rare that caregivers used only problem focused coping (Lin & Wu, 2014). Instead, most caregivers use either emotion-coping or a combination of both problem-coping and emotion-coping, which they categorized as hybrid-coping. There was a third group of caregivers who used few coping strategies, classified as unpatternedcoping. This last group also reported having fewer stressors than the other two groups even with little support from friends or relatives. In contrast, the hybrid-coping groups had the most stressors, engaged in much conflict with other family members, and had the most difficulties caring for their senior family members.

Lin & Wu's (2014) research demonstrates that family caregivers have different ways of coping with their caregiving situation and have different needs for support. Those caregivers with few difficulties and stressors (unpatterned-coping) need little outside support, whereas those who have many difficulties and stressors require much assistance. These caregivers use both emotion-coping and problem-coping, but these strategies often are not sufficient. These caregivers are the ones that need to be targeted for intervention. The research has also demonstrated that they are usually the adult children of the care recipients.

Other factors that can impact on stress and coping of caregivers are socio-cultural differences, such as ethnicity and nationality (Knight, Silverstein, McCallum & Fox, 2000). These sociocultural factors impact on the variables outlined by Haley et al (1987), and will be discussed below.

Diversity

Ethnic differences can impact on the caregiver's appraisal of caregiving as stressful, which then has an impact on the person's coping skills. (Knight, Silverstein, McCollum & Fox, 2000). African-American caregivers have lower appraisal of caregiving as burdensome (Pinquart & Sorensen, 2003), as caregiving is seen as a normative process. However, this can be counterbalanced by the use of emotion-focused coping (emotional control, self-blame) by African-American caregivers, thus increasing their emotional distress. Therefore, intervention with this population needs to focus on alleviating this distress. One study reported that when African-American daughters who were caregivers of elderly parents attended support groups, they had increased family involvement and increased positive coping (Jones-Cannon & Davis, 2005). Support groups can be helpful for African-American caregivers, such as Lisa in the case example.

Regarding diversity, some studies on caregiving that have focused on ethnicity have reported mixed findings regarding stress and coping methods in different ethnic populations. However, in most of the studies, the ethnic diversity was mainly AfricanAmerican (Janovic & Connell, in Chun, Knight, & Youn, 2001). When considering the needs of caregivers, a meta-analysis of ethnic minority groups in the United States produced the results that intervention needs vary among ethnic groups of caregivers (Pinquart & Sorensen, 2003); Asian-American caregivers tend to use less formal support, with language barriers speculated as a possible cause. Thus, language needs to be a consideration in providing intervention or support.

When examining caregivers in the East Asian population, one is focusing on a population with different traditions and values (Chun, Knight, & Youn, 2007) than those of Western societies. In East Asian culture there are strong values based on Confucian thoughts of filial piety and respect for the elderly. Moreover, East Asian societies have more of a community or collectivist orientation that differs from the emphasis on individualism which is strong in Western culture, especially in the United States. (Chun et al. 2007)

In a review of a research study on the East Asian population of Korean-American caregivers, one sees the importance of family values and filial piety. In the Chun et al. (2007) study, three different population groups of caregivers of elderly persons with dementia were compared, with regard to stress and caregiving processes. These were

Koreans residing in Korea, Korean-Americans and White-Americans. One common finding was that the care recipients' disruptive behavior had an impact on caregiver stress or burden, which in turn led to caregiver anxiety or depression. However, there were differences in the types of support that were important to the three groups, with the Korean caregivers wanting instrumental support and the Korean-American caregivers seeking emotional support. These outcomes are important to consider when designing support interventions for these populations; groups interventions for Koreans in Korea need to emphasize information and resources, whereas Korean-Americans may need groups that focus on emotional support.

Interventions for caregivers

As we have stated, most older adults desire the option of 'aging in place' which means staying in their own homes, and remaining involved in their own care. Supportive care to assist aging in place is expensive, so this often requires family members to step in, either directly to provide care or indirectly through the supervision of home healthcare. However, this family caregiver role can lead to higher levels of stress and tension which can affect the caregivers' physical and mental health (Lopez-Hartmann et al., 2012). Both caregivers and care recipients are at risk of isolation and its effects, and thus are both in need of support.

Intervention and research regarding caregivers for the elderly have largely focused on three types of support for the family caregiver: respite; information and technology; and psychosocial support – whether it is individual, family or group (Lopez-Hartmann et al., 2012). Social workers are the major providers of psychosocial support. Thus, the emphasis on aging in place challenges social workers to develop new models of support for elders who want to be part of the decision-making for their own care, and the care of their family. Sorensen and colleagues (2002) conducted a meta-analysis of 78 caregiver intervention studies. There were six types of interventions that were included in the meta-analysis: psychoeducation; supportive interventions; psychotherapy; respite/daycare; care receiver training; and multi-component intervention. Individual and group interventions were included and the results were positive for most interventions, leading generally to a decrease in caregiver depression, a decrease in caregiver burden, an increase in well-being, and an increase in ability or knowledge.

However, findings also indicated that group interventions were less effective at decreasing caregiver burden than individual or mixed interventions that included a combination of both group and individual programs . Sorensen et al. (2002) suggested that group interventions are effective ways to build support networks. Moreover, to improve caregiver affect and alleviate care receiver symptoms, then a combination of both individual and group interventions should be considered. In regards to group support, there were four major types of groups: education or training; support; social recreational; and psychoeducational.

Psychoeducational groups had the most consistent positive results. They are a structured group program to provide information on care recipients' illness, information on resources, and information and training on recipients' behavior and illness problems. This includes group discussions and written information. The goal of psychoeducational groups for caregivers is to help them with problems coping with stressful caregiving situations (McCallion & Toseland, 1995). Psychoeducational groups have been used with various types of caregivers, including those caring for persons with a serious mental illness (Lyman et al., 2014) and persons with cancer (Weis, 2003). In the field of mental illness some psychoeducational groups have included people with mental illness and their families together. These multifamily psychoeducation groups for families with mental illness have been used and studied for three decades.

In some models of multi-family groups for caregivers of persons with mental illness, the family members receive information, support and skill-building. In one model by Leff et al., (1982) families received education about the specific mental illness, and then participated in a multifamily group that included the family members with mental illness as well as the caregivers. In these groups, the members receive support from others in similar situations. A third component of this model was the availability of individual family sessions for those who needed them. Hence, this model provided support for family caregivers and for the person with mental illness, and was also flexible to provide educational support and individual support.

These multifamily psychoeducational groups for mental illness have been evaluated to have improved the problem-solving ability of the family caregivers and to have reduced their stress or burden (Lyman et al. 2014), and thus have proved to be effective interventions for support of persons and families coping with mental illness and for support for persons with cancer and their families (Weis, 2003). This type of group may, therefore, be helpful for older adults and their caregivers, especially for those who want to age in place.

The Latino population group has a high percentage of elders living with family. Latinos also have a greater longevity than whites and are the fastest-growing population among racial-ethnic population groups. To attend to the needs of this Latino population, Gonyea et al., (2016) conducted a culturally sensitive cognitive behavioral group intervention for caregivers of persons with Alzheimer's disease. This cognitive-behavioral group (CBT) was researched in a randomized controlled trial design and compared to a psychoeducational group (PED). Both groups were conducted for five weeks with 90 minute weekly sessions. Groups were interactive and didactic, and conducted in Spanish by culturally sensitive social workers.

The CBT group spent much time on teaching caregivers the specific skills of the CBT model, but also was attentive to specific needs of individual participants (Gonyea et al., 2016). The PED group focused on educating the caregivers about illness progression, community resources and caregiver strategies. Both groups had telephone coaching at three, six, nine, and twelve weeks post-group. Two thirds of the group members were female. Over one half of the participants in the groups were adult children and about one quarter were spouses. (Gonyea et al.,p. 297).

Results indicated that over the five weeks of intervention and three-month follow-up, the members of the CBT group experienced some improvement in self-efficacy and depression with the PED participants demonstrating little change over the six months (Gonyea et al., 2016). This was a small sample size and lacked a 'no treatment' group, but the results indicated the positive impact of the CBT group approach for caregivers. However, this group approach was also sufficiently flexible to consider the needs of individual caregivers. This flexibility is needed when intervening with different cultural groups. McCall and Toseland (1995) state that psychoeducation groups can be adapted to different theoretical approaches, and problem-solving has been demonstrated to be an effective approach for this type of group. Psychoeducation groups for older adults and their caregivers could use a CBT approach since this proved to be effective for a Latino population.

Discussion

In considering the needs of Lisa and Rae in the opening case example, we would suggest a multifamily psychoeducational group that provides both problem-solving and emotional support for Rae and Lisa. This model provides the flexibility to adjust to their needs and the needs of the other group members. This kind of group intervention is strengths-based; however, it is new to this field of seniors and caregiving, and thus requires evaluative research.

Values, beliefs and traditions all impact on how aging, health and illness are experienced and perceived by the elderly (Gonyea *et al.*, 2016). These factors need to be addressed in order to design group interventions that relate to the needs of different cultural groups. To achieve this more effectively, research is needed on group interventions with seniors of different cultural groups, with a particular focus on research on multifamily psychoeducational groups.

References

Ashford, J. B., LeCroy, C. W., & Lortie, K. L. (2006). *Human behavior in the social environment: A multidimensional perspective* (3rd ed.). Belmont, CA: Thompson.

Barusch, A. S. (2015). *Foundations of social policy: Social justice in human perspective.* (5th ed.) Stamford, CT: Centage.

California Health Care Foundation (2009). *There's no place like home: Models of supportive communities for elders.* www.chcf.org

Chun, M., Knight, B. C. & Yuan, G. (2007). Differences in stress and coping models of emotional distress among Korean, Korean-American and White American caregivers. *Aging in Mental Health, 11* (1), 20-29.

Gonyea, J. G., Lopez, L. M., & Velasquez, E. H. (2016). The effectiveness of a culturally sensitive cognitive behavioral group intervention for Latino Alzheimer's caregivers. *The Gerontologist, 56* (2), 292-302.

Haley, W. E., Levine, E. G., Brown, S. H., & Bartolucci, A. A. (1987). Stress, appraisal, coping and social support as predictors of adaptational outcome among dementia caregivers. *Psychology and Aging, 2,* 323-330.

Hooyman, N.R., & Kiyak, H. A. (2002). *Social gerontology: A multidisciplinary approach.* Boston, MA: Allyn & Bacon.

Jones-Cannon, S., & Davis, B. L. (2005). Coping among African-American daughters caring for aged parents. *The ABNF Journal 16*, 118-123

Knight, B. G., Silverstein, M., McCullum, T. J., & Fox, L. S. (2000). A socio-cultural stress and coping model for mental health outcomes among African-American caregivers in Southern California. *The Journal of Gerontology. 55*(37), 142-150.

Lazarus, R. S. & Folkman, S. (1984). *Stress, appraisal, and coping.* New York: Springer.

Leff, J., Kuipers, L., Berkowitz, R., & Eberline-Vries. (1982) A controlled trial of social intervention in the families of schizophrenic patients. *The British Journal of Psychiatry, 141* (2), 121-134.

Lin, I-F., & Wu, H-S, (2014). Patterns of coping among family caregivers of frail older adults. *Research on Aging, 36*(5) 603-624,

Lopez,-Hartmann, M., Wens, J., Verhoeven, V., Remmen, R (2012. The effect of caregiver support interventions for informal caregivers of community-dwelling frail elderly: A systematic review. *International Journal of Integrated Care. 12*, 1-15.

Lyman, D. R., Braude, L., George, P., Dougherty, R. H., Daniels, A. S., Ghose, S. S., & Delphin-Rittman, M. E. (2014). Consumer and family psycho-education. Assessing the evidence. *Psychiatry-online* http://dx.doi.org /10.1176/appl. ps.201300266.

McCallion, P. & Toseland, R. W. (1995). Supportive group interventions with caregivers of frail older adults. *Social Work with Groups, 18* (1), 11-25.

National Council on Aging www.ncoa.org/public-policy-action/elder

Pinquart, M. & Sorensen, S. (2005). Ethnic differences in stressors, resources and psychological outcomes of family caregiving: A meta-analysis. *The Gerontologist, 45* (1), 90-106.

Pinquart, M. & Sorensen, S. (2003). Differences between caregivers and non-caregivers in psychological health and physical health: A meta-analysis. *Psychology and Aging, 18*, 250-267.

Sorensen, S., Pinquart, M. & Duberstein, P. (2002). How effective are interventions with caregivers? An updated meta-analysis. *The Gerontologist, 42* (3), 356-372

United Nations. (2010). *Rethinking poverty: Report on the world social situation.* Retrieved from http://www.un.org/esa/socdev/rwss/docs/2110

U.S. Census Bureau (2010). *The next four decades: The older population in the United States: 2010-2050.* Retrieved from http://www.census.gov/ prod/2010pubs/p 25-1138.pdf

Weis, J. (2003). Support groups for cancer patients. *Supportive Care in Cancer, 11*(12), 763-768.

Wolf, R. S. (2000). The nature and scope of elder abuse. *Generations, 24*(11) 6-12.

Practicing gratitude:
Reflections on a community-based group in a supportive housing setting

Patricia Ki and Adina Muskat

Introduction

This paper describes a short-term, community-based group for women living in a supportive housing setting, offered through the Supportive Housing Program at the Jean Tweed Centre in Toronto, Ontario. The group, titled 'Practicing Gratitude,' focuses on the concept of gratitude and incorporates art and body-based components such as short walks in the community, mindfulness exercises, photography, drawing/painting, and collage-making. The following paper will discuss the context within which the group program was situated. Particularly, it will explore how the group demonstrated the use of creative strategies in responding to the needs and challenges of the specific setting and context, and supporting the participants to attend to the changes and challenges in their lives. It will also review relevant literature that informed the design and facilitation of the group, and reflect on the learning, challenges, and participant feedback from the group.

Setting and context

The Jean Tweed Centre (JTC) is a non-profit agency funded by the Ministry of Health and Long Term Care in Ontario to provide services to women and their families across the province who are experiencing challenges related to mental health, substance use and/or gambling. The Centre offers a range of services including supportive housing, day and residential programming, out-patient and outreach counselling, trauma counselling, and family support.

The JTC Supportive Housing Program operates in partnership with a women's organization that offers permanent supportive and subsidized housing units to individuals who identify as women and women-led families in downtown Toronto. A portion of the units are designated for women of Indigenous descent. Working from a trauma-informed approach, which is a way of practice that is informed by the complexity and multifaceted impacts of trauma, as well as a harm reduction, women-centred, and anti-oppressive framework, the JTC Supportive Housing Program offers on-site brief/drop-in and long term counselling, crisis intervention, service coordination, and group programming to tenants living with mental health and/or substance use issues. Some women also had involvement in the criminal justice system.

Over time, tenants in the housing program develop complex relationships and dynamics with each other. Tenants often express a desire to build positive, mutually supportive relationships with other women in the building; however, conflicts can develop over time regarding a variety of issues. Women have discussed obstacles in building positive relationships with other tenants due to difficulties they experience related to their mental health challenges and substance use, including maintaining emotional regulation and healthy boundaries. Through conversations with staff about their experiences in groups, tenants have shared they sometimes hesitate to participate in community engagement or group programming due to the discomfort of sharing confidential matters with their neighbours, and the concern that comments from groups would be shared throughout the building. Since many services and programming are offered onsite, a goal of the Practicing Gratitude group was to support tenants in connecting with resources outside of the building and expanding their support network.

Purpose and intentions

The development of the Practicing Gratitude group was shaped both by the context in which the supportive housing program was situated and participant feedback over time about the needs and concerns of the community. The design and facilitation of the group were further informed by relevant literature, as reviewed in the next section. The intentions of the group were set out as follows:

• To create opportunities for practicing gratitude in the context of the supportive housing community, and invite tenants to cultivate or consider alternative narratives or perspectives that support their well-being.

* To facilitate an activity-based group (rather than therapy/ processing) in consideration of the complexity of tenant relations and dynamics.
* To encourage creative self-expression through photography and other art-making activities.
* To create space for positive interactions and mutual support amongst participants through specific themes, guided activities and sharing.
* To use photography and art-making as a way for participants to give voice to what they value in their community.
* To decrease social isolation and support participants in exploring community both within and outside of the building, and foster an awareness of resources in the broader community, such as parks and green spaces for self-care within a large and busy urban centre.

Literature review

Photovoice

The development of the Practicing Gratitude group was inspired by the photovoice method, which is a research method with a strong focus on social action and the objective of creating policy changes that impact the lives of research participants (Wang & Burris, 1997). As part of the JTC onsite counselling services, the intentions of the Practicing Gratitude group primarily focused on the individual well-being of the participants. It did not have a political stance, nor was it a research project. Nevertheless, there were elements of the photovoice method that the facilitators were drawn to and inspired by in relation to the development of the group.

Wang and Burris (1997), the researchers who developed the photovoice method, suggest that photovoice "uses the immediacy of the visual image [...] to promote an effective, participatory means of sharing expertise and knowledge" (p.369). Wang (1999) further explains that "[images] contribute to how we see ourselves, how we define and relate to the world, and what we perceive as significant or different. The lesson an image teaches does not reside in its physical structure but rather in how people interpret the image in question" (p.186). The photovoice method therefore inspired the facilitators to create opportunities for tenants to tell their stories, share their knowledge, and connect with what is important to their well-being in their surrounding community through the medium of photography. Furthermore, the photovoice concept was originally developed with a group of Chinese village women to document their everyday health and work realities (Wang, 1999). It is rooted in feminist inquiry, with an appreciation and centralization of women's subjective experience. It "enables women to control the photographic process in order to express, reflect and communicate their every day lives" (Wang, 1999, p. 186) and "poses an alternative to positivist ways of knowing by listening to and learning from women's own portrayal of their lives" (ibid.). The Practicing Gratitude group strove to be a space that invited women to share and learn from each other about their realities and experiences. Therefore, while the group did promote a focus on gratitude, the design and facilitation intentionally shifted away from 'teaching' a particular way of thinking by offering simple, open-ended exercises that aimed to maximize opportunities for participants' narratives and creativity. As such, this group offered an alternative to the psycho-educational programming that is often offered through mental health services.

Gratitude

In research, gratitude is associated with "a worldview orientated towards noticing and appreciating the positive in life" (Wood, Joseph & Maltby, 2009, p. 443). It is therefore in contrast with the perspective that is commonly associated with depression, which is a negative view towards life and self (Wood et al., 2009). A longitudinal study shows that interventions involving gratitude led to increased levels of emotional well-being, and that the skills of using gratitude in everyday life and through difficult times can build psychological strengths that may protect against stress and depression (Wood et al., 2008). Particularly, a study in 2003 found that individuals who were assigned daily exercises focused on gratitude or 'counting their blessings' reported greater level of positive affects, fewer reported physical symptoms such as pain, more optimism, better sleep quality, and a sense of connectedness to others (Emmons & McCullough, 2003).

Feelings of gratitude are associated with a more positive view of the surrounding social environments and the supports or resources available, thereby leading to more ways of developing and utilizing social support that are helpful to the individuals (Wood et al., 2008). Gratitude involves the recognition that one has received something of value from another person or from a spiritual or non-human entity. It also stipulates that helping or giving can create positive impacts on people's lives. Practicing gratitude can therefore motivate individuals to reciprocate or 'pay it forward,' thus increasing their sense of social or self-worth, knowing that they have made a positive impact on others and feel valued (Grant & Gino, 2010). The feeling of gratitude and the reciprocal interactions between people are associated with feelings of empathy, trust, respect and admiration (Emmons & McCullough, 2003). Practicing gratitude can therefore be helpful in cultivating positive relationships and community-building.

Therapeutic quality of art-making

Theories in art therapy have suggested that art-making can serve as non-verbal ways for individuals to problem-solve and express feelings and ideas that are sometimes difficult to put into words (Hinz, 2006). For example, working from a trauma-informed approach, it can be understood that women may have a difficult time identifying their strengths and positive steps they have taken if they had experienced significant external and internal criticism as a result of interpersonal violence. Creativity and art-making engage different regions of the brain than the parts that articulate and filter thoughts and understanding through language (Hinz, 2006). With carefully designed, strengths-based activities, art-making can be used to support women in enhancing their self-awareness of their strengths and wisdom. Art-making can also serve as an opportunity for relaxation, play, and mindful engagement with the present moment through structured, tactile activities. Studies suggest that serotonin is increased during creative activities, and art-making can have mood-enhancing qualities, reduce anxiety (De Petrillo & Winner, 2005; Bell & Robbins, 2007), and produce a state of restful alertness that is similar to the mind state during meditation (Malchiodi, 1999). For these reasons, the Practicing Gratitude group sought to incorporate art-based activities into the group structure.

Implementation and overall structure

The group was promoted through posters in the lobby of the building complex. Interested tenants were invited to contact the facilitators directly and schedule a brief pre-group meeting, in which the facilitators shared the purpose and format of the group and the outing locations, and discussed practical preparations for the group according to individual client needs, such as dressing appropriately to the weather. It was explained that the group focused on exploring the concept of gratitude, rather than photography skills. Tenants were invited to discuss any accessibility, mobility, or safety concerns they may have about the locations of the outings, and to ask any questions they may have.

In keeping with best practice, working from a trauma-informed framework was imperative, regardless of whether participants had disclosed histories of trauma (Jean Tweed Centre, 2013). Working from a trauma-informed framework means that the clinician's practices and understanding of clients' experiences are informed by the understanding of the complexity and multifaceted impacts of trauma. Central to this framework is supporting clients' sense of safety and control through facilitating an environment that is nonjudgmental, collaborative, consistent and predictable, as well as supporting them to build skills in being aware of and regulating their emotions. This framework was implemented in the group through the ritual of beginning each session with a mindfulness or grounding exercise, the facilitators conveying an attitude of warmth, respect, acceptance, and calmness, and delivering activities in ways that were simple and open-ended, with the invitation to explore the theme or topic creatively, thereby minimizing the pressure to complete or follow the activities the 'right way.' Facilitators participating in group activities alongside the tenants and implementing participants' input regarding group activities also helped to create a collaborative and egalitarian atmosphere, and supported the women's sense of control and feeling of empowerment. While the group activities were open-ended and encouraged creativity, the basic structure of the group, such as the agenda for each session and outing locations, were consistent and predictable.

Two cycles of the group were held with six sessions in each cycle during fall 2016 and winter 2017. Each group session was two hours in length, and took place on a weekday afternoon. Seven participants confirmed attendance in the beginning of the first cycle, and six in the second cycle. In the first cycle, participants took short walks into the community and took photos in the first four sessions, and then worked on an art project using the photographs they took in the last two sessions. The art project was determined through participants' input and discussions, and involved transferring photographs onto wood panels. In the second cycle, there were alternating sessions of group outings and art-making, and the art-making sessions focused on creating coping cards according to the theme of the week. Coping cards involve collage, painting or drawing created on postcard-size paper that can serve as a reminder of one's inner strengths or capture encouraging and inspiring ideas that might support individuals in coping with difficult times (Hansen-Adamidis, 2014).

Session format

Each session began with a welcome and introduction, and brief explanation of the activities for the session. It was followed by a brief check-in or mindfulness and breathing exercise. If participants had taken photographs in the previous week, they would be invited to select and share with the group one or two photos that they took. The group would then begin their outing into the community or art exercise, and end with a brief check-out or sharing of artwork created.

Sample themes

Participants were invited to reflect on a particular topic or theme and some supporting questions when taking photographs or creating their artwork each week, including the following:

* Positivity & Joy – What brings you joy? What makes you smile?
* Finding Calm – What grounds you or brings you calm in the midst of busyness?
* Growth – In what area would you like to grow more? What supports your growth?
* Overcoming Challenges – Invitation to capture images that represent how you have overcome a challenge.

Evaluation methodology

Participants were invited to complete a mid-point evaluation in the third session of each cycle as well as a final evaluation in the last session. The mid-point evaluation was a qualitative questionnaire consisting of three questions:

- What should we start doing?
- What should we stop doing?
- What should we continue to do?

The final evaluation involved a questionnaire with both qualitative and quantitative questions, such as asking the number of sessions attended, a multiple choice question about different kinds of benefits gained, ratings of satisfaction about the group, and open-ended questions about what participants enjoyed, what could be done differently, and themes they would suggest for the group in the future.

Highlights from the evaluation

Seven of the eight evaluations received rated "satisfied" or "very satisfied" with the group. Participants who filled out the questionnaires attended between three to six sessions of the group. From the multiple choice questions about benefits gained from the group, "increases in positive emotions" was selected in all of the questionnaires completed, and "feeling less lonely and isolated" was selected in all but one questionnaire. Comments regarding what was helpful in the group included the group outings, photography, focusing on the present, discussions and reflections on positivity and gratitude, positive connection with other participants, and staff's facilitation style. Regarding elements of the group that they would like to see changed, participants identified issues including alternative activities for cold weather in place of an outing, better camera quality, and more structure and time management during participant sharing.

Three of the participants expressed interest in further sharing their experiences of the group to contribute to the facilitators' presentation at the International Association for Social Work with Groups

Symposium. The facilitators interviewed these participants, and the following themes were identified from the conversations: connections to community, creative self-expressions, focus on strengths, and mutual support.

Connections to Community

One of the participants shared about her experience of exploring areas of the community for her well-being: "[It] opened my eyes to realize the things that I had missed in my 'dark side,' past life. Gave me a chance to get out there and see what I've been missing [...] I learned to be more aware of the beauty of the world, take heed of things that I passed by and overlooked [...] I appreciate more." The facilitators also recall comments from group discussions about being able to find spaces for quiet time and self-care outside of the building through the group outings. One participant shared that she was new to Toronto, and learning about the greenhouse at a nearby park which she could freely access was helpful to her. In relation to group outings and the overall group structure, having clear and predictable expectations in programming contributed to a sense of safety from a trauma-informed perspective (Jean Tweed Centre, 2013), and participants expressed that these elements have been beneficial. For example, when asked what was helpful about the group, one participant shared, "enjoyed the breathing exercise [...] having objective for each class and knowing where we're going."

Creative Self-expressions

Participants discussed the experience of being able to express their perspectives through different creative lenses, including photography, discussions, and art-making. One participant explained a photograph she took of what appeared to be dark clouds, which she had titled "Before." She shared that the image represented "substance using days, bad days that would never end." She further explained that "before, I didn't have anybody to listen to, to listen to me. I never had a say in my life until now. [The photo is] hanging on my wall so I don't forget where I came out of. When I look at this picture: emptiness, darkness, dark, evil demons. Everything happens for a reason."

Another participant shared about her perspective on homelessness through a photograph she took: "Gratitude for physical home. Homelessness is right in our face but people don't want to look at it. Much bigger picture than black and white. Judgment of people with mental health issues. We're just one step away from being homeless. Took it in black and white for this reason, things are not black and white."

Focus on strengths

Conversations with participants indicated that, through the group activities, they were able to connect with their own knowledge, skills, and strengths rather than deficits. Particularly, a common theme of personal growth was regularly discussed in group sharing, and many of the women commented on past barriers and difficult times they have experienced and the ways they have overcome challenges in order to be where they are today. One participant spoke about a photograph she took of sunlight shining through the leaves and branches of a tree, and expressed pride in the quality of the photograph as well as the important life achievements that it represented for her. She shared, "looks like it was taken by a professional. Captures everything, Life is there [...] where I sit with thoughts now [...] How I feel: bright, colourful, happy, most of the time. Shows how far I've come [...] There is light at the end of the tunnel if you reach out for it and that's what I've done."

Mutual support

The facilitators frequently witnessed participants showing support for each other in the group. As discussed in the evaluation questionnaires, the participants described experiencing the group as an opportunity for positive interactions with others in the building. One example of positive interactions that the facilitators observed was when one participant was feeling tired and unwell, another participant encouraged her in practicing self-care and returning to the group after taking a break. The participants also reported socializing outside of the group. In the final few sessions, they had requested group photos be taken at an outing, and spontaneously created a group mural using their photographs, magazine images, and words to capture their experiences of the group and the connections they experienced with each other. The words that were written on the mural included "finding calm," "everyone matters," "joy," and "empowerment". One participant shared how this group was helpful, given her own trauma history: "Being with like-minded people is encouraging, sharing and talking about my gratitude [...] very positive experience, people didn't go there to talk about problems, it was about sharing gratitude [...] What I go through as indigenous woman [...] [I] appreciate different women coming together [...] everybody having courage, honesty [...] learning to see, knowing that everyone's gone through their own stuff."

Challenges and learning

Both facilitators and participants identified that cold weather and snow had an impact on camera functions and made the outings less enjoyable. Suggestions were made for alternative indoor activities for inclement weather. Group attendance was another challenge encountered by the facilitators. Half of the tenants who registered did not attend or attended inconsistently. The ongoing dynamics between tenants in the building may have contributed to barriers in attending the group. Indeed, two tenants shared that they had decided not to attend after registering because they would like to avoid the potential of coming into contact with particular tenants also in attendance. Facilitators also observed one participant raising her voice and reproaching another for appearing tired in the group, which the facilitators understood as stemming from a conflict that arose outside of the group. This interaction had led one of the participants to stop attending the group, despite the facilitators' invitation to talk about the situation and return to the group.

Differences in understanding about the intentions of the group also created challenges in the first cycle. Initially, basic photography tips were shared in the first group with the intention to support the use of the camera as a creative tool. However, while some participants shared that it was interesting to be introduced to different techniques and to look at ordinary scenes in various artistic ways, the facilitators noticed that it also created the expectation that the group would teach professional photography skills. One participant had expressed disappointment that the facilitators were not professional photographers who could teach these skills, and the facilitators observed that participants would focus more on how the photographs turned out rather than what the images meant for them. In the second cycle discussions about photography tips was omitted and, using discussion questions and art-making exercises, participants were encouraged to reflect on the meanings that they gave to their photographs, such as "what attracted you to the object/scene you took a photo of?"

Conclusion

The Practicing Gratitude group created space for tenants in the housing program to build mutual support and expand their skills for well-being. It also provided a valuable opportunity for the facilitators to deepen their understanding of how sense of safety, wellness, and community can be facilitated through creative means, and how activities focused on gratitude may be particularly helpful to those impacted by trauma, mental health issues, and substance use. Moving forward, the facilitators hope to continue evolving and implementing the group program in ways that best support women's well-being, personal growth, and self-efficacy.

Acknowledgement

Special thanks to Kelly Luminoso, Kathryn Mettler and Charlotte Bondy in supporting our work on the group program and this paper.

References

Bell, C. E., & Robbins, S. J. (2007). Effect of art production on negative mood: A randomized, controlled trial. *Art Therapy: Journal of the American Art Therapy Association, 24*(2), 71-75.

De Petrillo, L., & Winner, E. (2005). Does art improve mood? A test of a key assumption underlying art therapy. *Art Therapy: Journal of the American Art Therapy Association, 22*(4), 205-212.

Emmons, R. A. & McCullough, M. E. (2003). Counting blessings versus burdens: An experimental investigation of gratitude and subjective well-being in daily life. *Journal of Personality and Social Psychology, 84*(2), 377-389.

Grant, A. M. & Gino, F. (2010). A little thanks goes a long way: Explaining why gratitude expressions motivate prosocial behavior. *Journal of Personality and Social Psychology, 98*(6), 946-955.

Hansen Adamidis , P. (2014). Creative self-care. Retrieved from http://www.arttherapist.ca/art-therapy/creative-self-care/

Hinz, L. D. (2006). *Drawing from Within: Using Art to Treat Eating Disorders.* London: Jessica Kingsley.

The Jean Tweed Centre. (2013). *Trauma matters: Guideline for trauma-informed practices in women's substance use services.* Toronto: The Jean Tweed Centre.

Malchiodi, C. A. (1999). Art therapy and medicine: Powerful partners in healing. In Malchiodi, C. A. (Ed.) *Medical Art Therapy with Adults* (pp. 13-24). London: Jessica Kingsley.

Wang, C. (1999). Photovoice: A participatory action research strategy applied to women's health. *Journal of Women's Health, 8*(2), 185-192.

Wang, C. & Burris, M. A. (1997). Photovoice: Concept, methodology, and use for participatory needs assessment. *Health Education & Behavior, 24*(3), 369-387.

Wood, A. M., Joseph, S. & Maltby, J. (2009). Gratitude predicts psychological well-being above the Big Five facets. *Personality and Individual Differences, 46*(4), 443-447.

Wood, A. M., Maltby, J., Gillett, R., Linley, P. A., Joseph, S. (2008). The role of gratitude in the development of social support, stress, and depression: Two longitudinal studies. *Journal of Research in Personality, 42*(4), 854–871.

Māori student perceptions of group work in their social work degree

Donna Guy

Introduction

Few practitioners today would argue the value of group work as an effective teaching approach to enhance deep learning opportunities for social work students – but how many of us have stopped to wonder whether our students agree? This paper presents the findings from an interpretive study, using a mixed method approach to investigate students' perceptions of group work. A particular focus was the experiences of Māori students, as one of the frequently cited assumptions about Māori cultural teaching and learning preferences is that they are a communally-minded culture with a preference for group, rather than individualized processes and inquiry.

Māori are the indigenous people of Aotearoa New Zealand, comprising 15% of the population. Like many indigenous and colonized cultures, Māori have experienced ongoing oppression and practices of colonization resulting in significant disparities in social, economic status, education, health and wellbeing (Ministry of Health, 2015; Tertiary Education Commission, 2011). Māori are a large client group for social workers, and the profession is keen to ensure a strong Māori presence among the qualified practitioners to work alongside their own people. It is important, then, that teachers give Māori students in higher education every assistance to succeed.

The findings from this study highlighted a few surprises. Māori students revealed mixed and, at times, contradictory perceptions of the value of group work. As one participant revealed, "Group work can be really awesome but it can also be really stunting". While acknowledging a number of benefits, students emphasised peer influences and the role of the teacher as having a significant impact on whether group work was deemed a positive or negative experience. This paper discusses these, and other key themes related to positive and negative group work experiences, along with strategies students suggested to enhance their social work study experience. The paper concludes that generalizing about Māori, and/or possibly other indigenous cultures who naturally thrive in collective environments, does not mean we can assume they will thrive during group work in the higher education classroom. Finally, some reflections and implications for best practice are offered.

Research study

Background

The topic for this study is critical to all facets of my professional pedagogy. Both as a teacher and registered social worker, group work plays an integral role. I was surprised then, when evaluations completed by Bachelor of Applied Social Science (BASS) Social Work students highlighted a significant variety of perceptions around the ways that group work activities were experienced. A number of students expressed their dislike for group work, stating they could not understand how group work could in any way benefit their learning. Indeed, several wanted an 'expert' teacher to stand at the front of the classroom and deliver 'expert knowledge' and not waste their time with group work activities.

I was intrigued that some students appeared to prefer a traditional lecture style of learning. This was in direct contrast to the significant body of literature on student-centered learning and adult-learning principles which highlight the inclusion of experiential group work activities as key to effective engagement and achievement of adult students (Knowles, 1984; Kolb, 2015; Merriam & Bierema, 2014).

Research rationale and aim

Despite the volume of literature which highlights the possibilities and value of group work as a teaching and learning method, students' perceptions of such experiences remain relatively unexplored and under-researched. Student engagement and overall achievement have been investigated, but there appears to have been little research that has focused specifically on what students feel about participating in such learning experiences (Anderson, Sylvan & Sheets, 2014; Thondhlana & Belluigi, 2014).

Furthermore, most literature investigating student perceptions is quantitative, with relatively few studies that include qualitative methods (Welsh, 2012). When researching attitudes, values and beliefs, qualitative methodologies can increase the likelihood of rich data concerning participants' worldviews (Bell & Waters, 2014; Cresswell, 2014). The present study seeks to address this gap in the literature. As Struyven, Dochy, Janssens, and Gielen (2008) state, only through understanding student attitudes and beliefs can institutions of higher education provide the best teaching and learning experiences.

The aim of the study was to identify and explore the perceptions social work students hold in relation to group work as a method of teaching. By investigating students' perceptions and examining how students feel and think about group work as a strategy for learning, greater insight and ultimately new knowledge and understanding about group work in higher education settings may be generated.

Māori student perceptions have been extracted and analysed for the purpose of this paper. Curtis et al. (2012) speak of a lack of research investigating non-lecturing teaching methods such as group work in Aotearoa New Zealand and highlight, even "fewer studies have focused on representing indigenous student voice" (p. 5). As an educator of Māori students, it is pertinent to ensure Māori students' collective voice is shared in an effort to enhance best practice.

Research methodology

A mixed methods research design founded within an interpretive paradigm was selected. The study involved students enrolled in year two of a Bachelor of Applied Social Science (BASS) Social Work program within a higher education institution. Responses to an initial survey (comprising both quantitative and qualitative questions) were collected from 28 of the 33 students. Data generated informed the purposive selection of six participants to engage in semi structured interviews with the intention of expanding on ideologies and discourses revealed in the survey data. Participants who identified as Māori comprised 61% of survey responses and 67% of interview responses. Findings were then systematically and transparently analyzed using a thematic approach.

Context

Group work in higher education

A global shift to what can be termed non-traditional pedagogical approaches, emerging from social constructivist theory and founded in adult learning principles, informs the increasingly popular strategy of group work in the higher education classroom (Miller & Metz, 2014; Taqi & Al-Nouh, 2014). Group work, defined as learning by doing with others, is acknowledged as a significant, versatile and valuable learning approach (Kolb, 2015; Merriam & Bierema, 2013), in contrast to the traditional lecture. Group work positions learners at the center of learning experiences with the teacher taking the role of facilitator rather than the expert working in partnership with learners to explore and discover new meaning and understanding (Jarvis, 2010). The benefits of group work include: increased student achievement; better understanding of course content; development of inter/intra communication skills; ability to retain knowledge; critical thinking skills; opportunities for sharing ideas with peers and knowledge transfer of skills to future professions (Lom, 2012; Taqi & Al-Nouh, 2013; Jackson et al., 2014; Thaman, Saggar, Gupta & Kaur, 2013)

Notwithstanding the above benefits, group work also presents problematic concerns. Students often complain that peers lack commitment, are dominant, negative and do not participate (Smith & Cardaciotto, 2011; Sundrium & Kanasan 2013). Indeed, such interpersonal challenges have given rise to student perceptions of 'group hate'; the dread some students associate with participation in group work (Burke, 2011).

Group work in social work education

Group work is an essential component of social work education. Experiential group work ensures social work students experience not only an accumulation of knowledge (surface learning approaches) but also understand and have the opportunity to practice (deep learning approaches) (Hermida, 2014). Colby (2009) agrees that traditional education which focuses on passive lectures does have a place, but has limitations for preparing social work graduates for the reality of social work practice. Instead, group work affords students the opportunity to challenge, discuss, debate, articulate and negotiate others' ideas, leading to insight and increased knowledge they would not have gained through participation in a traditional lecture (Knight, 2014; Gibbons & Gray, 2002).

Context of Aotearoa New Zealand

Māori, the indigenous people of Aotearoa New Zealand, have been significantly impacted by colonization policies over the last 160 years. The consequences of oppression and discrimination have left Māori individuals, *whanau* (families) and communities as disproportionately represented across a range of disparities in social and economic status, education, health and wellbeing (Ministry of Health, 2015; Tertiary Education Commission, 2011). Such inequalities equate to Māori learners' experiences in higher education, often a difficult journey, too often marked by low achievement and completion rates (Bishop, Berryman, Cavanagh & Teddy, 2009).

As Māori currently comprise a large portion of social work clients, there is demand for educational institutes to produce Māori social work graduates who can return to their communities to support the social and emancipatory transformation of their families and wider communities. Therefore, it is imperative for teachers in higher education to pursue teaching methods which will enhance learning and achievement for Māori students.

Research emphasizes that traditional and more formal approaches to teaching pose significant issues for Māori learners (Curtis et al., 2012). Rather than an individualistic and competitive ideology, Māori identity is founded within the success and wellbeing of the collective (Durie, 2001). Put simply, group learning is intrinsic to *Te Ao Māori* (the Māori worldview). Research by Bishop et al. (2009) confirms that Māori students feel more at ease working in a small-group context with interaction and dialogue with their peers. Arini et al. (2011) agree that new attitudes to teaching, embracing the concept of the teacher as a facilitator of a group process rather than a knowledge expert, are required in higher educational institutions if we are to improve Māori learning outcomes.

In Aotearoa New Zealand, group work approaches where learners 'scaffold' and co-construct their learning with peers draws upon Māori pedagogies such as *tuakana/teina* (older/younger siblings) and *kanohi ki te kanohi* (face to face) (MacFarlane et al., 2008; Tangaere, 1997). From a traditional Māori worldview, *tuakana-teina* is a concept in which "older and more experienced siblings or relations have a responsibility for sharing their knowledge and skills with their younger or less-experienced siblings and relations" (MacFarlane et al., 2008, p. 110).

Moreover, Tamati (2005) and MacFarlane et al. (2008) point out that the pedagogy of *tuakana-teina* is intrinsic to the concept of *ako* (to learn as well as to teach). According to Pere (1982), and Pelling and McBride (2010) the concept of *ako* is "the inseparable, reciprocal nature and process of teaching and learning, where teacher and learner are partners in the 'conversation' of learning" (cited in Tahau-Hodges, 2010, p.10). In addition to each individual being valued and regarded as having knowledge and skills they can contribute to learning experiences, students are positioned as equal partners in the teaching and learning process. There are synergies here with the work of Paulo Freire (1970) who states "that in genuine dialogue, the teacher teaches the learners, who learn and teach the teacher as well" (cited in Jarvis, 2010, p. 188). As Winitana (2012) concludes, "The Māori *tuakana-teina* pedagogy has provided fresh energy in adult education, providing for more rewarding educational engagement between learner and tutor, and between learner and learner" (p. 33).

These concepts of *tuakana-teina* and *ako* align well with the global shift to group work founded in social constructivist approaches and notions around co-construction of knowledge This alignment with adult learning principles and student-centered learning approaches provides the platform from which New Zealand educators aim to ensure positive learning outcomes not only for Māori, but all students. As Bishop et al. (2009) discovered in their research, what is good for Māori learners is good for all learners.

Research findings and analysis

The choice of methodology provided a strong triangulation of key findings. Many themes identified in the initial survey were strongly reinforced by data generated in the semi-structured interviews adding to the validity of this study. Likewise, some contradictions in the data demonstrated the strength of the mixed method approach as it enabled more than a snap shot of students' perceptions to be gained. It was interesting and surprising that those students who proclaimed liking group work in the initial surveys shared negative aspects during interviews. Moreover, those who initially declared a dislike of group work expressed many positive attributes when given the opportunity to tell the story of how they arrived at their opinions. Such findings are not new to the literature, as Marks and O'Connor (2013) discovered, "there is no real consensus about whether or not students prefer to work individually or in teams [groups] – the results are truly mixed" (p. 149).

Regardless of liking /disliking group work, Māori students identified a number of benefits from group work related to their learning;

Social interactions

Māori students found peers' narratives and worldviews highly useful for promoting positive interactions. All participants saw social interactions as invaluable opportunities not only for learning but also for their social skill development (Beccaria, Kek, Huijser, Rose & Kimmins, 2014; Taqi & Al-Nouh, 2014). The students acknowledged that they were more at ease speaking and engaging in a group of four or five as opposed to a class of forty, echoing the findings of Bishop et al. (2009) and Greenwood and Te Aika (2008)

Increased understanding of course content

Group work as a teaching pedagogy is an efficient means of supporting increased understanding of course content for students (Lom, 2012; Hillyard, Gillespie & Littig, 2010). Māori students shared this view, enjoying group work activities in which they used visual and other tactile resources as opportunities to use their artistic and creative skills, thus enhancing understanding. All are essential elements previously found to enhance learning outcomes for Māori students (Curtis et al., 2012; Arini, et al., 2011)

Use of te reo Māori (language)

Findings indicate group work has proved useful for some Māori students to practice their *te reo Māori*. An older Māori student spoke of the shame she felt not understanding or being able to pronounce Māori words correctly. (Until the late 1980's, when a resurgence in *te reo Māori* emerged, colonial social policy banned the use of *te reo Māori* in schools in an attempt to eliminate the Māori language (Durie, 1998; 2001)). This student stated that small group work with trusted peers mentoring (*tuakana/teina*) provided a safe place in which she felt comfortable to practice and improve her *te reo Māori*.

Acknowledging competence

Māori students reported feeling empowered during group work when their life experience and prior knowledge supported learning for non-Māori students. For instance, although new to Māori models of social work practice, when encouraged by teachers to share their understanding of *Te Ao Māori*, Māori students found themselves in a natural leadership role. The power of these moments in which Māori students became leaders of learning cannot be underestimated. Participants stated they felt listened to and valued by both peers and teachers as they shared their prior knowledge and expertise. Research confirms that when teachers acknowledge the competence, the knowledge and understanding unique to their life experiences, Māori students' learning outcomes are enhanced significantly (Bishop, et al., 2009; Curtis et al, 2012).

Links to future social work practice

Of significance, all Māori students acknowledged that group work learning experiences are an essential element in their social work education. They highlighted the following ways group work contributed to their development as social work professionals:

Application of knowledge

The notion that group work provides students with the opportunities for deep learning, to put in practice knowledge accumulated, is well represented in the literature (Kiweewa, Gilbride, Luke & Seward, 2013; Smith & Davis-Gage, 2008).). Māori students reported role plays, simulations and case studies provided opportunities to gain an understanding of theory to practice and supported the development of skills and behaviors which could be transferred to their future practice.

Ability to work with future clients

Participants spoke of a range of inter- and intra- communication skills that group work provided which would enhance their future social work practice. For example, engagement in group discussions in which they were able to confront problems, discuss, debate, negotiate, and make decisions, increased knowledge and understanding of skills required to work effectively within the multidisciplinary field of social work practice (Sweifach, 2015; Pollio & Macgowan, 2010). Likewise, students felt such skills also increased their knowledge and ability to facilitate their own groups in the future.

In addition, students also stated group work experiences often evoked emotions and heightened their awareness of the vulnerability clients often face during social work processes. This aligns with Wolfe's (2006) study which advised, emotions created from such experiences encourages the development of insight and empathy in students. Students declared a need for more of these experiences in their degree programme.

Cognitive disequilibrium

Interestingly, Māori students revealed an awareness that difficult and challenging group work experiences did, in some instances, lead to strong learning opportunities. The literature refers to these experiences of discomfort as cognitive disequilibrium (Anderson et al., 2014). Several students recognized that experiencing resistance, fear, anger, frustration, and at times confrontation, are all 'real' experiences that will enhance their developmental knowledge and skills crucial for their future professional practice.

Essential elements for positive group work experiences

All on the same page

Māori students declared that in order to ensure positive group work experiences the most important thing was, "everyone being on the same page, that's the crucial part". When explored further, participants advised "being on the same page" comprised the following key elements:

- Peers who are: like-minded, hold a similar work ethic, keen to participate, of a similar level of academic ability, willing to share ideas and who demonstrate a desire to learn from each other;
- A learning environment where trust and a sense of belonging have been established.

Connection

This requirement for trust and a sense of belonging are recognized indicators for effective group work in higher education (Analoui, Sambrook & Doloriert, 2014). Māori students referred to 'connection' as a feeling of trust, safety, comfort, a sense of belonging and that all were critical for successful engagement with their peers. Inversely, when there is no connection in the group, Māori students struggle to participate or share ideas (Curtis et al., 2012).

Significantly, Māori students reported some teachers did not provide the time or space to establish a sense of connection and trust with their peers. As one student explained, meaningful and quality conversations only evolved once she felt a connection and that it was only from this place of mutual respect and safety that she was able to put forward her viewpoints and openly discuss/debate different opinions.

Elements contributing to negative group work experiences

Three key themes emerged in relation to aspects Māori students felt contributed to their negative group work experiences. In addition, students were asked to suggest possible solutions and/or ways teachers can look to enhance group work. Therefore, each theme in this section will conclude with strategies students feel can be implemented to ensure more positive group work experiences.

Group composition

An aspect of group work that often proves a challenge in higher education relates to the composition of group membership. There are primarily three ways groups are formed: students are randomly assigned to groups; students select their own group members; or a mixture of student assignment and self-selection (Hassanien, 2006). Findings revealed that most group work selections involved numbering off and/or were teacher selected. Without exception, Māori students expressed their strong dislike for the domination of random/teacher selection of group members with most insisting this made a significant difference as to whether they had a positive or negative group work experience.

The rationale for social work teachers randomly assigning group membership is to ensure diversity among participants for group work. However, as reiterated by one Māori student, "tutors want us to work with different people, but that does not work". The placement of diverse students into groups can in fact create significant disadvantages, lead to negative group dynamics and ultimately the effectiveness of the group in achieving tasks (Van Knippenberg & Schippers, 2010, cited in Beccaria et al., 2014).

Strategy: Let us pick our group members
Māori students were very clear that how groups are formed has a significant impact on their learning experiences. One student said, "Do not number us off ... I mean, just let us go in our own groups ... let us go in groups with people we know, those who we can work with, those who we can learn from".

Peer influences

Although highlighted by researchers as one of the most significant benefits, social interaction with peers is often regarded as one of the most problematic aspects of group work. It was very evident in the findings that Māori students identified peer behavior as a significant factor influencing their perceptions of group work. Three strong sub-themes emerged as follows:

1. Lack of commitment and participation

All participants struggled immensely with peers who demonstrated little commitment and would not actively participate in group work. Importantly Māori students highlighted the impact on their learning, as one clarified, "You can tell they have that mentality. When they get in a group they say, I don't have to do this! Why should I have to do this? And it's like *'agrrr'* we are all trying to do the same thing, it's very dysfunctional". These findings are consistent with studies by Thondhlana and Belluigi (2014) and Pauli, Mohiyeddini, Bray, Michie and Street (2008). Furthermore, participants considered that peers who did not want to participate but were instructed to do so by the teacher tended to make the whole group experience miserable for everyone else.

An alarming narrative shared by one Māori student revealed the impact of working for long periods with peers of this nature. Once a motivated and proactive class participant in group work, her frustration and annoyance with peers who would not participate impacted on her own contributions. She explained, "I try not to be the one who talks, not to be the one who puts the ideas in, because they depend on me to do it". This reaction, where a student pulls back from their contribution due to feeling other group members are taking advantage of them, is known as the 'sucker effect'. In some misguided way, the student decides that making minimal contributions to the group is a better option than doing all the work while others do not participate during class (Pauli, et al., 2008).

Strategy: Teach us the benefits of group work
Māori students suggest teachers need to provide evidence and research outlining how group work can support their learning. As one student stated, "I think if people can really see that group work is going to benefit them they will be more inclined to participate". By ensuring students are informed of the value of group work and the significant contribution it can add to their learning, there is more likelihood of student buy-in, thus increasing the possibility of students keen to participate in group work processes (Thondhlana & Belluigi, 2014).

2. Dominant and negative peers

It was very evident in the findings that dominant and negative peers were a problematic concern to all participants. Students spoke of peers who refused to listen to their ideas, and at times completely shut them down. Such findings are not new to the literature. In a study conducted by Thondhlana and Belluigi (2014) students declared the domination of peers and the impact this behaviour had on students was significant.

Negative and discouraging peer behavior also impacted significantly on Māori students' learning experiences and hence perceptions of group work. Dysfunctional behaviors noted in the literature and acknowledged by participants in this study included being bullied, put down, targeted, ignored and intimidated (Sundrium & Kanasan 2013; Taqi & Al-Nouh, 2014). One student explained:

"We had a really negative person who was just sitting there and shutting us down, everything we said, every bit of advice we offered, she just didn't have anything to offer except her bad remarks, her negative statements.

It was like this for our whole group time. The mood ... everyone was like ... was just a bad buzz".

Such behavior has a significant impact on students' learning and can lead to feelings of incompetence as well as being detrimental to the self-esteem and confidence (Heinstrom & Sormunen, 2012).

Chapman (2006) concurs adding this type of behavior and attitude within the group dynamic can lead to some "students feeling alienated and oppressed (cited in Beccaria et al., 2014, p. 1095). Certainly, this has been the experience of Māori students who expressed an air of hopelessness about having to work with peers who behave in this manner. In addition, Māori students advised, this day-to-day interaction with peers who are uncommitted, do not participate, are dominant and behave negatively takes a toll. Several spoke of how this disillusionment filters into the class mood/demeanor. Hillyard et al. (2010) supports these findings, offering numerous examples of peer interaction issues which have proven to be detrimental to positive group work experiences for some students.

Strategy: Teach us how to work in a group
Participants feel strongly that at times, they have been dropped in the deep end without the tools and/or skills to navigate the challenges group work dynamics brings to the social work classroom. "How do we work in a group? How are we supposed to know what to do when someone is being dominant and/or bossy?". Often, there is an implicit assumption by teachers that students will 'just learn' about group work skills by being engaged in group work itself, although Coers et al. (2010) suggest that such an assumption indicates teachers have a lack of understanding of the complexities of group work.

3. Teachers' role

Research, both international and specific to Māori learners, clearly highlights the role of the teacher as a critical indicator in the success of the group work experiences in higher education (Yazedjian & Kolkhorst 2007; Woodward, Colyar, & Woodward, 2009; Curtis et al., 2012). As aptly put by one student, "The teacher sets the tone". This insightful comment argues the impact of a teacher who is skilled in the facilitation of group work. Māori students' comments in this study clearly identified that while experiencing group work facilitated by teachers with a high level of group work skills, participants also identified teachers who had little skill in group work facilitation.

Furthermore, Māori students placed significant value on teachers making them aware of why they were doing group work. When activities lacked purpose and/or direction, participants perceived group work as just 'time wasting' by teachers who were not prepared for class. Lumpkin, Achen and Dodd (2015) state, the teacher must ensure students understand the learning objectives of all group work activities they will take part in. When clarity was not provided participants advised this encouraged disengagement and motivation loss. As one commented, "It becomes very easy to become disconnected when you cannot see the purpose or relevance of an activity".

In addition, as discussed earlier, the use of cognitive disequilibrium to activate deeper learning experiences is an important component of social work education. However, it is essential that teachers are skilled in the appropriate processes to ensure the safety of all class members. In some instances, Māori students found themselves in challenging situations, without a skilled teacher, and the consequences proved detrimental not only to peer relationships, but also to their individual confidence and self-esteem. According to Thondhlana and Belluigi (2014), in such circumstances group work becomes more of a negative than positive experience for students.

Strategy: Teacher's skill development
Participants suggested that some teachers require improvement in their facilitation skills. Aspects for skill development mentioned related to the management of group dynamics and ability to ensure group work activities have a clear purpose, are monitored throughout and debriefed appropriately.

Preferences for traditional lectures versus group work

Surprisingly, a number of Māori students expressed a strong dislike for group work. This is in contrast to the limited research conducted to date which suggests Māori students prefer to work in small groups within the educational setting due to their familiarity with collective ideologies

(Arini et al., 2011). When explored further during interviews, students commented that the whanau context in which Māori traditionally work in groups is founded on trust and meaningful relationships with clear lines of responsibility. For example, when engaging on a *marae* (meeting house), everyone knows their place, *tikanga* (tradition) and values ensure everybody knows and understands their roles and/or responsibilities. However, it appears that even in a culturally responsive classroom (Bishop et al., 2009; Curtis et al., 2012), group work in the social work classroom raises concerns and a number of dilemmas for Māori students.

One dilemma shared by several students related to an internal conflict around expressing opinions to peers older than themselves. One participant explained that, as a younger student, she did not feel able to express her point of view to more senior peers as this would be considered questioning an elder. She explained, "I would never speak to *Matua* (senior male) like that .... it was the same for *Whaea* (senior female) ... where I come from that is very disrespectful". In addition, another student added that older Māori students often used their elder status to dominate and shut down younger students when they tried to voice their opinions with statements like, *you are young what would you know?*

Undoubtedly, the expectation in social work education is that students will engage in those 'difficult conversations', those that inevitably lead to debate and in-depth analysis of one's values and beliefs. Such interactions are essential as they enable students to reflect, develop and grow both their personal and future professional practice (Cournyor, 2014; Sweifach, 2015). The classroom must be a safe space in which all students' viewpoints are valued and they feel able to express their individual voice. However, as expressed by several participants, it becomes complicated when you have teenagers and grandparents debating values and beliefs around a range of complex social issues (the cohort in this study comprised students aged from 19 to 60 years old). This is a significant dilemma requiring consideration by educators when using group work.

Conclusion

The aim of this research was to seek to understand Māori students' perceptions of group work in their social work degree. Often the assumption is made that Māori students like working in groups due to their inherent collective culture. However, the findings revealed Māori students hold mixed perceptions of group work. Experiences ranged from those that enticed responses such as, "Wow it was amazing!" to the, "Oh no, I just hate group work!"

Although perceptions can be deemed mixed, participants' narratives point to the possibility that group work itself was not problematic, rather the conditions in which groups are formed and implemented was more likely the problem. Contradictions were revealed: rather than liking or disliking group work or even having a preference for lecturer over group work, the manner in which group work unfolds in the classroom is critical. Both the findings and the literature overwhelmingly report that the way group work is planned and delivered, and the manner in which peers conduct themselves throughout the group process has a high impact on student perceptions.

The study highlights that placing students into groups and expecting them to function and achieve tasks with limited knowledge and understanding of the group work process is unlikely to produce quality learning experiences. In essence, the co-construction of knowledge during group work is not an automatic process. Teachers need to ensure students have not only the knowledge and understanding about group work processes but specific strategies to enable them to navigate the perils of group dynamics which will arise at some point.

Importantly, negative experiences appeared to influence students' overall perceptions of group work. This is not new to the literature, (e.g. Hillyard et al., 2010). For Māori students, this is a considerable concern due to their difficult educational journey. In the classroom, factors and variables must be addressed. Otherwise oppression and powerlessness in the mainstream education sector is amplified, as revealed by Māori students' reflections in this study.

Implications & recommendations

Importantly, most of the strategies Māori students offered align with research around effective group work. That students know what works best in their teaching and learning has been reinforced in this study, highlighting the critical need for higher education institutes to seek student voice in order to ensure optimal teaching and learning outcomes. Moving forward, the following recommendations are likely to improve Māori student experiences of group work and ultimately improve their learning outcomes, based on the findings from the present study:

- Teachers need to be more conscious of their decision-making as regards group composition. Randomly selected groups with diverse group membership can contribute to Māori students' negative group work experiences. Enabling self-selection may be a way forward to address some of the significant issues identified in this study;
- Student frustration and mixed views of group work will be ongoing until educators consider introducing students to group work processes as part of the curriculum. Group work must be given the same priority as other courses skills, competencies and knowledge;
- Educators need to carefully consider when group work skills are introduced to their social work programmes. New students require skill development around group work processes, especially in the management of group dynamics;
- Professional development for social work teachers in group work pedagogy is essential to ensure the delivery of safe and meaningful deep learning opportunities. Likewise, teachers require conflict resolution skills so they may address and prevent negative relationships within the class.

It is my hope that this study may go some way to informing and inspiring fellow colleagues teaching in higher education to pursue similar research. By doing so they will enable Māori students and other indigenous populations to engage in positive group work experiences and ultimately reap the rewards of their success into the future.

References

Analoui, B. D., Sambrook, S. & Doloriert, C. H. (2014). Engaging students in group work to maximise tacit knowledge sharing and use. *The International Journal of Management Education*, 12, 35-43. http://dx.doc.org/10.1016/j.ijme.2013.08.002

Arini, Curtis, E., Townsend, S., Rakena, T., Brown, D., Sauni, P...Johnson, O. (2011). Teaching for student success: Promising practices in university teaching. *Pacific-Asian Education*, 23(1), 71-90. Retrieved from http://hdl.handle.net/2292/13472

Anderson, M. L., Sylvan, A. L., & Sheets Jr, R. L. (2014). Experiential group training: An exploration of student perceptions. *In Ideas and Research You Can Use: VISTAS 2014. Retrieved from: http://www.counseling. org/knowledge-center/vistas/by-year2/vistas-2014/docs/default-source/vistas/article_35.*

Beccaria, L., Kek, M., Huijser, H., Rose, J. & Kimmins, L. (2014). The interrelationships between student approaches to learning and group work. *Nurse Education Today*, 34, 1094-1103. http://dx.doi.org/10.1016/j.nedt.2014.02.006

Bell, J. & Waters, S. (2014). *Doing your research project: A guide for first-time researchers.* (6th ed.). New York, NY: Open University Press.

Bishop, R., Berryman, M., Cavanagh, T., & Teddy, L. (2009). Te Kotahitanga: Addressing educational disparities facing Māori students in New Zealand. In *Teaching and Teacher Education* 25, 734-742

Burke, A. (2011). Group work: how to use groups effectively. *The Journal of Effective Teaching*, 11(2), 87-95.

Coers, N., Williams, J., & Duncan, D. (2010). Impact of group development knowledge on students' perceived importance and confidence of group work skills. *Journal of Leadership Education*, 9(2), 101-120

Colby, I. (2009). An overview of social work education in the United States: New directions and new opportunities. *China Journal of Social Work*, 2(2), 119-130. doi:10.1080/17525090902992339

Cournoyer, B. R. (2014). *The social work skills workbook* (7th ed.). Belmont, CA: Brooks/Cole.

Creswell, J. W. (2014). *Research design: qualitative, quantitative and mixed methods approaches.* (4th ed.). Thousand Oaks, CA: SAGE Publications.

Curtis, E. T., Wikaire, E., Lualua-Aati, T., Kool, B., Nepia, W., Ruka, M., Honey, M., Kelly, F., & Poole, P. (2012). *Tatou Tatou/success for all: Improving Māori student success.* Wellington, New Zealand: Ako Aotearoa,

National Centre for Tertiary Teaching Excellence.

Durie, M. (2001). *Mauri ora: The dynamics of Māori health*. Auckland, New Zealand: Oxford University Press.

Gray, M. & Gibbons, J. (2002). Experience based learning and its relevance to social work practice. *Australian Social Work*, 55(4), 279-291.

Greenwood, J., & Te Aika, L. H. (2008). *Hei tauria: Teaching and learning for success for Māori in tertiary settings*. Wellington, New Zealand: Ako Aotearoa.

Hassanien, A. (2006). Student experience of group work and group assessment in higher education. *Journal of Teaching in Travel & Tourism*, 6(1), 17-39.

Hermida, J., (2014). Facilitating deep learning: pathways to success for university and college Teachers. Boca Raton, FL USA: CRC press

Hillyard, C., Gillespie, D., & Littig, P. (2010). University students' attitudes about learning in small groups after frequent participation. *Active Learning in Higher Education*, 11(1), 9-20. DOI:10.1177/1469787409355867

Jackson, D., Hickman, L. D., Power, T., Disler, R., Potgieter, I., Deek, H., & Davidson, P. M. (2014). Small group learning: graduate health students' views of challenges and benefits. *Contemporary Nurse*, 48(1), 117-128.

Jarvis, P. (2010). *Adult education and lifelong learning: Theory and practice*. (4th. ed.) New York, NY: Routledge

Kiweewa, J., Gilbride, D., Luke, M., & Seward, D. (2013). Endorsement of growth factors in experiential training groups. *The Journal for Specialists in Group Work*, 38(1), 68-93.

Knowles, M. (1984). *Andragogy in action*. San Francisco, CA: Jossey-Bass

Kolb, D. A. (2015). *Experiential learning: Experience as a source of learning and development* (2nd ed.). Upper Saddle River, NJ: Pearson Education.

Lom, B. (2012). Classroom activities: simple strategies to incorporate student-centered activities within undergraduate science lectures. *Journal of Undergraduate Neuroscience Education*, 11: A64-A71.

Lumpkin, A., Achen, R. M., & Dodd, R. K. (2015). Student perceptions of active learning. *College Student Journal*, 49(1), 121-133.

Macfarlane, A.H., Glynn, T., Grace, W., Penetito, W., & Bateman, S. (2008). Indigenous epistemology in a national curriculum framework? *Ethnicities*, 8, 102-127. Doi:10.1177/1468796807087021

Marks, M. B., & O'Connor, A. H. (2013). Understanding students' attitudes about group work: what does this suggest for instructors of business? *Journal of Education for Business*, 88, 147-158. DOI: 10.1080/08832323.2012.66457

Merriam, S., & Bierema, L. L. (2014). *Adult learning: Linking theory and practice*. San Francisco, CA: Jossey-Bass.

Miller, C. J., & Metz, M. J. (2014). A comparison of professional-level faculty and student perceptions of active learning: its current use, effectiveness, and barriers. *Advances in Physiology Education*, 38(3), 246-252. DOI:10.1152/advan.00014.201

Ministry of Health (2015). *Tatau Kahukura: Māori health chart book* 2015 (3rd ed.). Wellington, New Zealand: Ministry of Health

Ministry of Education (2009). *Hangaia te mātāpuna o te mōhio: Learning foundations for Māori adults*. Wellington, New Zealand: Ministry of Education.

Pauli, R., Mohiyeddini, C., Bray, D., Michie, F., & Street, B. (2008). Individual differences in negative group work experiences in collaborative student learning. *Educational Psychology*, 28(1), 47-58.

Pollio, D. E., & Macgowan, M. J. (2010). The andragogy of evidence-based group work: an integrated educational model. *Social Work with Groups*, 33(2-3), 195-209.

Smith, C. K., & Davis-Gage, D. (2008). Experiential group training: Perceptions of graduate students in counselor education programs. *Groupwork*, 18(3), 88-106.

Smith, C. V., & Cardaciotto, L. (2011). Is active learning like broccoli? Student perceptions of active learning in large lecture classes. *Journal of the Scholarship of Teaching and Learning*, 11(1), 53-61.

Struyven, K., Dochy, F., Janssens, S., & Gielen, S. (2008). Students' experiences with contrasting learning environments: The added value of students' perceptions. *Learning Environments Research*, 11(2), 83-109. DOI:10.1007/s10984-008-9041-8

Sundrum, A. & Kanasan, M. (2013) Students' perception on the effectiveness of teamwork based activities in enhancing the learning process. *Eurasian Journal of Social Sciences*, 1(2), 52-60.

Sweifach, J. S. (2015). Has group work education lost its social group essence? A content analysis of MSW course syllabi in search of mutual aid and group conflict content. *Journal of Teaching in Social Work*, 35, 279-295. DOI: 10.1080/08841233.2015.1031928

Tahua-Hodges, P. (2010). *Kaiako Pono: Mentoring for Māori learners in the tertiary sector*. Wellington, New Zealand: Te Puni Kōriki & Ako Aotearoa

Tamati, A. (2005). "Ma tou rourou, Ma toku rourou": The concept of AKO: Co-construction of knowledge from a kaupapa Māori perspective. *Early Education*, 37, 23-31.

Tangaere, A. R. (1997). *Learning Māori together: Kōhanga reo and home*. Wellington, New

Zealand: NZCER

Taqi, H. A., & Al-Nouh, N. A. (2014). Effect of group work on EFL students' attitudes and learning in higher education. *Journal of Education and Learning*, 3(2), 52-65. DOI:10.5539/jel.v3n2p52

Tertiary Education Commission. (2011). *Ministry of Education. Part Two: Priorities Retrieved from* http://www.minedu.govt. nz/NZEducationPolicies/TertiaryEducation/PolicyAnd Strategy/ TertiaryEducationStrategy/PartTwoPriorities.aspx.

Thaman, R., Dhillon, S., Saggar, S., Gupta, M., & Kaur, H. (2013). Promoting active learning in respiratory physiology–positive student perception and improved outcomes. *National Journal of Physiology, Pharmacy and Pharmacology*, 3(1), 27-34. DOI:10.5455/njppp.2013.3.27-34

Thondhlana, G. & Belluigi. D. Z. (2014). Group work as 'terrains of learning' for students in South African higher education. *Perspectives in Education*, 32(4), 40-55.

Welsh, A. (2012). Exploring undergraduate perceptions of the use of active learning techniques in science lectures. *Journal of College Science Teaching*, 42(2), 80-87.

Winitana, M. (2012). Remembering the deeds of Māui: What message are in the tuakana-teina pedagogy for tertiary educators? *Mai*,1(1), 29-37

Wolfe, P. (2006). The role of meaning and emotion in learning. *New directions for Adult and Continuing Education*,110, 35-41.

Woodward, B., Colyar, J., & Woodward, J. F. (2009). IT group work: Undergraduate student perceptions. *Issues in Information Systems*, X, 1, 103-108.

Yazedjian, A., & Kolkhorst, B. B. (2007). Implementing small-group activities in large lecture classes. *College Teaching*, 55(4), 164-169.

P.re.turn:
Group practice approach for working with citizens returning from prison

Thomas Kenemore, Brent In, and Sr. Hien Nguyen

Introduction

This paper describes an idealized group process aimed at helping citizens returning from prison make a successful transition to freedom. The approach is applicable to individuals in prison, in a transitional arrangement, and on community supervision. The approach is responsive to the experience of these citizens, and takes into account how they understand and explain successful reentry. Current programming for the reentry population is, with some exceptions, extremely limited and fragmented, typically organized around specific skills, and aimed at reducing recidivism. Our approach is aimed at overcoming oppression and facilitating movement toward liberation. It recognizes the importance of a consistently supportive ecological context during the reentry process, a psychologically transcendent narrative, and a facilitative relational stance by those who help. 'P.RE. TURN' (In, 2017), a conceptual process, is explained as essential to an individual's progress toward successful to reentry.

Empowerment and restorative practice perspectives inform the development of a group approach that is relevant to the experience of returning citizens. The empowerment tradition is deeply embedded in Social Work practice ideology (Simon, 1994) and more broadly in an empowerment tradition that advocates liberation (Freire, 1970, 1992). More recent general progressive Social Work practice texts utilize these philosophical perspectives, aimed at enhancing Social Work's relevance to oppressed populations. An earlier publication summarizes the anti-oppressive perspective as it relates to the reentry population (Kenemore, 2014), and identifies the link between culture, social structure and social inequality (Houston, 2002). Applied at a micro-level, these practice approaches require bridging "the separation of existential freedom and socio-political liberty" (Mullaly, 2010, p. 223). Philosophical concepts of transcendence (Frankl, 1959, 1985) and empowerment are essential to the proposed model, as returning citizens need to be understood as experts of their experience, and, therefore, as arbiters and pilots of their own determined journey.

A restorative practice stance focuses on building social capital and achieving social discipline through participatory learning and decision-making, that enables people to restore and build community (Zehr, 2002; Pennell, 2006), and may include culturally restorative practices that address the impact of oppression on diverse communities (Akon, 2006). The stance utilizes restorative justice concepts, which can be defined as, "a process to involve, to the extent possible, those who have a stake in a specific offense and to collectively identify and address harms, needs, and obligations, in order to heal and put things as right as possible" (Zehr, 2002 p. 38). This philosophical stance is consistent with an empowerment approach, and in its application shapes the role of the Social Work practitioner as a facilitator of empowerment for returning citizens.

Reentry population

The United States has the highest incarceration rate in the world (Statistica, 2017), with over seven million individuals in some status in the correctional system (Kaeble & Glaze, 2016). The same Bureau of Justice Statistics (BJS) report indicated at the year end of 2015, nearly 2.2 million incarcerated and over 4.6 million under some form of community supervision, either probation or parole. Most of those incarcerated are released back into their communities. Members of the reentry population in the United States are, by definition, oppressed. They are distinct, yet largely invisible; the invisibility maintained by social, political, and cultural forces that, by design, relegate individuals in this category to a permanent under-cast, and by neglect. They are recognized for the remainder of their lives as having a criminal background, and experience significant barriers in their post-incarceration journeys (Alexander, 2010). The U.S. dominant culture, informed by a 'tough on crime' ideology and racism, encourages attitudes and arrangements that severely undermine re-integration of formerly incarcerated individuals into their communities. Thus, they are a population that should be a primary focus of Social Work policy and practice (Specht & Courteny, 1994).

Reentry experience

Qualitative findings from several studies (Kenemore & Roldan 2006; O'Brien 2001, 2001; O'Brien & Bates, 2005; Maruna, 2001) have begun to describe and explain the actual experience of individuals moving from prison to their communities. This experience can be characterized as moving from a highly controlled and dangerous environment in which passive compliance is required, to a highly uncontrolled and dangerous environment in which proactive and flexible planning and behavior is required (Kenemore, 2014). Coping with a confusing range of internal experiences and feelings is an immediate task. Internal experiences emphasize lack of preparation for leaving the structured, predictable prison environment. The returning citizens' perceptions of the broader community, and of institutions within the community, are more abstract and tend toward mistrust (Kenemore, 2006).

Successful reentry experience, as defined by those who are going through it, is roughly defined as 'staying straight' or 'making good', characterized by persistently moving forward and maintaining a hopeful attitude in spite of multiple, challenging barriers to forward movement. Experiences described as necessary for successful reentry include: having a change experience that alters one's narrative to include a positive self-image; having an ongoing experience of hope; having a mission; and having a spiritual or religious foundation (Kenemore & Roldan 2006; Maruna, 2001).

Current programing limitations

Primary aims of reentry programs have been to reduce recidivism, improve employability, and/or increase community support (Patterson, 2013). Unfortunately, with these conventionally defined reentry outcomes, successes are rarely experienced by most returning citizens who participate in reentry programs. Visher et al. (2005) conducted a quantitative meta-analysis and found that community employment programs for ex-offenders did not reduce recidivism. Similarly, Mulhausen (2015) found that many federal government funded employment-focused reentry programs were ineffective in reducing recidivism. Likewise, meta-analysis conducted by Ndrecka (2014) found that current national reentry programs reduced recidivism by only about 6%.

Most evaluations of reentry programs have focused on desistance from crime, using legitimate employment as the measuring stick (Mulhausen, 2015). Evaluators conclude that any programs considering desistance from crime should first address important concepts such as maturation, human agency, and psychological readiness. Paternoster et al. (2015) found that psychological readiness to give up crime and a desire to change must precede the turning points, or "hooks", such as employment and marriage, to effect desistance from crime.

In contrast, Sampson and Laub (2016) addressed the models of using the offender's narrative to understand the offender's mind, as a precursor to theorizing about human agency and identity. However, they concluded that a person's "articulated motives and self-reported reasons for action are rife with ambiguity" (p. 329). They based this conclusion on studies from cognitive science and behavioral economics. Instead of asserting that willful action of returning citizens brings about necessary changes in their life, they posited that "desistance by default" (p.328) is more consistent with the findings from behavioral economics and cognitive science. These authors supported the idea that small interventions can have large effects, which is in direct contrast to people first deciding to change before actual change happens. They believed that behavior changes identity, not the other way around. By altering the choice structure, offenders can then be "nudged" toward desistance from crime. The policy implication was that instead of focusing only on offender's agency at individual levels, more should be done on the informal social controls (life-course trajectories) to nudge offender's desistance from crime.

A study by Hlavka, Wheelock and Jones (2015) discovered that metanarratives offered insights into the factors that promoted successful reentry. This study concluded that one-size-fits-all models of reentry assistance are not prudent, echoing Petersalia's (2004) concern that too much focus has been placed on programs that reduce recidivism instead of looking at the psychological factors that promote long-term reintegration. Overall, inefficacy of current reentry programs in reducing recidivism, as an evaluation measure, prompts review of what factors are missed.

Sharing this concern, this paper seeks to explore reentry, not through the lens of tangible outcome measures, but as a "group process" that promotes empowerment and autonomy. We present a broad group relational approach that we believe needs to be in place whatever programming individuals participate in, to enhance the potential for transitioning individuals to make use of the programming and move toward real, stable community membership.

Relevant theoretical and practice perspectives

Perspectives considered foundational to the proposed group approach include established ecological system, meaning making, narrative reconstruction, and relational theories. Ecological system theory is "above all a relational perspective" in which "the person and environment are unceasingly, intricately, thoroughly (and more or less successfully) reciprocally sustaining and shaping one another" (Rothery, 2007, p. 91). Group process with individuals must take into account the changing reciprocal relationship between the individual in transition from prison to a relatively free and unstructured community.

Reentry interventions centered on helping returning citizens understand the meaning-making process and the meanings made as a result of traumatic or troubling events, such as imprisonment, can facilitate forming a new narrative identity (Saari, 1991) . This process presents as a promising intervention in improving the reentry outcomes by increasing the returning citizen's optimism and generativity. Global meaning, or a global view, indicates beliefs, goals, and feelings that guide an individual from early life. Situational meaning and appraised meaning are meanings attached to specific situations and stressful events. Park (2010) suggests that meaning making's purpose is to reduce the stressful discrepancies between global and situational meanings. However, when faced with highly stressful events, many individuals were not able to comprehend the meaning making and the meanings made (Park, 2010). A study by Yeager et al. (2014) on self-transcendent purpose for learning, which is based on Victor Frankl's book *Man's Search for Ultimate Meaning* (Frankl, 1959, 1984) found that discovery of purpose for learning lead to finding meaningfulness in mundane and challenging tasks. McLean and Pratt (2006) found that meaning making was correlated with generativity and optimism from narratives of mortality experiences and redemptive story sequence. Meaning making was found to be an important part of narrative identity.

An individual change theory that is relevant to the reentry experience is narrative reconstruction. The goal of a narrative approach is to help clients to understand the stories, which have shaped their lives, and then to challenge and expand them. In this process, clients are able to see other alternatives, and discover additional strengths and coping skills they possess. White and Epston (1990), in explaining a narrative approach, positioned themselves within the epistemological umbrella of *social constructionism,* of which the foundational claim is that it is impossible to know with complete certainty the nature of reality. A narrative approach provides awareness into linking the problems people face, their connections with the larger society, and their own heritage. It establishes links with the past and the desired future. Its emphasis and focus of analysis cuts across the individual, group, family, and macro-social systems. It uses the supports available so that people can "re-author" their existence (Abels & Abels, 2001). In that regard, knowledge is a product of social interchange. What we call knowledge is basically what we agree to call truth (Berger & Luckmann, 1967). People's view of the world reflects their interests and values. There is space to consider other conceptions and epistemologies; however, our views are culturally specific (Baert, 2005).

According to Kelley (2002), the social worker does not design an intervention to do something "to" the client, rather takes a role of active listener to better understand the client's perceptions of the problem and the meanings given to it. White made famous the idea that "the person is not the problem; the problem is the problem" (White & Epston, 1990). Narrative therapy asks the therapist to listen 'de-constructively' (attending to the meaning assigned to the narrative, challenging embedded negative meanings, and considering alternative meanings) to peoples' stories. People create meaning as they present their stories and the facilitator engages in questions and summarizing; as he or she does this, the clients can reconsider their own meanings and modify them. Facilitators listen and pay thoughtful attention to new constructions which may be emerging. When listening, therapists ask themselves questions such as "what is problematic here? What is the nature of this problem? What does it feel for this person to have this problem in her life? What is keeping this person from having experiences she would prefer? There is a *re-authoring* process in which people come to experience themselves in new ways as they concentrate on previously neglected, avoided or "un-storied" aspects of their lives (Freedman & Combs, 1996). In addition, narrative therapy places strong emphasis on social justice and oppressed groups. Challenging dominant narratives that are oppressing has been a focus of the narrative framework, and it has a political nature in its advocacy for liberation from dominant familial and cultural stories (Kelley, 2002).

Another relevant perspective, that is compatible with both ecological and narrative reconstruction is relational theory. Relational theory offers a potential means of circumventing the clearly failing current pattern of either authoritarian or avoidant practices that reentry individuals ordinarily face. Emerging from psychoanalytic object relations theory and self-psychology (Goldstein, 2001; Meissner, 1979), this theory provides a general model for enacting a facilitation process with returning citizens. In an earlier publication (Kenemore, 2014), Social Work practice with a reentry population is elaborated emphasizing application of a relational approach to individual work. A psychoanalytic theorist, Nancy McWilliams, summarizes the relational process as being attuned to people who "...need to talk to someone who will let that process happen without trying to cheer them up, distract them, join them in their denial, or minimize their pain (McWilliams, 1999, p. 59). This attuned relational approach is consistent with what people in reentry say they need (Kenemore & Roldan, 2006), and is applicable to group process.

These theoretical positions, including ecological system, meaning making, narrative reconstruction, and relational theories, together inform the P.RE.TURN change process we recommend as essential to sustainable change in the returning citizen's psychological readiness to successfully adapt to freedom.

Change process

Praxis of Revenant's Empowerment and Transcendence Using Re-Narrations (P.RE.TURN) is a central conceptual scheme utilized in this approach (In, 2017). This theoretical construction is being developed by the author to provide a framework for understanding the steps necessary to achieve sustainable internal individual changes in the reentry process. It recognizes the complexity of the change believed necessary for managing expectable setbacks and continuing progressive adaptation. Preturn (the movement that leads to a turn) is a set of specific minor pre-movements that are conducted prior to, and as a setup for, full committed execution of a desired movement.

> *A baseball batter might shift the leading foot in anticipation of a good pitch to establish optimal body posture prior to full execution of a bat swing. Without the preturn, the body mechanic will cause unnatural torque to one's knee during execution of a full bat swing.*

In the group process developed for the reentry population, 'P.RE. TURN' indicates those psychological processes that are introduced to facilitate readiness for the transition from a structured prison or jail environment to a challenging free community. Praxis, the first component, is considered most relevant to the beginning engagement in changes facilitated by group involvement. Revenant's Empowerment, the second component, characterizes the repeated exploration of one's negative narration and reconstruction of that narrative to incorporate empowerment. This component is emphasized in the middle, or working, phase of group process. Transcendence Using Re-Narration, the third component, refers to practicing application of the changed narration to one's life and challenges going forward, and leading to a transcendent and sustainable change in identity. Failure to preturn in the reentry process can result in disappointments and setbacks among returning citizens who are often not psychologically ready for the reentry process.

> *A case in point is a man in his early thirties with an impressive physique, who confidently asserted that he worked as a landscaping crew chief at a federal prison camp. Based on his claims of work experience and knowledge in landscaping he was assisted in getting a job as a supervisor of a landscaping crew in Chicago. Unfortunately, he did not last more*

than the morning of the first day on the job, because the work was too fast paced. He was not psychologically ready for the intensity of the job.

Through the group process incorporating P.RE.TURN, the participants develop changes in their cognition, emotion, and behavior that lead to transformation of their values and beliefs. The transcendence that sustains this shift from their revenant selves to new identities is achieved through continued engagement in the praxis of change and transformation, reinforced by narrative interchanges among group members.

Group approach

A group approach to services for this population is recommended as potentially both efficient and powerful. Groups serve several individuals simultaneously, thus enabling less costly and more efficiently structured service. The power of group dynamics has long been recognized (Yalom, 2005; Tosone & Rivas, 2009). Yalom's proposed therapeutic factors embedded in the group experience provide a theoretical grounding for the reentry group experience. Of particular relevance are instillation of hope, altruism, universality, interpersonal learning, mutual aid, and self-understanding. Yalom considers cohesiveness as a primary curative group factor in group therapy, and a necessary precondition for effective therapy. If group members feel connected to one another and there is group cohesion, then they will try harder to influence other group members, be more open to be influenced by other members, be more willing to listen to other members, be more accepting, feel a greater sense of security and relief from tension in the group, and will self-disclose more (Yalom & Leszcz, 2005). This sense of "belonging to the group" only occurs when everyone in the group values the group and feels valued and unconditionally accepted and supported by the other group members. Only when individuals are in a "real" relationship with each other, can they benefit and attend to life challenges (Rogers, 1961).

The idealized group practice approach we describe assumes continuity of group contact over the reentry process, including: anticipating release, actual release, transitioning from prison to freedom, and settling into a community. Recognizing the fragmented nature of reentry services, and the extremely limited access to those services, the practical barriers to the possibility of establishing small groups for individuals while in prison that would continue throughout the reentry process is unlikely. We recommend that current practitioners refer to the described approach as an ideal reference, and maximize relational continuity where possible.

Case example

The composite case example described below will be utilized to illustrate application of the proposed model in each phase of group practice.

In 2008, four federal probations officers from the Northern District of Illinois incubated a promising reentry program that later became a model for other adjacent federal districts. Based on their collective experience in supervising the federal supervision cases, the program's primary mission centered on helping prerelease detainees (federal inmates in halfway housing prior to full release to community) and unemployed individuals under active supervision to receive job training and placement. Toward that end, group activities were formed and facilitated to address job readiness, preparation for job interview, and job retention.

Beginning phase: Praxis

During initial group engagement Praxis is most relevant, ensuring that the facilitator and group members engage in discussions, using the real experience of participants, that demonstrate how revenant identity experiences inform behaviors and patterns that keep individuals from creating a more positive engagement in the community. The beginning phase involves creating an empathic milieu, clarification of roles and power arrangements, normalizing experience, and establishing norms that differentiate group relationships from ordinary social relationships with peers and institutional staff. The facilitator may introduce the need to develop a group contract regarding group norms and goals, including specific individual objectives representing successful reentry. A group agreement about members helping each other establish these objectives and practical plans may be suggested to solidify a common, shared theme among group members.

The group facilitator needs to try to see and know the person who lives beneath the apparent problems, bad decisions, and self-defeating behavior. Typically, they have adapted to a prison environment with defensive posturing and compliance, and are mistrustful and uncomfortable in sharing vulnerabilities. Group members will often initially state global goals that suggest a desire to avoid repeating difficulties that they believe caused their incarceration, including spending time with people who are a 'bad influence', or utilizing established illegal ways of surviving. Absent are often specific, practical objectives or ideas about steps toward achieving 'good citizenship'.

Reentry group facilitators need to recognize the value of the shared experience of the participants. They must quickly establish norms that challenge the initial defensive stances, and allow for sharing of experiences, and non-judgmental support. Alliance with group leaders in establishing norms can enable more reluctant members to comply. The group facilitator is required to establish a synthetic, or dual stance, combining authoritative and therapeutic elements, to guide group alliance development. The typical mandated supervision status of the reentry person requires a significantly different relationship dynamic with the facilitator than a voluntary clinical relationship. A mandated, dual-role, relationship (Skeem et. al, 2007) must not only develop a therapeutic alliance, but must also take into account the procedural justice factors. This facilitator stance is characterized as "firm but fair", and is consistent with what reentry individuals have defined as the kind of relational help they need, which is based on care, straight talk, trust, and authoritative but not authoritarian relationships.

The returning citizens assigned to the group viewed federal probation officers as adversarial authorities, and any mandatory participation only exacerbated the adversarial relationship. Therefore, extra care and effort were needed at the start to establish empathic working relationships that were based on respect and trust, and clear boundaries. From the first encounter, the officers modeled prosocial cognition, emotion, and behavior for the returning citizens to emulate throughout the group process and beyond. One of the first groups was an informational meeting held at a Salvation Army halfway house. The meeting started off with an introduction of the unique role of the officer who greeted the attendees with "Welcome home, everyone. We are glad you are back home. We are here to help you succeed in your return home. We will help you navigate through the maze of all the resources out there, so that you get what you need for successful reentry. We will work as a group and talk about what is important to everyone and how you can satisfy the supervision requirement". This set the tone for the rest of the group and future meetings.

It was emphasized that officers were not looking to find faults in order to re-incarcerate them, but instead wanted to understand their struggles so best strategizes could be developed and implemented for their successful reentry. However, the officers explained that they were going to be lenient, but would be honest in holding them accountable in a firm and fair manner. This instruction set apart the group as different from their day-to-day experience in prison and in the transitional facility. This praxis of honest and empathic reflections through a group was reinforced so that the participants could continue processing on their own.

Middle phase: Revenant's empowerment

In this phase the Revenant's Empowerment is a key concept, insisting that the negative narration is exposed, explored and reframed, and that more positive narrative content is to some degree integrated. The middle phase involves normalizing shared stories and experience, deconstructing and reconstructing narratives through meaning making (Frankl, 1959, 1984) to incorporate turning points, hope, spirituality, and enacting one's mission; and building supportive and sustaining alliances among group members. From sharing within a supportive milieu, participants revisit their individual revenants (traumatized and scarred selves from the past that continue to haunt them). By bringing to surface these revenant selves, cautious reflections can begin, reframing the traumatized and scarred past with the group's help and validations, then attempt to re-narrate their past selves into more empowered selves. This process of empowerment will require repeated attempts with acceptance that each attempt will require further recollections, deeper reflections, creative reframing, and authentic re-narration. All the while with the group's realistic affirming support and corrections.

This is the phase in which the practitioner facilitates

operationalization of the development of steps for each individual member to achieve realistic objectives, and for the members to engage together in preturn exercises and explorations, to enable integration of a readiness to face barriers, experience fall back, and regroup. It involves normalizing shared stories and experiences, deconstructing and reconstructing narratives to incorporate turning points, hope, spirituality, and enacting one's mission; and building supportive and sustaining alliances among group members engaging life experiences. Normalizing shared experiences, refers to "disconfirmation of a client's feelings of uniqueness" (Yalom &Leszcz, 2005, p.7). When group members are listening to one another's stories, they may be able to step back and decode or explore their own experiences in the same type of story, which may have been hidden or unheard (Freire, 1970). So, hearing others' similar stories can motivate re-narration of one's own story. Group members are inspired by other members (Yalom & Leszcz, 2005).

Furthermore, the cohesion of the group provides a supportive relationship to individuals, allowing them to explore their inner and buried experiences, which can be painful (Rogers, 1961). By applying such a disciplined focus, however, members learn to become curious, clear, accepting, and nonjudgmental observers of their thoughts and feelings and to reduce anxiety and vulnerability to depression (Yalom & Leszcz, 2005). Also, acceptance yields hope for transcendence and the potential for a continuing relationship after reentering back into the community. "The instillation of hope requires restoration of security in attachment relationships, which serves not only to ameliorate distress but also to restore the self-worth and self-confidence essential for exploration and growth" (Allen, 2013, p. 303). Hence, in the middle phase, group members are engaged in self-discovering, and deconstructing and reconstructing details of their own stories and experiences. They learn to view and interpret their experiences in a transformative way. Along with this, the group approach helps clients to maintain their hope and be psychologically ready for their return to the community.

Officers emphasized the praxis of honest and empathic reflections by encouraging participants to share their struggles with the group for mutual learning benefit. While initially hesitant, most participants began finding assurance and validation through sharing of common struggles that normalized their troubling experiences. Initial caution eventually transformed into chorus of complaining, mocking, and shared concerns.

Officers facilitated deeper discussions by summarizing, reframing, and further probing. However, both helpful and dangerous suggestions and solutions were shared by the participants. In response, officers did not hold back on confronting troubling issues by holding participants accountable with immediate corrections, encouragement, and sanctions. Officers were authoritative (firm and fair), but not authoritarian (petty and controlling). Paradoxically, this approach alleviated trust issues and elevated the working relationship through deeper discussions.

In another series of group meetings based on a cognitive behavioral therapeutic curriculum, the participants were led through class discussion exploring their patterns of antisocial thinking patterns and how these problematic thinking patterns have led to a cycle of poor decisions resulting in same poor consequences. Most participants lacked understanding of how their thinking patterns were garnering cycles of poor outcomes even though they were hoping for alternate positive outcomes. The cognitive and emotional awareness involving problem identification and solution development, and pro-social decisions and communications and follow-through required many hours of working on vignettes shared by the participants. These vignette group discussions prompted recall of past events, reflection of decisions made and consequences faced. Further exploration led to reframing the events based on new meanings found, and re-narrating the events to incorporate new resolve, identity, and hope for oneself.

Layers of forgotten past failures were shared and the group members helped each other to unravel and find possible solutions to the problems. Yet, the greater group accomplishments were found in how the group members were able to break down very big insurmountable problems or goals into small, realistic, and manageable strategic steps, thus to better understand the problems in discussion and realization of goals. Such deeper discussions engaged more silent participants to begin to share their reentry issues. Through this praxis of honest and empathic recalling, reflecting, reframing, and re-narrating their failures, participants were able to find shared solace in their struggles and find the motivation to continue the praxis so as free up current paralysis in their current station of life. The praxis was repeated throughout the workforce development program through group discussions, challenges, and facilitator/peer modeling.

Ending phase: Transcendence using re-narrations

This final phase of the group process emphasizes Transcendence Using Re-Narrations, so that individual participants are able to explore and anticipate how to respond to opportunities and challenges, using newly developed and empowered self-narratives. This phase emphasizes, in part, preparing group members for ending participation, dealing with members' reactions to the group's ending, systematically evaluating goal achievement and unfinished business, and helping members utilize new knowledge and skills in their lives outside the group. For the returning citizens, the end phase involves stabilization, enhancing hope, anticipating social and psychological challenges, dealing with barriers, and facilitating establishment of support systems beyond the group. The focus is on understanding the individual's process of reentry success, rather than on fulfillment of programmatic aims (Hong et al., 2014: Hong et al., 2015). The group approach enables individuals in the reentry process to envision current and future obstacles to successful reentry.

The end phase involves stabilization, enhancing hope, anticipating social and psychological challenges, and dealing with barriers. The focus is on understanding the individual's process of reentry success, rather than on fulfillment of programmatic aims (Hong et al., 2014; Hong et al., 2015). This reentry process requires herculean efforts that may feel like enactment of Sisyphus rolling a boulder uphill in Hades. Disappointments abound from missed opportunities and failed attempts. Barriers unexpectedly mutate while strengths evolve. One may have struggled finding gainful employment due to felony drug conviction, but upon employment, the excess money in pocket lead to relapse and eventual loss of job. The returning citizens may find difficulties in access to stable housing, employment, substance abuse treatment, and mental health treatment services, and a general lack of support networks. These are essential to making a successful transition from prison to community (Roman, Wolf, Correa, & Buck, 2007; Travis, 2005).

The ending phase should involve clarification and sharing of specific changes in narratives that incorporate empowerment and resilience, and a readiness to recoup from inevitable disappointments and failures. Ideally, the group approach should continue support when individuals return to the community, until they have achieved some degree of stabilization in the new environment. The group facilitators can keep in touch with their group members and provide continuing supports by connecting them to key resources. Also, group members can engage in continued mutual support and networking, to sustain them through a most vulnerable transition from incarceration to freedom.

For many, recalling and reflecting the past mistakes was not an easy exercise. These traumatic events and ensuing consequences limit how quickly, deeply, and completely one can explore and revisit the past. However, once others began sharing the floodgates opened for the more reluctant. Later, they were able to better organize and articulate their thoughts and emotions, and also accept their disappointments, frustrations, and then the real hurts, with the support and validation from others in the group. What kept this recall, reflection, reframing, and re-narration (four R's) process moving forward was the earlier praxis of building relationships with others and with renewing self. Without this praxis, the four R's became impotent exercises and futility that led to an old pattern of antisocial thinking, once the individual confronted major external barriers in the community.

It was important for the group members to keep reminding themselves of who they are, what they have to do, and how and when they must to do it. Repeated reminders redirected them toward realistic goals. They became focused on simple, measurable, and achievable tasks with a sense of urgency, and not entertaining delusional aims that would backfire and result in more harm. The graduates of this workforce program helped each other become job ready by providing peer feedback on mock job interviews, especially on how to explain the conviction record and long gaps in employment history. They helped each other on how to dress for an interview, how to address potential employers, how to effectively network for job leads, and so on. They even participated in team approach to job searches and created job banks to share openings that group members might benefit from. During the graduation ceremony, they participated in acknowledging and celebrating the group members' achievement of small successful steps that could potentially lead to greater success if they kept doing what was discussed in the group.

Effective group cohesion is not without problems. One of the groups had a small faction that was found discussing how to smuggle in large shipments of marijuana from Mexico. This was a faction that got caught. Without effective facilitation, there could easily have been more who successfully used the group sessions to plot and hatch lucrative criminal acts. Despite these expected failures, the vast majority of participants were able to graduate from the workforce development either with a job or enrollment in community job training program which they would not have been able to avail themselves without participation in the workforce development program.

Many participants expressed how difficult it is to remain law-abiding upon release from prison. Some equated the reentry to "hell", and they were just waiting to be burnt again for trying to survive, and to be sent back to prison. They saw no way out of this revolving door. This hopelessness led in a few to an inability to attempt anything meaningful. In this paralysis, many opportunities were missed, or never seen as a realizable goal. However, in most instances the participants achieved a more empowered re-narration and embraced a newer identity based on profound meanings they found in their lives. Transcendence that sustains these changes and transformations was achieved when the participants supported each other in integrating their revised narratives. Repeated praxis better prepared the participants for a world ripe with barriers and traps that they have now been taught to recognize.

Conclusion

We have presented an idealized group practice approach for work with individuals in transition from prison to community that is developed from a beginning understanding of a typical thematic experience of citizens going through that transition. It is informed by ecological, meaning making, narrative and relational theories, and grounded in a philosophical foundation that assumes reentry individuals are fully functioning members of an oppressed population, and that change toward successful citizenship requires empowerment and a restorative practice stance by those committed to helping them. The group practice approach further insists that achievement of sustainable changes to one's narrative to include an empowerment world view is achievable through focused group attention to psychological readiness to overcome severe internal and external challenges and barriers that are expected to confront these returning citizens.

It is our hope and expectation that Social Workers and other practitioners who work with members of this population during their transition from incarceration to freedom will consider utilization of the group approach presented, with its attention to Praxis of

Revenant's Empowerment and Transcendence Using Re-Narrations (P.RE.TURN), as explicated and illustrated, and with its recognition of the power of group process and support, as a general guide to their work. The approach described is conceptual, and not yet validated by evidence-informed application. It is, however, solidly grounded in, and responsive to, the experiences of individuals who have successfully navigated the transition from prison to freedom, and continue to do so. In addition, this conceptual group intervention model is informed by several decades of direct practice with the criminal justice/reentry population.

References

Abels, P. & Abels, S. (2001). *Understanding narrative therapy: A guidebook for the Social Worker,* Springer Publishing Company.

Akon, A.A. (2006). The racial dimensions of social capital: Toward a new understanding of youth empowerment and community organizing in America's urban core. In S. Ginwright, P. Noguera, & J. Cammarota (Eds). *Beyond resistance: Youth activism and community change,* 81-92. New York: Routledge.

Akon, A.A., Cammarota, J. & Ginwright, S. (2008). Youthtopias: Towards a new paradigm of critical youth studies. *Youth Media Reporter, 2*(4), 1-30.

Alexander, M. (2010). *The new Jim Crow: Mass incarceration in the age of colorblindness.* New York: The New Press.

Allen, G.J. (2013). Hope in human attachment and spiritual connection. *Bulletin of the Menninger Clinic,* 77 (4), 302-331. DOI: 10.1521/bumc.2013.77.4.302.

Baert, P. (2005). *Philosophy of the social sciences: Towards pragmatism.* Malden, Massachusetts: Polity Press.

Berger, P. L., & Luckmann, T. (1967). *The social construction of reality.* New York: Doubleday.

Frankl, V. E. (1959, 1985). *Man's search for meaning.* Boston, MA: Beacon Press.

Freedman, J; & Combs, G. (1996). *Narrative therapy: The social construction of preferred realities.* New York, NY: W.W. Norton Company, Inc.

Freire, P. (1970). *Pedagogy of the oppressed.* New York: Continuum.

Freire, P. (1992). *Pedagogy of hope*. New York: Continuum.

Hlavka, H. Wheelock, D. Jones, R. (2015). Ex-offender accounts of successful reentry from prison. *Journal of Offender Rehabilitation*, 54:6, 406-428.

Hong, P.Y.P., Hodge, D., & Choi, S. (2015). Spirituality, hope, and self-sufficiency among low income jobseekers. *Social Work, 60*(2), 155-164.

Hong, P.Y.P., Lewis, D., & Choi, S. (2014). Employment hope as an empowerment pathway to self-sufficiency among ex-offenders. *Journal of Offender Rehabilitation, 53*(5), 317-333.

Houston, S. (2002) Reflecting on habitus, field and capital: Towards a culturally sensitive Social Work. *Journal of Social Work*, 2(2), 149-167.

In, B. (2017). Personal communication.

Kaeble, D, Glaze, L.E. (2016) Correctional Populations in the United States, 2015. *Bureau of Justice Statistics*, December 29, 2016. NCJ250374 Retrieved from https://www.bjs.gov/index.cfm?ty=pbdetail&iid=5870

Kelley, P. (2002). Narrative therapy. In A. R. Roberts & G. J. Greene (Eds.), *Social workers' desk reference* (pp. 121-124). New York, NY: Oxford University Press.

Kenemore, T. (2014) Social Work practice with reentry from incarceration. In, J. Rosenberger (Editor), *Relational Social Work Practice with Diverse Populations*. New York: Springer, pp. 239-260.

Kenemore, T. & Roldan, I. (2006) Staying straight: Lessons from ex-offenders. *Clinical Social Work Journal*, 34 (1) 5-21.

Maruna, S. (2001). *Making Good: how ex-convicts reform and rebuild their lives*. Washington, DC: American Psychological Association.

McLean, K. C., & Pratt, M. W. (2006). Life's little (and big) lessons: Identity statuses and meaning-making in the turning point narratives of emerging adults. *Developmental Psychology, 42*(4), 714.

McWilliams, N. (1999). *Psychoanalytic case formulation*. New York: The Guilford Press.

Muhlhausen, D. B. (2015). *Studies cast doubt on effectiveness of prisoner reentry programs*. Heritage Foundation. No. 3010.

Mullaly, B. (2010). *Challenging oppression and confronting privilege: Second Edition*. Oxford University Press.

Murphy, B. C., & Dillon, C. (2011). *Interviewing in action in a multicultural world*. Australia; United States: Brooks/Cole Cengage Learning.

Ndrecka, M. (2014). *The impact of reentry programs on recidivism: A meta-analysis*. (Doctoral dissertation, University of Cincinnati).

O'Brien, P., & Bates, R. (2005). Women's post-release experiences in the U.S.: Recidivism and re-entry. *International Journal of Prisoner Health, 1*(2), 207-221.

O'Brien, P. (2001) Just like baking a cake: Women describe the necessary ingredients for successful reentry after incarceration. *Families in Society: The Journal of Contemporary Human Services*, 82(3), pp. 287 – 295.

O'Brien, P. (2001). *Making it in the free world.* New York: State University of New York Press.

Park, C. L. (2010). Making sense of the meaning literature: An integrative review of meaning making and its effects on adjustment to stressful life events. *Psychological Bulletin, 136*(2), 257.

Patterson, G. T. (2013). Prisoner reentry: A public health or public safety issue for social work practice? *Social Work in Public Health.* 28: 129-141.

Pennell, J. (2006). Restorative practices and child welfare: Toward an inclusive civil society. *Journal of Social Issues,* 62(2), 259-279 .

Petersilia, J. (20004). What works in prison reentry? Reviewing and questioning the evidence. *Federal Probation,*68 (2), 4-8.

Pfaff, J (2017). *Locked in: The true causes of mass incarceration—and how to achieve real reform.* New York: Basic Books.

Rogers, C.R. (1961). *On Becoming a Person: A Therapist's View of Psychotherapy.* Boston: Houghton Mifflin Company.

Roman, C. G., Wolff, A., Correa, V., & Buck, J. (2007). Assessing intermediate outcomes of a faith-based residential prisoner reentry program. *Research on Social Work Practice, 17*(2), 199-215.

Rothery, M. (2007). Critical Ecological Systems Theory. In. N. Coady, & P. Lehman,. *Theoretical perspectives for direct Social Work practice.* New York: Springer Publishing Company.

Saari, C. (1991). *The creation of meaning in clinical Social Work.* New York: The Guilford Press.

Sampson, R. & Laub, J. (2016). Turning points and the future of life-course criminology: Reflections on the 1986 criminal careers report. *Journal of Research in Crime & Delinquency,* 53 (3).

Simon, B. (1994). *The empowerment tradition in American Social Work: A history.* New York: Columbia University Press.

Skardhamar, T., & Savolainen, J. (2014). Changes in criminal offending around the time of job entry: A study of employment and desistance. Criminology, 52(2), 263-291.

Skeem, J. L., Louden, J. E., Polaschek, D., & Camp, J. (2007). Assessing relationship quality in mandated community treatment: Blending care with control. Psychological Assessment, 19(4), 397.

Specht, H. & Courteny, (1994) M. Unfaithful angels: How Social Work has abandoned its mission. New York: The Free Press.

Statistica (2017). Countries with the largest Number of Prisoners, as of July 2017. Retrieved from https://www.statista.com/statistics/262961/

countries-with-the-most-prisoners/

Tosone, R. & Rivas, R. (2009). An introduction to group work practice. Sixth Edition.

Travis, J. (2005). But they all come back: Facing the challenges of prisoner reentry. Washington, DC: The Urban Institute Press.

US Department of Justice, FBI, *Uniform Crime Reports*, www.bjs.gov/, accessed 2017.

White, M., & Epston, D. (1990). *Narrative means to therapeutic ends.* New York: WW Norton & Company.

Visher, C.A., WInterfield, L., Coggeshall, M.B. (2005). Ex-offender employment programs and recidivism: A meta-analysis. *Journal of Experimental Criminology,* 1:295-315.

Yalom, I., & Leszcz, M. (2005). *The theory and practice of group psychotherapy* (5th ed.). New York: Basic Books.

Yeager, D. S., Henderson, M. D., Paunesku, D., Walton, G. M., D'Mello, S., Spitzer, B. J., & Duckworth, A. L. (2014). Boring but important: A self-transcendent purpose for learning fosters academic self-regulation. *Journal of Personality and Social Psychology, 107*(4), 559.

Zehr, H. (2002). *The little book of restorative justice.* Intercourse, PA: Good Books.

A conversation begins:

Using teach-ins to begin a dialogue about racial justice

Samuel R. Benbow

Overview of the Teach-in about Racial Justice

During the fall of 2016, in response to ongoing racial tensions, acts of intolerance and community concerns, Shippensburg University Social Work & Gerontology department planned a day-long teach-in event. The event was entitled "Teach-in about Racial Justice." The teach-in called for the suspension of all social work classes for the day, and bringing all program students to one large central location for the purpose of creating a space for real and in-depth conversations.

In the format and tradition of group work, content regarding race relations was presented in an experiential-based manner, directly connected to recent race related incidents which occurred on our campus as well as ongoing across the nation. LePeau, Morgan, Zimmerman, Snipes, and Marcotte (2016) suggests that "building a better environment occurs on the individual and systemic level as well. If one individual has a better experience, feels supported, and is retained on the institutional level, then the environment is better for that individual" (p.121). What resulted was an excellent example of group work used in a community to tackle challenging topics in a proactive way.

Historical context

According to the Southern Poverty Law Center (2017), in 2009 hate groups, hate propaganda, acts of violence, and acts of intolerance dramatically increased throughout the United States in the wake of the election of President Barack Obama. While the cause of this increase cannot and should not be solely attributed to one specific event or incident, there were several notable ones that negatively impacted race relations throughout the United States. These include but are not limited to the following events:

1. The Support Our Law Enforcement and Safe Neighborhoods Act, better known as *Arizona Senate Bill 1070*. According to Wallace (2014) Senate Bill 1070 "criminalizes failure to carry proof of legal immigration status as a state misdemeanor; requires the police to determine the immigration status of a person detained in a lawful stop, detention, or arrest if there is a reasonable suspicion that the person might be undocumented; and prohibits local and state officials from limiting or restricting enforcement of federal immigration laws." (p.1)
2. The killing of Trevon Martin in February 2012 by George Zimmerman. Martin, an unarmed teen, was shot by Zimmerman, who was acting as a neighborhood watch coordinator in Sanford, Florida, and he was subsequently acquitted on the grounds of self-defense.
3. The ongoing fatal shootings or killings of unarmed Black men by police officers which in the vast majority of cases resulted in no charges pressed or acquittals. These outcomes intentionally or unintentionally sent and reinforced the message that Black men's lives are less valued than their white counterparts. Quah & Davis (2015) chronicled a list of Black men killed by police officers beginning April 2014 thru April 2015. The following list is not all inclusive, however was featured on many news outlets and social media venues nationally and internationally.

    *   Dontre Hamilton, April 2014, 31 yrs. old, Milwaukee, Wisconsin
    *   Eric Garner, July 2014, 43 yrs. old, Staten Island, New York
    *   John Crawford III, August 2014, 22 yrs. old, Dayton Ohio
    *   Michael Brown Jr. August 2014, 18 yrs. old, Ferguson Missouri
    *   Ezell Ford, August 2014, 25 yrs. old, Florence California
    *   Donte Parker, August 2014, 36 Victorville California
    *   Akai Gurley, November 2014, 28 yrs. old, Brooklyn ,New York
    *   Tamir Rice, August 2014, 12 yrs. old, Cleveland Ohio
    *   Rumain Brisbon, 34 yrs. old, Phoenix Arizona

- Jerame Reid, December 2014, 36 yrs. old, Bridgeton New Jersey
- Tony Robinson, March 2015, 19 yrs. old, Madison Wisconsin
- Philip White, March 2015, 32 yrs. old, Vineland New Jersey
- Eric Harris, April 2015, 44 yrs. old, Tulsa Oklahoma
- Walter Scott, April 2015, 50 yrs. old, North Charleston South Carolina
- Freddie Gray, April 2015, 25 yrs. old, Baltimore, Maryland

While it might be expedient to examine the above list from an individual case-by-case basis, it is important to consider the systemic nature of the collective. The list represents diversity in ages, educational achievement, employment/non-employment status, city and state, economic levels, faith systems and so forth, with the two constants being sex and race.

The hate-filled rhetoric, attitude and behaviors of then Presidential nominee Donald Trump through his present tenure as President of the United States. His statements, tweets and actions served and continues to serve as a venue to embolden white supremacy, ableism, sexism, racism, classism, heterosexism, ageism and religious oppression. Messages such as *"Make American Great Again," "Build that Wall"* and *"Lock Her Up"* reverberated at several of President Trump's rallies that were nationally televised. Individual blatant acts of intolerance through prideful aggression continue to occur across the nation. In June of 2015, for instance, a 21-year-old self-proclaimed white supremacist, Dylan Roof, entered a predominantly black church in Charleston South Carolina and killed nine people during a prayer service with the intent of starting a race war.

1. Acquittal of police in the killing of Freddie Gray, who was a 25 year-old Black man from Sandtown-Winchester, in Baltimore, Maryland. On April 14, Freddie led police on a foot chase through his inner-city neighborhood. Once caught, he was arrested, and then placed in the back of a police van. Five days later, he died as a result of injuries to his neck and spine while being transported by police. Baltimore's impoverished and oppressed community rioted in response to the yet another unarmed Black man killed by police (Herman & Cox, 2015).
2. The above-mentioned events and many more acts of hatred, intolerance and bigotry entered the national consciousness as they were streamed across the nation via social media outlets. Shippensburg University is less than a two-hour drive from

Baltimore and therefore the local television stations, along with other media outlets showed graphic and detailed footage of the events leading up to the killing as well as the riot itself.

About Shippensburg University and the Social Work and Gerontology Department

Shippensburg University of Pennsylvania, located in Central Pennsylvania, is one of fourteen Universities within the Pennsylvania State System of Higher Education. The university is considered a mid-sized institution with an enrollment of 6, 550 undergraduates, 998 graduate students, 100 undergraduate programs and 57 graduate programs. The student/faculty ratio is 20 to 1, and consists of 77.5% (White), 11.5% (Black), 4.5% (Hispanic) and 3.2% (Multi-racial) students.

The Social Work and Gerontology Department was established in 1974, and has a current student enrollment of more than 250 undergraduate students in its campus-based program, a cohort-based degree completion program, and a Gerontology minor. Additionally the department offers an MSW degree as a joint program with Millersville University of Pennsylvania. Finally, there are 10 tenured-tracked faculty members which have all earned advanced degrees, and less than 10 adjunct part-time faculty members. (Shippensburg University, 2017).

Impetus for the Teach-in about Racial Justice

On September 26, 2015 the campus of Shippensburg University was placed into a windstorm of emotions and activism not seen or experienced before. An undergraduate student used Facebook as a vehicle to express his thoughts on Shippensburg University's enrollment practices regarding students of color. He stated:

"There's a lot of dark meat on our campus this semester. Inner city garbage rolled in because the university wants to look "diverse". A lot of them wear BLM shirts to classes. I'm gonna enjoy their faces when I start wearing my Baltimore City Police hoodie to classes in the colder days." (Eckstine, 2016)

The screenshot of his post immediately entered the social media world and within a matter of hours the hate-filled, racist message was seen and or heard far beyond the quiet community of Shippensburg. Within 48 hours of his Facebook posting, the student was asked to leave the university. Shortly after his departure, he submitted a letter of apology stating he was sorry for his:

"words of hate" which were "borne out of anger, ignorance, selfishness and bitterness" and claimed to take full responsibility for what was said before concluding by asking for "forgiveness from my peers and all who were affected by this" (Driscoll, 2016).

Despite the student's apology and departure from Shippensburg University, the pain, hurt and damage caused lived on. The university community, our Social Work and Gerontology department faculty, and students believed these incidents, amongst others in the neighboring community, were being called to action to address the Facebook post and its aftermath. Racial injustices, hate and intolerance were no longer down the street or around the corner, but had returned again to our campus. The famous quote from Martin Niemöller posted in the U.S Holocaust Memorial Museum states:

First they came for the Socialists, and I did not speak out—
Because I was not a Socialist.
Then they came for the Trade Unionists, and I did not speak out—
Because I was not a Trade Unionist.
Then they came for the Jews, and I did not speak out—
Because I was not a Jew.
Then they came for me—and there was no one left to speak for me.
(Niemoller, n.d.)

The university's initial response presented as tempered, lukewarm and inadequate to the point of nonexistent. University students, alumni, and commentators from news organizations and on social media outlets such as Facebook and Twitter demanded the university take a stronger, more decisive stance towards rejecting racial intolerance, and acts of intimidation on the campus of Shippensburg University.

The university had nowhere to hide, could no longer marginalize the statement or its impact, nor ignore that these types of incidents have occurred on our campus. Like the final line in Niemoller's (n.d.) statement, "then they came for me-and there was no one left to speak for me." Students were bringing their frustrations and concerns into the classroom, campus-based student affairs events, residence halls, and to faculty, staff and administrators.

During the Social Work and Gerontology department's biweekly faculty meeting immediately following the incident, time was taken to process personal and professional feelings amongst the faculty. We abandoned the previously set agenda and instead shared our thoughts and feelings, provided support to each other, and strengthened our resolve as a group to social justice. Within the 90-minute time frame of our meeting, the design of a teach-in was completely formed to focus specifically on race relations.

The concept of a "teach-in" has its roots in events at the University of Michigan at Ann Arbor in late March 1965. At that time, the intent of a teach-in led by faculty and students, was to protest the Vietnam War. With opposition from the University President, the Governor and the Michigan legislature, the faculty and Students for a Democratic Society (SDS) organized the event in a way that did not take away from the educational responsibilities of the faculty, but sent a clear message regarding the opposition to the United States' involvement in the Vietnam War.

It was reported that the event was attended by more than 3,500 individuals and consisted of lectures, movies, and musical performances focused on protesting the war. Regular classes were canceled, and rallies and speeches went on for more than 12 hours. The teach-in was viewed a success by its organizers because it effectively created a nonviolent protest against the Vietnam War on a college campus reaching thousands and sparking teach-in style protests across the nation. (New York Times, 1965).

At Shippensburg University, our goal for the teach-in was to engage in experiential-based learning opportunities focusing on creating space for dialogue about race relations on our campus, in the local community and throughout the nation. We wanted students to hear each other, understand others' experiences that were different from theirs, and learn about how our community experiences racial tensions. Most importantly, we wanted to teach students various ways to become actively involved in addressing racial inequality and tensions within our campus community.

Design and implementation of the Teach-in about Racial Justice

As previously stated, the idea of the teach-in was formed during the biweekly faculty meeting, which commonly consists of updates (Department Chair, BSW and MSW programs, Gerontology minor, and Field Coordinator), and reviews of faculty professional development accomplishments, university policy updates, and student concerns. The agenda for the meetings are e-mailed out to all faculty in advance of the meeting as a way of preparing for the meeting as well as potentially adding to the agenda.

The meeting started with the approval of minutes from the previous meeting and then very quickly moved to the need to process what was happening on our campus, with our students and the seemingly increase in acts of intolerance locally, regionally and nationally. We were compelled to take a stand! We were compelled to help our students express their thoughts, feelings and experiences in a way that was constructive and empowering. The agenda was abandoned and the remaining 80 or so minutes of the meeting was dedicated towards developing a framework for a teach-in. The framework included clarifying the purpose and focus of the teach-in, the intended curriculum, date for which we would be able to capture the largest number of students, and the time needed to carry out our goals.

A synthesis of the six major points for the teach-in were as follows:

First: When, where and how long?

Four sessions lasting 75 minutes per session would be facilitated by two or more faculty members with a 10-15 minute break in between. Sessions would be held in a central location on campus that would support large and small group work as well as provide the technology resources needed.

Second: Take a definitive stand

A letter was created and signed by all of the faculty members in the department, then emailed to all program students, and administrators. The letter served to reaffirm the department's commitment to inclusivity of and for all, which directly aligned with our social work values and principles.

Third: "All In"

All faculty committed to adjust their teaching schedules and content to implement the teach-in, thus requiring all students who would be in class during the time of the teach-in to attend. All students majoring in social work and others connected to the department were invited to participate and highly encouraged to attend.

Fourth: Essence of group work

Based on professional and personal interest as well as expertise, faculty members teamed up to design their 75 minute session based on the agreed-upon focus, goals, and implementation strategies. Teams shared content, activities and focus with other teams to ensure overlap and consistency of message. It must be noted that several of the 10 faculty members served on more than one team, and thus facilitated more than one session.

Fifth: Creative group work strategies for change

Purposeful planning to create opportunities for individual, small group, and large group experiential-based learning. Intentional use of power point, videos, music, lecture, participant led discussions, questions and answers, and take away tools/skills were built into all the sessions.

Sixth: No one-time event

A commitment was made that the teach-in would be an annual event during the fall semester with a specific focus on race relations. A spring event would be dedicated towards increasing cultural awareness and sensitivity through select field trips such as the National Holocaust Museum, the National African-American Museum, and the National Native American Museum to name a few.

Content of the Teach-in about Racial Injustice

Shippenburg's "Teach-in about Racial Justice" focused on micro-aggressions, the history of racism in the United States, past and present-day policies which serve to influence racism and oppression, the power of privilege, and understanding the culture of "whiteness." These culminated in the identification and development of practical tools to combat racial injustices within one's own sphere of influence.

Throughout the event, which included more than 150 students throughout the day, opportunities were provided for discussion, reflection and increased awareness of the ongoing racial injustices within the criminal justice system, employment practices, housing, and in higher education. It was reinforced to the students that as social workers, we are equally committed to understanding our roles in either perpetuating the racial inequalities or in working towards improving access to opportunities which foster physically and emotionally safe environments that are free from hate and discrimination.

As previously stated, the teach-in was a one-day, four session event. Each session lasted 75 minutes in total with a 10- 15 minute break between sessions for students, faculty, administrators and guests to engage in further discussion. Students who were originally scheduled to attend a class at that time, were required to attend the session offered at the same time. Additionally, all students in the major as well as those interested in possibly majoring in Social Work, were encouraged to attend the teach-in. Students, campus faculty, administrators and guests were able to attend all or parts of sessions based on their interest and availability.

A brief synopsis of each session follows:

Session #1: Silence in the face of injustice is not an option in the social work profession.

The session focused on participants learning how to have authentic, courageous conversations about racism. Participants worked with a partner and then in small groups and responded to prompts such as 'discuss something positive about your race or ethnic background', 'share messages you learned /were shown/saw about your own racial group': (a) 'in your family', (b) 'in your community' and (c) 'in society at large'. Participants then engaged in a debriefing and were asked to share about 'questions that stood out and or challenged you. Why? What will you remember most about this activity? What did you learn about yourself from this activity? From others? About racism?'

Session #2: Historical Foundation: A walk down the historical lane for Black people in the United States.

The session focused on providing a glimpse of the racial injustices experienced by Black people from a historical perspective. Participants were shown videos that included "A hole in a head" – a true story of a childhood survivor of radiation testing, the 1955 Alabama Church Bombing, the Tuskegee Study, and the Emmet Till Story. Examples of questions presented during the session to engage in courageous dialogue were: 'Does Black Lives Matter? Where do social work core values come into play for you? And where do we go from here?' Participants were then taught about the concept of an action continuum that included identifying where they found themselves on the continuum and where they wanted to move towards. The categories of the continuum were (a) Actively participating via jokes and acts of discrimination, (b) Denying there is a problem, (c) Recognizing and taking no action, (d) Educating self by taking action.

Session #3: Policy influence on racism and oppression: Past, present and future.

The session focused on participants learning about the levels of oppression in relationship to policy design and implementation from a past, present and future perspective. Policy discussion focused on Stop and Frisk in New York City, the Real I.D. Act of 2005, Lynching in America, Dyer Anti-Lynching Bill, and the Civil Rights Act of 1957. Participants engaged in small group and large group discussions about the influence of such policies on creating a safe and inclusive environment in the United States.

Session #4: White Privilege: What does Whiteness mean to you? Growing up White and not knowing anyone different or being exposed to difference.

The session focused on participants learning the importance of acknowledging White privilege and understanding each person's ability to use their privilege to impact change. In addition to White privilege, other concepts addressed were micro-aggressions, the power of trust, the fallacy of colorblindness, taking a stand, social justice and advocacy. Participants shared their understanding of these concepts, and their experiences on campus and in their home communities on how to deal with racism and acts of intolerance. The format for the session was small group discussion, applying concepts to video presentation of case scenarios, and the development of action plans to be implemented after the teach-in.

Cost and benefits of the Teach-in about Racial Injustice

How much did it cost? During the presentation with Dr. Clements at the 2017 Symposium, several attendees specifically asked about the cost of implementing such an event. While our response that "there was no financial cost" was true and accurate, it was not a complete answer. To fully answer the question of cost, it is important to start off with the realities that no monies were needed to secure the meeting place on campus. The space provided enough room to effectively seat the 150 participants in small round tables that seated eight persons per table, allowing for the use of technology to display power point as well as video clips. Finally, no food or drink was provided, however sustenance was plentiful.

There was also an unmeasurable moral and ethical cost to us as educators, social workers, faculty members, and practitioners if we knew something was critically missing or needed in our program and chose to do nothing. Our decision was to create space for genuine conversation about biases, micro-aggressions, and oppression in a way that extended the depth of discussion beyond the classroom environment. We felt committed to make a difference and move from talk to action.

How much time did it take to pull it all together? It took 80 minutes to decide on the teach-in, commit to it, and then design it. After the 80 minutes, the curriculum building and implementation design occurred within small work teams. Yes, we all had content we needed to cover in a certain period of time within our department meetings and classes. Yes, we all had committee work that needed our attention and time. Yes, we use group work for mutual aid and task completion as common tools in our courses. Yes, we as faculty members participate in group work within the social work department, through the college on various committees, during our community outreach work and in our personal lives. Yes, we as educators talk about getting involved and being activists. Yes, we were able to accomplish a great deal in 80 minutes when we were all intentionally in the moment. Yes, it is my sincere belief that we have become closer as a faculty in a way unlike other semesters and or other work related experiences. Yes, an 80 minutes mutual aid group did that!

What were the benefits of the teach-in? Our department created a space for real dialogue for students and faculty, students were able to apply the Code of Ethics and Social Work values to real life experiences, we collectively increased activism through advocacy amongst social work students, we as faculty served as role models for active civic engagement, and we unintentionally increased the visibility of our Social Work and Gerontology program throughout the college, university, community and region. Students provided feedback about their growth, increased understanding, and continued interest in ongoing dialogue about race relations.

Conclusion to the Teach-in on Racial Injustice

In response to a racially charged act of intolerance on the campus of Shippensburg University, a teach-in about racial injustice was designed and implemented within the Department of Social Work & Gerontology. The goals of the teach-in were to create space for department faculty and students to safely express their feelings regarding the incident, become educated about the historical oppressive practices in the United States, and to learn proactive ways to effectively address racial intolerance.

We were successful in creating an opportunity through small groups for program students to share their thoughts, experiences and feeling about acts of racial intolerance in their personal lives, as well as in their roles as college students. They were provided a historical foundation of racism and oppression in the United States that in many cases filled in the gap of past educational teachings, while further developing ways to identify and effectively work through acts of racial intolerance. The initial decision to conduct a teach-in, cancel all classes for the day of the teach-in, design and fully commitment to the process occurred within 80 minutes of a bi-weekly department meeting.

Acknowledgement

While I am the author and co-presenter of the presentation at the 2017 Symposium, it's very important to emphasize the fact that this was and continues to be a team effort. Thank you *Dr. Deborah Jacobs, Dr. Liz Fisher, Dr. Jen Clements (co-presenter), Dr. Jayleen Galarza, Dr. Marita Flagler, Dr. Michael Lyman, Dr. Dara Bourassa, Dr. Charlene Lane, and Dr. Dorlisa Minnick.*

References

Driscoll, P. (2016). Public statement to Shippensburg University Community.

Eckstine, C (2016, September 28). Students Facebook post sparks backlash, petition at Shippensburg University. ABC 27.com News. Retrieved from http://abc27.com/2016/09/28/students-facebook-post-sparks-backlash-petition-at-shippensburg-university/

Herman, P. & Cox, J.W. (2015, April 28). A Freddie Gray primer: Who was he, how did he die, why is there so much anger? Washington Post. Retrieved from https://www.washingtonpost.com/news/local/wp/2015/04/28/a-freddie-gray-primer-who-was-he-how-did-he-why-is-there-so-much-anger/?utm_term=.d43734ded4bc

LePeau, L. A., Morgan, D. L., Zimmerman, H. B., Snipes, J. T., & Marcotte, B. A. (2016). Connecting to Get Things Done: A Conceptual Model of the Process Used to Respond to Bias Incidents. *Journal of Diversity In Higher Education*, 9(2), 113-129.

MICHIGAN FACULTY CREATED TEACH-IN; 49 at University Staged the First Vietnam Protest. (1965, May 9). *The New York Times,* p. 43. Retrieved January 20, 2017.

Miller, B. (2016). You don't expect it on a college campus: Shippensburg students on racist post. Retrieved from http://www.pennlive.com/news/2016/10/shippensburg.html

Niemoller, M. (n.d.) Martin Niemöller: "First they came for the Socialists..."Retrieved from https://www.ushmm.org/wlc/en/article.php?ModuleId=10007392

Quah N. & Davis L.E. (2015, May, 1). Here's A Timeline Of Unarmed Black People Killed By Police Over Past Year From Arizona to New York, the cases have added to national outrage over deadly force used by police. Buzzfeed. Retrieved from https://www.buzzfeed.com/nicholasquah/heres-a-timeline-of-unarmed-black-men-killed-by-police-over?utm_term=.sw6Y4me8j#.xgZG1A8L4

Shippensburg University (2017). About Shippensburg University. Retrieved from http://www.ship.edu/about/

Southern Poverty Law Center (2016) Hate Groups 1999-2016. Rise of Hate Groups. Retrieved from https://www.splcenter.org/hate-map.

Wallace, S.J. (2013). Papers Please: State-Level Anti-Immigrant Legislation in the Wake of Arizona's SB 1070. *Political Science Quarterly* 129 (2), 261- 291.

Passing the baton:
Revitalization of an IASWG chapter

Maria Gandarilla, Cheryl D. Lee and Mei Kameda

Introduction

The IASWG organization, formerly known as the Association for the Advancement of Social Work with Groups (AASWG), was founded in 1979 through the efforts of academics and group workers who felt that group work was being forgotten in social work education with the advent of the generalist model (Ramey, 2009). Currently, the IASWG has 18 chapters throughout the world, and this number continues to grow. IASWG chapters are an essential element to the sustainability and functionality of the organization as a whole. Through chapter efforts, the organization promotes its mission to further the practice, teaching, and research of the group work practice method in different communities, and it maintains a vibrant and diverse membership.

The Southern California Chapter

The IASWG Southern California Chapter is located in Long Beach, California, where it conducts most of its chapter efforts. The chapter is composed of social work students, practitioners and academics. It includes members who are registered with the larger organization, as well as attendees who have some interest in group work or a meeting topic and are curious about the organization. Those who attend meetings often become involved in planning and attending chapter events. The emeritus president of the chapter is a professor at the California State University, Long Beach (CSULB) School of Social Work; therefore, outreach has often been conducted on campus. Students make up the largest group of participants, though most are not registered members. The chapter's leadership is formally structured as an elected board, though currently, the chapter leadership functions as a planning committee that includes elected board members and regular chapter members. The chapter's co-chairs and the emeritus president are responsible for setting up and initiating meetings. The planning committee decides on the events to be hosted by the chapter.

Chapter history

The Southern California Chapter of IASWG became active in the 1990's and at that time was located in San Diego, California, USA. The leaders in the chapter were: Dr. Jean Gill and Dr. Joan Perry. Dr. Gill had a tremendous passion for activity based group work and for the international group work organization. Dr. Perry wrote a book about social group work and left funds to IASWG in her will. Dr. Paul Abels, a member of the Southern California Chapter, was one of the initiators of IASWG. He helped organize its first symposium in 1979 when he was a professor at Case Western Reserve University in Cleveland, Ohio (Ramey, 2009). When Dr. Abels later took a teaching position at California State University, Long Beach (CSULB), he became involved with the Southern California IASWG Chapter. He mentored Dr. Cheryl Lee, a new group work professor at CSULB in 2000, and asked her to drive with his wife Sonia, also a group worker, to San Diego (a two-hour drive from Long Beach) to attend IASWG chapter meetings. Dr. Lee soon became bonded to the chapter, its founders and later the international organization. Dr. Abels encouraged Dr. Lee to attend the Brooklyn, New York Symposium in 2001 and that incredible symposium experience sealed her commitment to IASWG. Later she served on the international board. Although the Southern California Chapter, which was based in San Diego was small, it attracted members from Los Angeles, Northern CA, and Arizona. True to the saying that a small group can accomplish a lot, the Southern CA Chapter under the guidance of Jeannie Gill hosted two international group symposiums in San Diego, one in 1995 and one in 2005.

In 2005, Dr. Lee reached out to students in her classes to see if they would be interested in forming a group work club as an extra-curricular university activity. Students expressed interest, and a group work club was initiated. The Group Work Club, which had many diverse members (students, practitioners, and academics from a variety of cultures) became a strong task group providing education, support, networking and research opportunities to its members (Lee, Montiel, Atchisson, Liza, Flory, & Valenzuela, 2009). In fact, it became such a cohesive force that when the San Diego Chapter members were aging and not able to keep up the activities of the IASWG Southern California Chapter, the Club united with them and kept the chapter going (Lee & Montiel, 2013). Dr. Gill happily turned over the chapter's responsibilities to the CSULB Group Work Club, which in essence became the chapter and was chaired by Dr. Lee. In 2006 Dr. Lee and several club members presented research about the club's value in supplementing group work instruction at the Annual Program Meeting of the Council of Social Work Education (CSWE) in Philadelphia. In 2008, members of the Club/Southern California Chapter went to Germany to present at the IASWG symposium in Cologne. The Southern California Chapter officially moved to Long Beach and grew. Vanessa Shaffer, LCSW, who helped start the group work club as an undergraduate social work student, became the chapter chair. In 2011, Dr. Lee and Ms. Shaffer co-chaired the IASWG international symposium on the Queen Mary in Long Beach. This symposium put the chapter on the map as IASWG members attended from around the world and reported a memorable time. The symposium was titled "All in the Same Boat" by the brilliant and personable Steve Kraft. He was the IASWG international president at the time of the symposium and provided a lot of support and assistance to the chapter even coming to our chapter planning meetings from New York to help make the symposium a success.

Unfortunately, the chapter's chair Vanessa Shaffer left California due to her husband's serious illness; however, before leaving, she turned over the leadership position to Maria Gandarilla, the current chair. Not surprisingly, Maria and Vanessa met at a chapter meeting, and Vanessa helped Maria secure a new career as a hospice worker in her agency. Maria has been very successful guiding the chapter with her enthusiastic democratic leadership style. She also was elected to the international board. This past year the chapter, besides offering a meaningful, well attended holiday symposium for the community, attracted Mei Kameda, a graduate student who has a passion for intergenerational group work. Cheryl Lee, now an emeritus CSULB faculty and Chapter Board Member, is constantly amazed how brilliant angelic people become involved in our chapter. She recognizes it relates to the spiritual/mutual aid nature of group work.

The revitalization begins

Following a chapter hiatus in 2015, resulting from the chapter chair leaving the board due to a family emergency, the Southern California Chapter had few actively involved members remaining. Through the remaining leaders' efforts, a plan was established to recruit a new leadership group and develop a series of events to revitalize the chapter's work. The first event was a hosted chapter meet-and-greet, which was marketed at the university, through classroom presentations, fliers and posters, as well as in the community through social media and emails. In addition, informal recruitment was completed through word of mouth. Goals of the event were to introduce the IASWG and the Southern California Chapter to community members with an interest in group work and to recruit new members. In accordance with the tradition of establishing a comforting environment, the meet and greet was hosted in one of the chapter leader's homes. An agenda for the event was created to guide the night's activities though the pace was set by attendees. The event was potluck style, with raffles and ice breakers hosted throughout the night to keep the tone light hearted and fun. All 13 attendees, composed of social work students, faculty, and practitioners, sat in an informal circle in the family room area. After introductions and a presentation of the chapter and organization, much of the time was devoted to attendees getting to know one another and later, brainstorming future chapter endeavors. Members openly shared their ideas and provided helpful feedback to each other. At the end of the night, the room was filled with palpable excitement as members had meaningful conversations and shared their vision for the chapter. Following this event, several attendees expressed interest toward chapter involvement. Some attendees registered with the organization following the event, and some quickly emailed the chair requesting to be considered for a leadership role. To capitalize on the momentum generated by the first meeting, a work meeting was organized a few weeks after, inviting those who expressed interest to attend.

Prior to the second meeting, the chapter leaders (which included the authors of this article) debriefed on the meet and greet event. They also discussed their leadership style, their goals for the chapter, and their vision for how they wanted to lead the group. It was decided by the leaders that a shared leadership approach would be utilized as this type of leadership allows for the distribution of responsibility and influence, and it can result in improved team performance and valuable outcomes (Barnett & Weidenfeller, 2016). Furthermore, the authors felt that a shared leadership approach would allow committee members to offer, within their comfort and availability, their expertise and strengths to move along the group's work. In this way, members share responsibility and do not bear the onus of all activities under the umbrella of a specific role. The authors were also intentional in their design of the meeting agenda to include activities that fostered a supportive environment before the group's work began. A supportive environment, among other conditions, influences the impact of shared leadership on team performance (Barnett, & Weidenfeller, 2016).

The meeting, which followed the meet and greet, was held at the CSULB School of Social Work with ten people in attendance. Half of the attendees were students, and the other half were social work faculty and practitioners. The main goal of the meeting was to develop an idea for the chapter's first event. The chapter provided pizza and refreshments, and the meeting began with introductions, an icebreaker and member check-ins. This took approximately 20-30 minutes of the 1.5 to 2-hour agenda. Similar to the first event, the ice breaker and member check-ins created a sense of community, inclusivity, and safety. Attendees briefly shared their daily challenges, and members offered feedback and support to each other. The first part of the meeting was wrapped up by the co-chair who summarized the discussion and identified themes. Themes included the desire for a safe and supportive space, a desire to strengthen group work skills, a motivation to serve the community and a desire to connect with others. As the group prepared to begin the chapter's work, the room was filled with excited energy. Ideas were free flowing and members were respectful and constructive throughout the brainstorming session.

From this energy, the group reached consensus on the first chapter event- *Hope for the Holidays*. The purpose of the event was to invite group workers, social workers, and community members to participate in talking circles to discuss what the holiday season represents to them. To plan for the event, the planning committee members chose to meet on a weekly basis for about 4 to 6 weeks. Meetings were hosted in the same format that included an icebreaker, a member check-in, and then attention to the group's work. Though this format at times made the meetings long (about 2 to 2.5 hours), planning committee members left the room excited and expressed their satisfaction with this format. Throughout the meetings, the group dynamic and supportive environment remained consistent. The number of attendees, approximately eight to ten, also remained consistent, though due to the group's open ended nature, there was an occasional change of attendees. Although changing members can result in a lack of group cohesion (Corey, Corey & Corey, 2014), it was observed that new members were welcomed and quickly integrated themselves into the group. This may have been because the group environment was inclusive and supportive, and included ice breakers and other activities, which can lead to increased group cohesion (Pelech, Basso, Lee, & Gandarilla, 2016). Different committee members took leadership by volunteering to lead tasks (i.e identifying and securing an event location, marketing the event, securing donations, etc.). As members volunteered for tasks, they held themselves and each other accountable for task completion. Members quickly completed their tasks and reported to the group via email. At times disagreements arose amongst the group, with the biggest disagreement regarding the target population for the event. Because of the cohesion and trust among the group, as well as the leaders' inclusive approach that embraces diverse opinions (Pelech et al, 2016), members were able to openly express their points of view in a respectful manner. The leaders facilitated the discussion by summarizing the views presented and refocusing the committee on the event's purpose and desired outcomes. Through this, consensus was reached. Through the committee's concerted effort and thoughtful planning, the first event was successful. Following is a snapshot of the event.

Hope for the Holidays

The Hope for the Holidays event was hosted at CSULB and had 30 participants including: community members, practitioners, academics, and students. Attendees were split into three talking circles, each with co-facilitators who had varying experience facilitating groups, and who had been briefly trained on how to facilitate a talking circle. During the circles, which lasted an hour and a half, members were welcomed to discuss what the upcoming holidays meant to them. Two social work practitioners were available for crisis intervention, as the planning committee recognized that the topic could potentially elicit strong emotional responses. Supportive literature on topics pertaining to the holidays (i.e coping with grief during the holidays, holiday traditions, etc.) and resources were also available for members. At the end of the night, a larger debrief circle was made, allowing members to reflect on their experience. Members were asked to summarize their experience in one word. This was powerful, with attendees using words such as "inspired", "motivated", "community," and "supported". Following the event, several attendees, many of whom were new to the organization, spoke to the chapter chairs expressing their interest in being involved with the organization. Additionally, some community members who had experience facilitating groups offered to share their expertise in future workshops. Other members inquired about the next event and how to join the organization.

To continue the momentum of the Chapter, a holiday party/meeting followed two weeks later to debrief the *Hope for the Holidays* event, celebrate the chapter's progress and plan for the future. The meeting had a similar structure as previous meetings. Fifteen people attended and a rich discussion ensued on the Hope for Holidays event. Because of the group's cohesion and inclusive environment, members critically yet respectfully evaluated the strengths and areas for improvement of the event. Following this meeting, it was decided by a few of the members that a fundraiser would be organized to secure money for travel scholarships to the international symposium in New York and to assist an individual member's project. Below is a snapshot of the planned event and the planning process.

Cake Pop Fundraiser

The Cake Pop Fundraiser was spearheaded by one of the chapter board members who was currently working on raising funds for her non-profit organization. The purpose of the event was to raise funds with a cake pop making class led by a professional chef, and to give community members the opportunity to decorate cards for incarcerated women. The funds raised would be split between the member's non-profit organization and the chapter. The decision to have this event was made by only a few board members; therefore, the planning process was done by these board members with minimal efforts to include other chapter members. Planning took place through email with some attempted phone call meetings. A list of tasks was immediately created, with three board members splitting the tasks, and a date for the event was set. Initially some of the tasks were completed; however, a lack of communication regarding expectations, task completion, and work yet to be done, led to the postponing of the initial desired date.

Examples of the issues that arose included: lack of clear deadlines, poor communication among the planning team (i.e. members were unaware of each other's progress and did not check in or move forward on their tasks), and a lack of accountability.

The chapter's co-chair reached out to the small group of planners to schedule a conference call and face to face meetings to integrate the entire chapter's board and membership into the planning process. There was minimal interest in the project, possibly because the full chapter membership did not partake in the decision to pursue this project. Members still showed some willingness to help plan. As more members became involved, they identified issues with the pre-set details of the event and even brought up reconsidering holding the event. Since the smaller group of original planners had tight schedules and some had competing agendas, certain details of the event could not be changed and thus the plan for the event remained. In order to support the group's endeavor, members actively took on tasks. The planning process mostly continued via email and conference calls due to the challenge of scheduling face to face committee meetings within the short timeline. Conflict arose with simple tasks, mostly involving marketing efforts and often consensus was not reached. For the purpose of time, members often chose the option resulting in least conflict. It should be noted that some of the board members spearheading this event were not involved in the planning of the Hope for the Holidays event, and therefore their relationship with the planning committee was limited, lacking cohesion and trust. As the event drew closer, the specifics of the event were finalized, though the event had not been marketed aggressively to garner the desired participation. The small planning committee members had a conference call to determine the best route to take, and it was decided that due to the low sign up, the event should be cancelled. A debrief was completed by the chapter's board following this. It was discussed that the less inclusive leadership approach significantly impacted the planning process and outcome of the event. The board recognized that the Cake Pop Fundraiser lacked an inclusive planning approach that promoted cohesion and collaboration by integrating board leaders and committed chapter members from the beginning. Although the chapter co-chairs attempted to rectify this later in the planning process, the competing agendas, limited flexibility of schedules, and the lack of member "buy in" made it difficult to salvage the event. Recognizing that this leadership format was ineffective, it was decided that future events would be more effectively planned with an inclusive and shared leadership style. Although the canceled cake pop event did not contribute toward membership growth or increased community recognition of the chapter, the lessons learned were invaluable to the chapter and its leadership.

Discussion and implications

Leadership plays a vital role in the planning and revitalizing of a chapter. This paper reflected on the revitalization efforts of the IASWG chapter in Southern California and focused on two main events that illustrated how leadership and planning impacted these efforts. In the first example, the chapter utilized a shared leadership approach, in the form of a committee composed of elected chapter board members and chapter members, and found this leadership style to be effective in increasing member participation and engagement. Particularly, in planning meetings, shared leadership allowed a natural emergence of leaders as members freely contributed their identified strengths, and volunteered to take leadership roles to complete diverse tasks. Along with this leadership structure, the authors found that frequent meetings and structuring the planning committee's purpose to integrate both a task focus and mutual aid were effective in maintaining member engagement, commitment, and task completion. Additionally, group cohesion, bonding, and a sense of safety within the task group allowed members to be creative, take risks, and hold each other accountable, furthering the group's work. The high level of commitment and efforts by the committee members determined the quality of the group work outcome (Joo & Dennen, 2017). Ultimately, the culmination of these conditions led to a successful event that achieved the committee's mission to revitalize the chapter.

In the second example, the event and planning lacked clear leadership and direction. Kurland (2008) emphasized the lack of knowledge of the planning process and preparation by professionals while developing a group significantly impacts desirable outcomes of a group. Although the members did not necessarily lack knowledge of the planning process, their inability to adhere to best practice standards while preparing and planning significantly impacted the desired outcome. Furthermore, the small cake pop planning committee had different agendas, some of which did not necessarily tie to the IASWG chapter's mission and purpose. Competing agendas have been found to impact a group's task completion (Pelech et al., 2016).

The planning committee for the *Hope for the Holidays* event developed a strong, inclusive planning process. When group workers identify shared goals, it leads to exchanges in information, new perspectives, and distribution of tasks, which creates new solidified shared goals, called backing up behavior or collective effectiveness (Joo & Dennen, 2017; Abdellatif, Arjoun, Belhadj, & Belhabib, 2015). This was not present in the planning of the *Cake Pop Fundraiser*. When a project or an event is presented in a disorderly manner through lack of preparation and communication among leadership, it may be a challenge for members to have a sense of meaning behind the group itself. Although members asserted their commitment to the group by taking on tasks and working toward achieving the intended goal, they were not fully engaged or invested as they did not have a say in the decision to host this particular event from the beginning.

The *Hope for the Holidays* event was successful because it was grounded on collaborative decision making and consensus building. Conversely, for the planning of the *Cake Pop Fundraiser* event, consensus building was sacrificed for the sake of time. Particularly, members made decisions that resulted in the least amount of conflict, even when those decisions were not the best course for the intended outcomes.

The *Hope for the Holidays* planning committee was observed to have a strong group structure that considered the strengths of the group and the mediating role of the leaders to influence the group's decisions and successful outcomes (Ghavami & Taleai, 2017). Strong leadership which includes group processing is necessary for sound decisions to go forward. Leaders are not to be the sole decision makers; however, it is those leaders who are able to foster a trust-building relationship within the group decision-making process that move the group forward (Platow, Haslam, Reicher, & Steffens, 2015). Finally, in order for strong strategic planning of an event, the group leader along with group members need to identify specific goals/strategies to measure group success and coordinate group roles to utilize strengths of group members. This creates collective efficacy during the group process which also leads to member satisfaction (Winton & Kane, 2016).

Limitations

Some limitations include that the research only reflects a single chapter's experiences toward revitalization through a short time frame of six months. In addition, there are possible biases of the authors who were also involved in the chapter events and leadership components. Lastly, the group composition of the chapter became a challenge. The chapter members include mostly students and students who are also full-time professionals, which may have contributed to inconsistent momentum of the chapter's development due to members having competing responsibilities outside of the chapter.

Recommendations

One of the common challenges identified among IASWG chapter leaders is the difficulty of maintaining a thriving chapter, particularly when there is a loss of a leader. Given this phenomenon and the recognized importance of leadership to a chapter, it may be beneficial for the organization to include in its chapter development efforts a focus on leadership development. Investing energy in developing and maintaining an infrastructure that promotes leadership development has been identified as helpful in growing leaders in an organization (Shekleton, Preston, & Good, 2010). Utilizing shared leadership may be helpful to identify future leaders as this type of leadership encourages the emergence and flow of leadership from task to task. Early identification of future leaders, paired with a program that promotes the development of these leaders, could result in better preparation for transfer of leadership, allowing chapters to continue to thrive as leadership changes.

It is further suggested that to address the normal changing of chapter leadership, it may be helpful for the organization to create more opportunities for IASWG chapters to connect and share experiences with current chapter leaders, as well as aspiring chapter leaders. Through this, chapter leaders could gain skills and ideas from one another to continue to develop strong chapters across the globe. Having a panel presentation or discussion at a future symposium may be a valuable opportunity for seasoned, new, and revitalizing chapters to identify and address issues, some of which may include geographic or language specific issues.

Lastly, it is recommended that more research and writing about chapter development and growth be completed, so that information is shared among diverse chapters to strengthen the IASWG organization.

References

Barnett, R. C., & Weidenfeller, N. K. (2016). *Shared Leadership and Team Performance. Advances in Developing Human Resources, 18*(3), 334-351. doi:10.1177/1523422316645885

Abdellatif, N.B., Arjoun, A., Belhadj, S., Belhabib, N. (2015). The relationship of the collective effectiveness with the leadership in a group work: A project in the field of health. *European Researcher, 95(6), pages 429-441.*

Corey, M. S., Corey, G. & Corey, C. (2014). *Groups: Process and practice* (9th ed.). Belmont, CA: Brooks/Cole.

Ghavami, S., & Taleai, M. (2017). Towards a conceptual multi-agent-based framework to simulate the spatial group decision-making process. *Journal of Geographical Systems, 19*(2), 109-132. doi: 10.1007/s10109-016-0243-9.

Joo, M. & Dennen, V.P. (2017) Measuring university students' group work contribution: Scale development and validation. Small Group Research, 48:3, 288-310.

Kurland, R. (2008). Planning: The neglected component of group development. *Social Work with Groups, 28*(3/4), 9-16.

Lee, C.D. & Montiel, E. (2013). The Metamorphosis of a University Social Group Work Club. *The 31st Annual International Symposium of the Association for the Advancement of Social Work and Groups, Chicago, Illinois Proceedings.* London: Whiting and Birch.

Lee, C.D., Del Carmen Montiel, E., Atchison, J., Flory, P. Liza, J., & Valenzuela, J. (2009). *An innovative approach to support social groupwork: A university groupwork club. Groupwork 19*(3), 11-26. doi: 10.1921/095182410X505848.

Pelech, W., Basso, R., Lee, C.D., & Gandarilla, M. (2016). *Inclusive group work.* New York, NY: Oxford University Press.

Platow, M.J., Haslam, S.A., Reicher, S.D., & Steffens, N.K. (2015). There is no leadership if no-one follows: Why leadership is necessarily a group process. *International Coaching Psychology Review, 10*(1), 20-37.

Ramey, J.H. (2009). The association for the advancement of social work with groups, inc., An international professional organization (AASWG). Gitterman, A. & Salmon, R. (Eds.) *Encyclopedia of Group Work.* NY: Routledge.

Shekleton, M., Preston, J., & Good, L. (2010). Growing leaders in a professional membership organization. *Journal of Nursing Management, 18*(6), 662-668. doi:10.1111/j.1365-2834.2010.01152.x

Winton, S.L., & Kane, T.D. (2016). Effects of group goal content on group processes, collective efficacy, and satisfaction. *Journal of Applied Social Psychology, 46*(2), 129-139. doi: 10.1111/jasp.12336.

Shifting contexts:

Transforming and sustaining professional identities using group work

Mary Wilson and Deirdre Quirke

Introduction

The traditional focus of social group work education in Ireland has been on meeting service user needs. Research into its use in ongoing professional education has been less well documented. Doel's (2006) work on post qualifying and continuous professional development has encouraged us to research its relevance and application in current post qualifying education in Ireland. Traditionally, approaches to teaching student supervision-field instruction have focussed on meeting the needs of the individual practitioner and her/his student Hawkins and Shotet (2000) and Morrison (2001). We support Smith's focus on the place of groups in developing conversations about professional practice,

> "the primary concern is the learning of the whole group, not just understanding of the individual whose practice provides the focus" (Smith, 2009:56).

As a result of teaching a group work module to field instructors at University College Cork (UCC) and the National University of Ireland Galway (NUIG), the Authors re-discovered the *secondary advantage* of (Mullender & Ward 1991); whereby participants began using the module as a method of peer mentoring and support. In this paper we provide a contextual overview of the model's evolution and the challenges of its implementation in practice. The results are discussed and supported by the voices of course participants from their collective explorations of practice challenges and ethical dilemmas.

Current context of social work supervision

Social work in common with other professions have been subjected to public scrutiny as a result of public enquiries that emerged from the 'crisis of trust' in professionals. The resulting fear of public opprobrium and criticism has resulted *"in an increased focus...on issues of accountability and proper management of cases in both social work practice and supervision"* (Halton, Powell & Scanlon 2015:92). This is reflected in global trends focussing on

> "issues relating to performance measurement, case management, resource allocation and the control of risk, with consequential lowering of emphasis on the more educational and formative elements of supervision" (ibid: Hawkins & Shotet, 2000; Morrison, 2001).

So how do practitioners currently come to voice about their practice? There are a number of accepted ways including formal one to one supervision, talking informally with peers, individual consultancy, debriefing, writing and journaling, conference presentations and publications, and assessing or contesting standards of best practice. Many of these are privatised and individual, focussing on compliance-social control. Privatising reflection which has become the dominant intellectual activity has contributed to a failure to develop understandings that locate and value the lived experiences of practitioners and their students. Models of clinical supervision draw heavily on psychodynamic insights and focus on isolated situations, considering problems as individual pathology. Research suggests that social workers have become overly aligned with the work system that employs them, to the neglect of the professional endeavour. Managerialism has become the dominant discourse in agency supervision to the exclusion of dialogue and bridge building between practitioners and students (Halton, Powell and Scanlon, 2015).

We contest that world view by offering more creative and inclusive forms of engagement that seek to work collaboratively with students, and by implication service users, to challenge the dominance of existing individualised approaches. Appreciation of the social reality of shifting relationships and imbalances in the contexts in which we work, require that professional issues need to be addressed as both personal and collective concerns in making judgments about what constitutes *the common good.* This is the rationale for collective explorations of practice. Our model encourages workers to take responsibility for their practice, to work autonomously (CORU, 2011), while discovering their existing practice frameworks and developing awareness of their creative and professional potential. We believe this scaffolds a practice that is both ethical and sustainable.

Rationale

We are heartened by our experiences on the post qualifying practice teaching programmes at Universities in Cork and Galway, Ireland, which incorporate group work as a core module in the education and training of fieldwork instructors. Our brief was to *'teach group work'* to field instructors, to facilitate their students with the group work practice analysis module- which is a requirement of the fieldwork placement. Our initial engagement with course participants revealed that they had a 'basic' knowledge of group work and the students' requirements. They identified their learning need as the use of group work for peer mentoring and as a forum for collective exploration of the issues and dilemmas that were arising from student supervision. We draw on our Meitheal Model to illustrate the process in which the group becomes the context and the means of delivering supervision skills and peer mentoring; achieving a synthesis of knowledge building and skills development. The word *Meitheal* is the Irish expression of the ancient and universal appliance of cooperation to social need (Lordan, Wilson & Quirke, 2002).

Introducing the Meitheal Model

The core aspects of sustainable professionalism concern the duality inherent in knowledge building and skill development for existing field instructors and their students through collective-critical-creative exploration of practice issues and dilemmas. This process involves the action- reflection- action cycle (Kolb, 1983) and reclaims *the social* using group work as the central component in transforming professional identities and delivering sustainable professionalism. Group supervision and peer mentoring is based on an emancipatory approach to social work. At its core are principles of social justice, creativity and peer support. The group work modality builds capacity for professional transformation and offers a challenge to current models of supervision, whose elements may be regarded as typically hierarchical and unsupportive of the practitioner needs. We agree that

> "group supervision, is a process of ongoing dialogue for the purpose of reflecting upon professional practices. The goals, experiences, resources of the supervisee, and supervisor, indeed the group process itself- all make their contribution towards the goal of providing quality services as well as meeting the needs for skills development in this learning community" (Berteau & Villeneuve, 2005: 45).

We propose a group work model which involves a continuous process of critical enquiry questioning the dominant discourse of individualised responses (Wilson & Quirke, 2009).

Principles for professional practice

- The essential ingredients of the Meitheal Model are that it builds a learning community, is person centred and strengths based; involves collective explorations through critical conversation and mindfulness of the needs of the end user; reclaims the social often using creative means; and challenges the dominant discourse of privatised reflection. From this the principles that underpin it emerge:
- Person Centred: The person is multifaceted and requires a holistic focus. The person is embedded in citizenship and human rights. Good practice always reflects the view that the person is wholly valuable and unique.
- Strengths Based: By recognising the positive potential of each member the emphasis is placed on the person's contribution through the opportunity to work in an environment where their worth is both recognised and utilised. Good practice reflects the belief that capacity equals power
- Collaborative Working: The group process connects with peoples'

primary concerns and liberates the energy for mutual aid and peer endeavour.

- Creativity: New ways of being and doing are achieved by combining dialogue and aesthetic practices.
- Challenging Xenophobia: Identifying and acknowledging the worker's own value base becomes a pre-requisite for ethical practice.
- Person is Political: Deconstructing power relationships facilitates the development of action strategies that redresses balances of power and generates a helix of transformation (Lordan, Wilson & Quirke, 2002, pp. 158-159).

Specifying the process

The collective exploration that occurs in group supervision and peer mentoring is also the means used to reclaim *the social.* Charting the movement from *I to We,* is achieved through the group work modality and is essential to the process of critical enquiry and reflection. It is paralleled by the group process that unfolds through the encounter whose foundation principles and values were discussed above. This movement from *I to We, is* a process that encompasses the following stages:

- Self+
- Known Professional Self+
- Developing Professional Self+
- Ongoing Professional Development+
- Assessment+Self realization

Forming and building trust to discover self

Self-discovery begins with engagement in the process of disclosure about oneself. Understanding self, through examination of how one's belief systems, values and past experiences is necessary to establish commonality and facilitate the choice of entry into the learning cycle (CORU 2011: Domain 4.1a). In the Meitheal Model participants are introduced to the process via a case study scenario. This is co-constructed from their own experiences of a challenging fieldwork instruction scenario that posed an ethical dilemma and determined the assessment outcome. Members pair initially to identify and discuss their experiences. Then they move to trios and quartets to agree on the overarching issue(s) that the group will address in their deliberation of the ethical and practice issues concerning professional formation and subsequent assessment. One of the challenges associated with good peer supervision is trust building which helps to develop a cohesive team structure…"*it takes a lot of trust, that's the only thing….*" (Halton, Powell and Scanlon 2015:116).

Norming and facilitation reveal roles and tasks of the Known Professional Self

On-going support for the known professional self is essentially a work in progress. The group focus on workloads/tasks; skills/methods; roles and responsibilities re-enforces communality and identification of purpose. The role of the facilitator-supervisor here is to clarify purpose, objectives and expectations, while supporting and encouraging participation. At this stage the group experiences peer and supervisor feedback as validating and begins to adapt to the new opportunities for practice consultation that arise. (CORU 2011: Domain 5. 4).

Storming towards Conflict Resolution unmasks the Developing Professional Self

To develop the professional self, feedback is essential to meet the duty of care-accountability. The collective approach encourages exploration of practice dilemmas and conflicted positions

> "Professional judgements often involves making decisions about complex and often competing agendas associated with safety, risk, need and availability of resources (Halton, Powell and Scanlon 2015:126).

Facilitation that reviews existing skills for their effectiveness and suggests new strategies is part of the action-reflection-action process that lies at the heart of reflective practice in group and peer supervision. Dealing with challenge in groups can be an easier than face to face in the one to one encounter. Fears about challenge are natural and essential for issues of risk and uncertainty to emerge. However, the frame of reference of the group and expectations of participants, established at the earlier stage, are important in creating a safe learning environment where constructive challenge is experienced as professional discourse rather than a personal attack!

> "peer supervision allows practitioners to talk about difficulties that are coming up in cases or difficulties that are coming up for them.....”(ibid: 117).

A caveat however is that groups have the potential to become cosy or induce a false sense of security .....group think!! The role of facilitation, to encourage diverse opinions is critical to achieving balance and perspective (CORU 2011: Domain 2.2).

Performing re-enforces Ongoing Professional Development

Ownership of one's own practice and a willingness to share it means being open to giving and receiving feedback through engaging in critical enquiry. At this stage the group has become a reference point as well as a forum of mutual aid. Members realise the interdependence of group and selves to create a system of mutual support and problem solving characterised by creativity and spontaneity (Berteau & Villeneuve 2006:50) This represents complete engagement in the group supervision-peer mentoring process, where members demonstrate openness to new learning and incorporate new ways of being and doing (CORU 2011: Domain 4.1).

Ending in Self-Evaluation-Assessment of Sustainable Professionalism

Self-assessment has the potential for creating the conditions for critical reflection and the development of emancipatory knowledge to sustain the professional in transformative practice. Here we acknowledge strengths and achievements of connecting the personal and professional in an integrated practice wisdom. In teaching field supervision, the challenge is to provide an evidence based assessment that will be rigorous, transparent and that reflects professional accountability. At this stage we understand what others can teach us and how it can be applied in practice teaching. There is also an awareness of our purpose and responsibility as professionals to maintain standards and safeguard the public interest (CORU 2011: Domain 5.1a +4.a). To respond to demands for evidence of performance and productivity as well as advocating on behalf of vulnerable populations requires the elevation of *'agency'* and the subjugation of *'compliance'* to ensure that professional judgement includes a moral and ethical perspective of what makes for the *'good'*.

De-constructing the process

We actualised the Meitheal principles with the two groups of field instructors. The following gives a 'flavour' of their responses to the approach.

Building learning communities

The learning community is a form of engagement that provides opportunities for examination within and across different communities of practice. Such explorations allow for the generation of grounded theory and ways of making sense the concerns and actions of workers in different areas. In turn these can be used to deepen discussion and understanding across occupational boundaries

> *"the students are given time to familiarise themselves with the legislation, roles and responsibilities of the agency and other allied services... students are closely monitored and supported by all staff". (Field Instructor, UCC: 2016).*

> *"I had to ensure that the student was challenged in her thinking and practice and was not complacent. As a field instructor you have to challenge preconceived ideas and ensure that the student sees the role*

of social work in agency includes responsibilities. You're expected to guide, protect, challenge and support the student" (Field Instructor, NUIG: 2016)

Group members on both courses indicated the usefulness of this form of engagement for developing and transferring knowledge from college to practice context. Thus developing a new paradigm and encouraging a new world view.

Developing practitioner identities

Public explorations of practice helps to build practitioners' confidence and ability to inform an occupational identity. This experience of sustained exploration of practice with peers and recognition of ones' capacities in this area supports their understanding of themselves as *professional*. The group provides the environment as well as the means of processing these issues.

"I became more conscious and more reflective of how I portrayed myself- both professionally and personally" (Field Instructor, UCC: 2016)

"I found it difficult to keep on top of student as well as carrying out my own work and found that this challenged my own identity as a competent worker open to imparting my knowledge to my student" (Field Instructor, UCC: 2016).

Operating out of more than one context is experienced by the field instructor, and consequently by the student, as challenging the old identity and providing an incentive for developing a new professional persona.

Generating frameworks for practice

The group provides a structure for asking questions and exploring other ways of being and doing. Participants use these tools to analyse a piece of work or a practice dilemma-thus operationalizing the principle of 'inside out and outside in'. Through the group experience, other frames of reference emerge from the questions that group members pose and these shift from the individual to a shared enquiry of the social work discourse.

"I never thought of it like that before" (Field Instructor, NUIG: 2016).

"I was struck by the sentiment and thoughtfulness of the two presenters. There was a depth about their observations and engagement that is so often missing from day to day practice" (Field Instructor, NUIG: 2016).

Expanding practitioners repertoires

Additionally, the group allows the people to store images, ideas and examples adding to their repertoire, developing a bank of knowledge and metaphors which can be worked with (Lordan, Wilson & Quirke, 2002). This *working with* can be argued as constituting *'good practice'.*

Here the field instructors struggled with the duality of their role in relation to the personal and professional ethical issues that arose. An example from the Galway group illustrates this dilemma. The field instructor discovered that her student was initially unaware of the implications of her assessments for ethical decision making in the context of *the common good.*

"With regard to what I will bring to my practice, the discussions that took place in terms of what I can bring to the deal as a Field Instructor highlighted the need for a greater awareness of the personal traits-values I bring into my professional practice. It was beneficial to hear other people's views on what they bring to the role and how each person shows/hides various parts of their personality in the role" (Field Instructor, NUIG: 2016).

Using the group for peer support, she reported how she initiated a conversation with her student which opened the latter's understanding of the interdependence of personal-professional in the delivery of services.

A further example of the group's engagement in collective dialogue is illustrated in the use of journaling as a repertoire enhancing tool.

"Completing journal entries was insightful and I believe that in cases in my own supervision and when supervising students this is a practice

that I will develop in order to assist with self-reflection and observation of my own practice. Journaling is also something that I have used with service users and from revisiting the practice; it is something I hope to incorporate more into my practice. Journaling is something that I will incorporate into my role as a field instructor" (Field Instructor, NUIG: 2016).

Supporting Life Long Learning

Life Long Learning builds on the learner's prior life and work experience. In the field instructor relationship, identifying one's own and the student's learning style and point of entry into the learning cycle is central to successful outcomes. The Meitheal Model provides opportunities for collaborative ways of working which leads to active engagement with and in the learning process.

> *" I recognise that each student has their own learning style and try to tap into this at beginning of placement to support and enhance their learning for professional life" (Field Instructor, UCC: 2016).*

One field instructor's dilemma hinged on the absence of structural discourse on disability and consequent critical conceptualisations. She found her student to be *deficient* in these areas and thus needed to assume the role of teacher (text) in addition to her role as field instructor (context).

> *"The provision of quality services offered with honesty, energy and commitment to both clients and agency requires a small and a big picture outlook....this was achieved by myself and others, in ongoing research" (Field Instructor, UCC: 2016).*

Working creatively to support alternative paradigms

As social work educators and practitioners we believe in parity of esteem for educational initiatives that value cognitive, affective and intuitive processes. The question is how to construct a bridge between the conceptual and the participatory chasm that emerges when a student is on placement. Working creatively encourages us to *be and do* differently.

"I achieved a heightened awareness of role play and its use in group supervision" (Field Instructor, NUIG: 2016).

"I would have liked to have more creativity in my approach to instruction. I found that a combination of my lack of creativity, time constraints as well as the reluctance of the student to veer from her own wishes impeded my ability to practice teach creatively" (Field Instructor, UCC: 2016).

Using creative means allows us to work in partnership with each other to develop an inclusive practice and pedagogy to support the reflexivity necessary for addressing the post-modern dilemmas of uncertainty, chaos and crisis that are everyday events in the lives of social work practice teachers and their students (Wilson & Quirke, 2009).

Understanding group processes and working collectively.

The intensity of the experience and the anxiety around explorations of one's own work creates a rich store for critical reflection.

"We worked together and collaboratively, but some sessions fell flat... on seeking collaborative solutions we moved from own performance to that of care for the other, the common good" (Field Instructor, UCC: 2016).

"I was surprised that one of my colleagues began with the more difficult areas and worked from there. On reflection this has shown me that we all approach tasks differently. This will be important to remember if my student does not always do things as I would but the end result may be the same or better" (Field Instructor, NUIG: 2016).

Group reflection on members' experiences enhances understanding of group processes in general and cultivates the experience of working collectively. In the current climate where there is an emphasis on Multi-Disciplinary Teams and Teamwork in agency, this is a no brainer!

Dual process and analysis

The initial objective to teach group *work* was realised using a model of group supervision and peer mentoring that provided course participants with the conceptual and applied tools for knowledge building and skills development in the context of their continuing professional development. By exploring the key dimensions of the experience, the following themes emerged and were reflective of those identified by Smith (2009).

Managing boundaries

Establishing and maintaining boundaries from the onset are critical to successful outcomes. Field instructors reported the ongoing challenge of identifying and managing professional boundaries during the placement. As these can be contested and in their absence can generate unforeseen consequences for the end user either professional or service user-where issues of duty of care/fitness to practice are at issue, or in the words of one participant "...*being too willing and overburdening herself required boundaries and my role here was challenging"* (Field Instructor, UCC: 2016). The student's personal needs took priority over her social work student role. She wanted a therapist rather than a teacher! Modelling the appropriate behaviour became a feature of teaching the balancing issues of risk and safety; rights and responsibilities.

Being a facilitator

The task of facilitation is crucial to the process of collective enquiry and conversation. Firstly there is a need to establish a democratic mutual aid system and secondly there is the actualisation of purpose (Glassman & Kates 1990: 105; Mullender & Ward: 1991).

> *"It was more daunting than I thought to being responsible for assessing the student's fitness to practice, which I questioned initially at the beginning of the placement, particularly in the area of interpersonal skills"* (Field Instructor, NUIG: 2016).

The group needed to establish the 'exact framing of the task' -by engaging in it! This was achieved by asking questions and exploring themes and issues and by supporting each other about the focus of the discussion.

Focusing on work rather than on person of worker

Work rather than the character of the worker becomes the centre of attention in the collective exploration. The entwining of personal and professional identities involves a double paradox for workers...... involving the separation of the person from the worth of the deed. This leads to questions of ownership....of who and what we are? This splitting is a risky business but can be contained by the focus on the work. The central question concerns the appropriateness of our actions....as members of a community of practice. *"I found that my own work commitments interrupted my availability at times to carry out my fieldwork instructor duties. I found this frustrating and found this limited my role..."*(Field Instructor, UCC: 2016).

Being prepared to challenge and accept challenge

Dealing with challenge in groups can be an easier than in the face to face of the one to one encounter. However, groups have the potential to become cosy or induce a false sense of security that all is well. *"..Challenge myself to challenge the student and not be too nice..."* (Field Instructor, UCC: 2016). Fears about challenge are natural and essential. However, the frame of reference of the group (ground rules-contract making) and expectations of participants are important in providing the support for creating a safe learning environment where constructive challenge is experienced as professional discourse rather than a personal attack. This focus helps to ground the giving and receiving of critical- constructive feedback, as a group norm thus contextualizing it to the task under consideration.

Exploring and attending to group process

Using the collective modality enables dialogue to open up about what happened, what is happening....the reflection *on* and reflection *in* action. The nature of the interaction is the important factor with the focus on practitioner processes. It is an exploration of the group for informed committed action and an examination of the worker's thinking and behaviours. Thus all may share in the learning.

The movement from the individual to the collective is experienced as awareness of how individuals function in the group and how the group itself functions. This represents a shift in using the group as a context for interaction, instead it becomes an instrument where members are able to work as a unit to explore and exploit the communal resources to which they have access (Douglas 1993:31). Using this lens enables members to reflect and focus on the 'sensitive issues' and getting to the *nitty gritty*. As the group progresses members are able to flip between these two polarities and use understandings about one to inform the other. *"..keep quiet and don't fill the silences"* (Field Instructor, UCC: 2016).

Recording

> *"I found that the student's own focus on doing her portfolio and ticking boxes is difficult... and found this at odds of my own experience of being a student"* (Field Instructor, UCC: 2016).

The group identified the need to record and agree the key issues for further exploration. This encourages the process of enquiry and reflection upon which sustainable peer support is built.

Outcomes

- Through utilising group work, collective and critical enquiry is facilitated. This represents a sustainable and social form of professional engagement for those who make assessments of practice. As social workers are mandated to deal with matters relating to human well-being, their instructors need to engage in systematic assessment to uphold and re-enforce professional standards.

- Grounded theory occurs organically within these peer mentoring-supervision groups, enhancing understanding and appreciation of the processes that lie at the heart of social work. What emerges is a shared framework for thinking about things and a validation of practise wisdom.

- Forming and engaging in a community of practice develops and sustains the practitioner identity. It facilitates articulation of what is done to and for others- social workers in training, service users and the public at large. This aims to support an appreciation of issues of openness, transparency and accountability while actualizing the concept of the *common good* through group work.

- Ethical Practice underpins text and context in social work. Actualising principles of human rights, social justice and dignity and worth of all persons furthers the democratic process and ideas of what makes *for the good.*

- Cost benefit analysis. In the current climate of austerity and diminishing resources in the human services, the Meitheal model of group work is appealing as it responds to exigencies of value for money while building social capital.

Conclusion

In providing a conceptual overview of the issues and challenges of developing and implementing the Meitheal model with field instructors on continuing professional development courses we focussed on the themes and narratives that informed its practice evolution. In summary, the group supervision-peer mentoring community is a form of engagement that provides opportunities for examining interventions within and across different communities of practice. Such explorations allow for the generation of grounded theory and ways of making sense of concerns and actions of workers in different areas. In turn these can be used to deepen discussion and understanding across occupational boundaries. These collective explorations of practice hold great potential. The power does not simply lie in the notion that the greater the number actively engaged in the task, automatically results in the possibility of knowing more. Rather what occurs is the connection with something more fundamental about practice. It reveals that practice is a social process involving ideas of what makes for the good. As such it is lost without collective exploration!

References

Baldwin, M. (2004) 'Critical reflection: opportunities and threats to professional learning and service development ins social work organisations' in N. Gould and M. Baldwin (eds) in *Social work, critical reflection and the learning organisation*, Aldershot: Ashgate

Beck (1992& 1999) argues that "changing ideologies created even greater problems for professionals whose work is centrally involved with issues of risk and uncertainty" Beck, U. (1999) *World Risk Society*, Cambridge: Polity Press

Berteau, Ginette and Villeneuve, Louise (2006) 'Integration of the learning process and the group development process in group supervision' in Groupwork, 16, 2, 43-60

CORU (2011) Code of Professional Conduct and Ethics for Social Workers, Dublin: CORU Available at:http://www.coru.ie/uploads/documents/

Davy, A. and Beddoe, L. (2010) *Best practice in professional supervision: a guide for the helping professions*, London: Jessica Kingsley

Doel, M. (2006) *Using Groupwork* Abingdon : Routledge

Fook, J. 2011. 'Uncertainty: the defining characteristic of social work', in V. CREE (ed) *Social Work: a reader*, London: Routledge

Freire, P. (1996& 1972) *Pedagogy of the oppressed*, New York: Seabury

Gibbons, N. (2010) Roscommon Childcare Case, Report of the Enquiry Team to the Health Care Executive Available at: http://www.oneinfour. ie/content/ resources/Roscommon ChildCareCase pdf (Accessed June 2017).

Halton, C., Powell. F., and Scanlon, M. (2015) *Continuing Professional Development in Social Work*, UK & Chicago: Policy Press

Hawkins, P. and Shotet, R. (2000) *Supervison in the Helping Professions*, Buckingham: Open University Press

Jones, D. & Normie, G. (2002). *Life's Rich Pattern*, UK SCUTREA

Kadushin, A. (1992) *Supervision in Social Work*, (3rd Edn), New York: Columbia University Press

Kolb, D.A. (1984) *Experiential Learning, London*: Prentice Hall

Laming, H. (2009) The protection of children in England: a progress report.

London: The Stationery Office.

Lorenz, W. (1994) *Social Work in a Changing Europe*, London: Routledge

Morrison, T. (2001) *Staff Supervision in Social Care: making a real difference for staff and service users*, Brighton: Pavilion

Munro, E. (2011) The Munro review of child protection, Final Report: a child centred system, London: The Department of Education

Rath, A. (2010) 'Reflective Practice as conscious geometry: portfolios as a tool for sponsoring, scaffolding and assessing reflective enquiry in learning to teach', in N. Lyons (ed) *Handbook of reflection and reflective enquiry: mapping a way of knowing for professional enquiry*, New York: Springer

Saleeby, D. (2006) *The strengths perspective in social work practice*, MA: Pearson Education

Schon, D. A. (1991) *The reflective practitioner: how professionals think in action*, Aldershot: Ashgate

Smith, M. (2009) 'Developing Critical Conversations about Practice' *Groupwork Research*, Oded Manor (ed) London: Whiting and Birch

Wilson, M. & Quirke, D. (2009) 'Promoting Partnership and Empowerment through Groupwork: the way forward for social work education', in *Social Professional Activity*, Dorrity, C. & Herrmann, P. (eds) New York: Nova Science Publishers

Team-based learning: A classroom approach for teaching group work skills

Kristina Lind

Introduction

There is evidence that while the use of groups is on the rise for baccalaureate level social workers, opportunities for acquiring group skills in BSW and MSW group specific courses are on the wane. Some BSW programs continue to offer group work courses, but the transition to a generalist approach to social work education has eroded such specificity in course offerings. As a result, we are seeing fewer group courses being listed in social work course catalogs. The challenge for social work educators is in finding ways of teaching group work skills outside of an actual group work course. One such opportunity is through a team-based learning pedagogy. The following provides both a description of the team-based learning process and adaptations to the model as a means of promoting an experiential platform for the acquisition of group work skills.

How do we, as social work educators, assist students in developing the group work practice skills that will help them stand out when competing for jobs upon graduation? Teaching content in the classroom does not sufficiently prepare students to successfully facilitate groups in the workplace. There is some evidence that baccalaureate-level students do not learn requisite group theory, group concepts, or group skills through group courses (Hessenauer & Lind, 2013). Rather, students indicate they acquire group skills through group experiences during internships and through campus club experiences (Hessenauer & Lind, 2013). While field instruction can partially fill this gap, this too can be a flawed approach unless augmented with more guided group opportunities. Applying a team-based leaning (TBL) pedagogy to social work courses can offer one means for expanding student group work skill learning opportunities.

Overview of team-based learning

Team-based learning was introduced as a small-group teaching pedagogy in the late 1970's by Larry Michaelsen, who was encountering teaching challenges due to larger classroom enrollments. He questioned the efficacy of more traditional teaching approaches in helping students acquire the skills required by their places of potential employment (Sweet & Michaelsen, 2012). For the past 30 years, TBL has been primarily used in teaching within the health sciences, such as medicine, nursing, and physical therapy (Clark, Nguyen, Bray, & Levine, 2008), in business courses, and in engineering programs (Gullo, Ha, & Cook, 2015). The model has just begun to enter the teaching domain of the social sciences. In social work, evidence exists for the use of TBL in teaching research methods courses (Venema, Meerman, & Hossink, 2015), in human behavior in the social environment courses (Macke, Taylor, & Taylor, 2013), and in introduction to social work courses (Taylor & McLendon, 2013). It is interesting to note that the use of TBL, which is defined as a "small-group" pedagogy, has not received more attention within the social group work literature.

The team-based learning framework is made up of four component parts, each essential to the success of the model. The first, *strategically formed permanent teams* refers to small groups made up of five to seven students who are required to remain intact as a small group throughout the semester (Michaelson & Sweet, 2011). A key feature of the permanent team is that its membership is instructor determined and not left up to students. This eliminates the potential issue of friends working together which can decrease productivity in small groups and create a greater potential for subgrouping phenomena. The permanence of these small classroom groups is one of the major differentiations between this model and what is observed in more traditional educational practices where groups are established primarily for the completion of a temporary academic task within the semester and without attention to group composition. The advantage of a semester-long group membership is in team members being afforded the opportunity to move through the natural stages of group development over time (Griffin & Dunham, 2015).

The second phase of the model, *readiness assurance,* has students prepare for class through reviewing the assigned readings as homework much in the same manner as with flipped classrooms (Bishop & Verleger, 2013; Michaelsen & Sweet, 2011). Students may understand all or part of the readings and some may understand none, all of which is acceptable. Within this model, the effort invested in preparing for class and the level of understanding the material are assessed through readiness assurance tests which then help guide instructor lessons.

Readiness assurance structures the way students are assessed on their understanding of content. This is achieved through taking short, multiple-choice tests on the content individually in class. Immediate feedback is provided on individual test performance. The identical test is then re-administered to each team with intra-team dialogue on each question expected prior to reaching group consensus on the answers. Again, students receive immediate feedback. Both scores are entered, with the team score awarded higher value than the individual one. If the team disagrees with the answers marked as incorrect, the team may engage in a formal appeals process (Gullo, Ha, & Cook, 2015; Michaelsen & Sweet, 2011).

Instructor lectures are geared towards the concepts students seem to struggle with as determined by the results of the assurance tests. These lectures tend to be short and highly focused. The instructor does not review instructional material that students have grasped on their own or through discussion within their teams (Michaelsen & Sweet, 2011), thus not wasting class time on review of known material and risking losing students' attention.

The *application phase* follows readiness assurance. This entails applying material and concepts assessed during the previous phase to instructor developed 'real' problems or cases to be completed by each small group. Each group then presents their learning to the class (Michaelsen & Sweet, 2011). The onus is on the instructor to facilitate the ensuing discussion intended to promote critical thinking and maintain student engagement.

The final phase is *peer evaluation*. The evaluation process, consisting of both formative and summative feedback, is essential to the TBL model as it creates an expectation that team members are responsible for providing each other the feedback necessary to make changes that will facilitate a more productive group process (Lane, 2012). The originators of this model place the responsibility for developing evaluation criteria onto each group (Lane, 2012). While the formative evaluation can be processed at any point during the life of the group, the summative evaluation tool is meant to be completed at the end of the semester as a means of awarding final grades for the work (Lane, 2012).

Group work and TBL

As social work educators, we are well-aware of the decreasing emphasis on group work instruction in schools of social work (Simon & Kilbane, 2014; Sweifach & LaPorte, 2009). The number of actual courses currently offered in baccalaureate and masters level social work programs is shrinking but more alarming is that students are not learning sufficient group work concepts and skills when they do have an opportunity to enroll in a group work course (Hessenauer & Lind, 2013). Furthermore, students frequently complain about their previous small group classroom experiences which result in their resistance to future small group involvement. When asked about these previous experiences, they state, "Negative, negative, negative"; "I always end up doing all the work"; "Can get nasty"; "Dread it"; "I hate it"; "Don't want to do it"; and "Not enough structure" (SW 4020 students, personal communications, February, 2015). The primary reason rests on instructor focus on content and not maintaining a dual focus on content and process which is a perspective specific to social group work (Steinberg, 2004). Without processing group dynamics during the life of the group, conflicts do not get resolved, hurtful communication patterns remain unidentified, and dysfunctional roles impede successful task completion. Students emerge from such experiences feeling stressed, angry, taken advantage of, offended, and are left dreading future classroom group experiences. Thus, being able to identify a teaching pedagogy that utilizes a small group framework presents as an opportunity to teach specific group concepts and skills. TBL, with some modifications, lends itself to teaching group work through an experiential lens. What follows here are two categories of adaptations to the TBL model with the purpose of accomplishing two simultaneous goals; teaching prescribed course content in a more engaging and motivating manner and teaching group work skills and process experientially.

The TBL literature encourages the formation of heterogeneous groups (Liu & Beaujean, 2017; Michaelsen & Sweet, 2011). The first challenge with any new class is to become acquainted with students, getting a sense of their individual strengths, and discovering any areas of concern which may interfere with their academic and interpersonal success. Each student is provided a short instructor-developed survey which is shared only with the instructor. It asks for areas of academic strength and weakness, group work experiences, and level of comfort with public speaking. This information, coupled with previous instructor knowledge of the student, helps determine the strategically designed groups which maximize diversity such as in academic skill, major area of study, and life experience. Groups, according to the TBL model, need to be established within the first two weeks of the semester and they must retain their same membership throughout (Liu & Beaujean, 2017), making instructor directed group membership an essential process.

As an instructor encouraging students to engage in group work, safety within the classroom environment becomes a primary concern. Many of the elements helping to transform the classroom as a safe space for students to be themselves and be vulnerable in front of their peers are dealt with in a discussion of classroom expectations while reviewing the course and syllabus on the first day as transparently as possible. This discussion needs to continue in the small group's first session with structured discussion points established by the Instructor.

Adaptations to the TBL model

The first two sessions are planned according to beginning stage of group tasks. This includes icebreaker activities, finding commonalities between members, and forming a group identity. The instructor structures a series of tasks allowing group members to become acquainted and forming connections with one another (Garland, Jones, and Kolodny, 1978). This is achieved by asking each group to complete the following: introduce themselves to the group, including a discussion of individual self-identified academic strengths, creation of a meaningful team name that in some fashion incorporates commonalities among group members, and finally have time to decorate and/or individualize team folders which are repositories for daily class quizzes and application materials. Once completed, each group is asked to share the team name and its significance with the larger classroom group. Examples of team names include "The Fall Ciders", as all members of one group loved the fall and the fall products northern New England is famous for. Another group chose the name, "Unity and Diversity" as these reflected members' commonly held values. Once names are established, teams are referred to by the team name only as a means of reinforcing small group identity. Each group is then instructed to develop group rules, decide on a decision-making process, and create a system for communicating outside of class. It is helpful for the Instructor to check in with each group to ensure they are moving through this process and to facilitate a discussion with the group if they are struggling to progress with the assigned tasks. In the three years of implementing this model, there has never been an occasion requiring instructor intervention during the early formation of the group. Group development early in the semester has been met with enthusiasm and students have appeared eager to get to know one another in a new way.

One caveat is related to students with disabilities. Their placement in a group requires thoughtful consideration. Placing them in a group which will offer accommodations and ensure inclusivity and equal opportunities for participation is critical. In one TBL oriented course, a student exhibited a severe challenge in her language skills. She required a significantly protracted processing time, spoke with hesitancy, and noticeably struggled to find the correct words to express her ideas, all of which resulted in group tasks taking longer than was experienced by the other groups. With a patient and caring group, this student experienced a sense of success for having her intelligence, sense of responsibility, and her preparedness valued by group members. She gained confidence in her abilities and became a valued member of both her group and the class as-a-whole. Had she been placed in a group of students who exhibited impulsivity, who struggled with learning empathy skills, and who were exuberantly outspoken, this student might have had less opportunity to expose her strengths. Given the limited time of a 16-week semester, this approach, rather than having the group work this through as a potential learning opportunity, was deemed the most appropriate and expedient.

The stated goal for each group is to complete the assigned tasks competently and for most of our students this translates into receiving a good grade for the course. Thus, in this model, there is an investment in working productively with team members. The stronger the sense of belonging to the group, the greater the potential for cohesion between all members (Sweet & Sweet, 2008). When members prevent the group from working optimally, as through issues with attendance, active participation, and adequate preparation, the more strained the relationships will become. This is no different from what might transpire in any social worker facilitated group. For these interpersonal issues to be dealt with, the group may be called upon to use the skills of confrontation, conflict resolution, assertiveness, negotiation, and attention to group process. All present as challenges to the novice social worker. Therefore, the instructor, in the role of group facilitator, should observe the dynamics of each group and assist the group in dealing with the process as it emerges, particularly when it begins to interfere with optimal group performance. The use of the peer evaluation process with an expanded design helps move TBL from strictly a means of dealing with content to also attending to process issues as they emerge in the small groups.

Eliminating iRAT

The traditional TBL model calls for delivering both an individual and a team test to assess students' understanding of the day's content. To focus exclusively on group process, the first adaptation is to eliminate the individual readiness assurance test (iRAT). Students are expected to enter class, pick up their group folder, which is identified with group name rather than with individual student names, and take it to their part of the classroom where they arrange their desks so that eye contact and interpersonal connections are possible. Once the class is ready to begin, each group is expected to open their folders and begin taking their team readiness assurance test (tRAT). The students do so independently with prompting from the Instructor rendered unnecessary.

The role of the instructor, also different from the traditional TBL model, is to move from group to group, answer group questions, assist the group's progress by asking questions which help guide its thinking, sometimes encouraging a quieter member who seems tentative about sharing opinions, and to give some cue to the group when they are veering off base completely. Students' participation tends to be active, loud, argumentative, and enthusiastic. These are all signs of engagement although differences between groups certainly exist. Some function quite cohesively and get through the tasks quickly. Others find they have barriers to task completion which get dealt with in another adaptation to the TBL model.

Students are provided with a multiple-choice assessment system, IF-AT, (http://ww.if-at.com) which requires each response to be scratched off to receive immediate feedback. Students receive the highest points for finding the correct answer on the first attempt. The point value decreases with each subsequent attempt to find the correct answer. Students state this process is highly stressful, although exciting. Many groups keep a "lucky" penny and some even use "lucky" quarters, that they clip onto their folders for use during each tRAT. Their fingers tend to hover over the answers. The student chosen to record the answers on the team assessment form usually turns to the group for a consensus response as a means of sharing blame in the event of an incorrect answer. This dynamic reinforces the importance of the group weighing in on each multiple-choice item on the test. Again, the role of the Instructor is to move between groups to assess which answers the majority of students seem to grasp and which they struggle with as only the latter are included in the mini-lectures which follow the administration of the tRAT. Students claim this part of the model is their favorite which is borne out by the rise in volume, laughter, and at times complete silence as group members watch the "responder" uncover the answer on the feedback form. Students tend to be highly focused, engaged, and energized during this phase of the TBL model.

Use of peer evaluations

A peer evaluation process can be a powerful tool if it is used to reinforce elements promoting successful group functioning while simultaneously laying bare the barriers to productive group performance. The TBL model utilizes peer evaluations, usually at the end of the course as a means for students to provide feedback to group members (Michaelsen & Sweet, 2011). A common approach to the use of pre-designed evaluation tools follows a sequence which includes collating the data, summarizing the feedback, and submitting the summary feedback to students. With group process as a focus, peer evaluations are designed and delivered strategically.

Peer evaluations should be completed minimally twice a semester with ample time available for students to incorporate the feedback effecting positive changes to their group functioning. The first evaluation is delivered to students approximately one third of the way into the semester. By this time, students within each group know each other well. They also have had enough time together for patterns of behavior to emerge which in some fashion, effect the functioning of their group. For groups in which a strong group identity is already established, trust between members and a shared sense of efficacy assist group members to work together cooperatively and collaboratively (Druskat & Wolff, 2001). For groups without a strong sense of group identity, it is not uncommon to observe problems with attendance, timeliness to class, and unresolved conflict. The group grappling with these commitment issues tend to be less productive and members less satisfied.

The use of peer evaluations in its original form had a dual purpose. The formative section of the evaluation was left for each group to develop to match each group's culture, values, and desired behaviors. The summative section of the evaluation was administered to students at the end of the semester as a means of assessing a final grade for each student. An adaptation to this approach is key if the TBL model is used to help students process their group. In its adapted format, an evaluation form, with both summative and formative components, is instructor developed and administered to students. The aggregated feedback is returned to students where they are expected to begin a discussion of the feedback. Students are directed to use the feedback as a guide to plan for increasing group functioning, increasing collaboration and creating a quality work product. Groups, who are successfully collaborating, are asked to discuss roles, qualities, and processes they believe are effecting the group's productivity and ability to collaborate. This exploration does not happen in a vacuum as students can be hesitant about confronting behaviors lest they hurt others' feelings. It is incumbent on the instructor to initiate the exploration process when they observe a group struggling to begin. The instructor can move from group to group and facilitate a discussion by asking key questions such as, "how satisfied are you all with the way your group is functioning? What seems to be getting in the way? Is there anything you feel you might be doing that is keeping the group from working cohesively and collaboratively?" Or, "Do you feel that you are all contributing equally to the final work product? How would you describe who is doing what on this project?"

Two examples of how peer evaluations have been used in small groups with instructor facilitation are offered here. One group using TBL in a social work research course struggled with subgrouping. Every time the four group members were observed, two sets of students appeared to be completing the tests and application activities independently of one another. Instructor observations of the subgrouping phenomena were not initially shared with the group. A few weeks into the semester, the instructor received a visit from one of the two subgroups. The students began complaining about the lack of cohesion within the group and the unfairness of one subgroup being left to complete all the work. The students were encouraged to share their feelings with their larger group and to write their observations and feelings in the peer evaluations which were being distributed that week. They wrote up their peer feedback and when they received the aggregated results, were asked to meet to discuss the new information with each other. They were hesitant to start the discussion which is a common occurrence. With the instructor as facilitator, feedback related to subgrouping was pointed out. Specifically, two subgroups existed rather than one group functioning cohesively to complete the assigned tasks. The student with the highest number of missed class days spoke up and stated she had been unaware that her attendance issue was so upsetting to her group members. She also stated she was quite unaware until it was pointed out to her, that she was on her smart phone as much as she was. Unbidden, she took full responsibility for not having done her fair share in the group and asked the group if they would help her stay away from her electronic devices. She indicated she needed their help as she reached for her smart phone without any self-awareness. This was a clear example of mutual aid. The same student also committed to attend class more consistently and to do a larger share of the final project to make up for her lack of effort on the first few projects. The second member of the same subgroup also stated she would benefit from the group's help in keeping from using her electronics. She added that she now understood that having side conversations with one other member of the group was detrimental to the collaborative nature of working on tasks the group was responsible for. The student commitments were revisited during the next peer evaluation to assess progress.

As part of the debriefing, students in this group reviewed the difficulty they shared in confronting each other on behaviors interfering with a sense of group cohesion. They also recognized that by eventually doing so, they could change the climate of the group, the norms of the group, and the success of the group's final product. Group work concepts were identified, defined, discussed, and then related to their small group examples. In a sense, the small group became the laboratory for learning about group processes and practicing new skills.

In another TBL group, one student complained tearfully, that she was left to complete the final project without much input or communication from the other four group members. She also stated she did not deserve the less than optimal grade the group received as she should not be penalized for being part of a group that did not perform well. She was asked to speak to her group to process her feelings about the inequity of the workload and the lack of communication amongst members. This did not happen.

The remaining four students were observed crying in the hallway outside of their classroom, refusing to enter as they did not "feel safe" participating in the group. They stated they could not and would not deal with the tension within the group that existed between the strong, outspoken group member and the less assertive ones. They were frightened of anger being directed their way and being accused of underperforming. Assumptions and misunderstandings abounded. Clearly, there were strong feelings, assumptions about motivations, and numerous misunderstandings about what had transpired in their group. Because of the level of anger, lack of sense of safety, and the possibility of accusations being thrown around, the instructor facilitated this group where ground rules were established and agreed upon before any discussion could commence. The rules were basic, such as each student being granted an opportunity to share their perspective without interruption, each would speak with "I" statements, and the group having a time-limit. Additionally, the goal of the group was established, that of developing a mutually agreed plan for how this group could continue to work together in a safe, equitable, and collaborative fashion. Not only did individual members take responsibility for at least one behavioral change to enhance group functioning, they also learned a great deal about one another. They explored each other's strengths and how these influenced the group in either positive or challenging ways. The outspoken student for example, came to realize that her need to excel academically, her natural leadership skills, and her outspokenness were viewed as "dictatorial" by others and alienated less assertive group members. Another student expressed how she is conflict avoidant which causes her to shy away from confrontations. She allows others to have their ideas predominate as she fears "stirring the pot" and having others angry with her.

Yalom (2005) wrote about one therapeutic factor of groups being that of the importance of interpersonal relationships and groups providing opportunities to correct interpersonal distortions. This group, whose focus was on completing a series of tasks in collaborative fashion, ended up being a venue for increased self-awareness of interpersonal functioning within a group format, especially in a group composed of members with characteristics very different from one-another.

Summary

For both facilitated groups, concepts related to group work were discussed with examples from their own experiences. Concepts discussed included but were not limited to mutual aid, maintaining a dual focus, attending to process, conflict, cohesion, mutual support and demand, stages of group development, the importance of group purpose, group climate and norms, and communication patterns. Having students process their academic group experiences using a group work lens brings intangible and sometimes puzzling group concepts to life. Each group experience can be identified, labeled, explored, and then more richly understood when the instructor takes the time to meet with the group and use it as a teaching moment. It is a time-consuming investment which requires group work knowledge and skill. More than that, it takes a belief that offering social work students with group work experiences that have a dual focus on content and process is valuable to their development as social work professionals. Having group work skills internalized not through sitting through lectures or reading texts but rather from experiencing actual groups as members, coupled with opportunities to discuss the process, gives social work students a distinct advantage as they begin their professional journeys.

References

Bartolomeo, Francis (2009). Boston model, In A. Gitterman & R. Salmon, (Eds.). *Encyclopedia of social work with groups* (103-106). New York, NY: Routledge.

Bishop, J. & Verleger, M. (2013). The flipped classroom: A survey of the research. 120th American Science for Engineering Education Annual Conference and Exposition, Paper ID #6219, 1-18.

Druskat, V. & Wolff, S. (2001). Building the emotional intelligence of groups. *Harvard Business Review,* Reprint R0103E, 81-90.

Garland, J., Jones, H., & Kolodny, R. (1978). A model for stages of group development. In S Bernstein (Ed.), 17-71., *Explorations in group work: Essays in theory and practice.* West Hartford, CT: Practitioner's Press.

Griffith, B. & Dunham, E. (2015). *Working in teams.* Thousand Oaks, CA: Sage Publications.

Gullo, C. Ha, T. C., & Cook, S. (2016). Twelve tips for facilitating team-based learning. *Medical Teacher,* 819-824

Hessenauer, S. & Lind, K. (2013). Preparation for group work: Perceptions of bachelor level social workers. *Journal of Baccalaureate Social Work, 18,* 141-156

Jakobsen, K., McIlreavy, M., & Marrs, S. (2014). Team-based learning: The importance of attendance. *Psychology Learning and Teaching, 13/1,* 25-31

Lane, Derek (2012). Peer feedback process and individual accountability in team-based learning, 51-62. In M. Sweet & L. Michaelsen, (Eds.), *Team-based learning in the social sciences and humanities.* Sterling, VA: Stylus

Liu, Sin-Ning & Beaujean, A. Alexander (2017). The effectiveness of team-based learning on academic outcomes: A meta-analysis. *Scholarship of Teaching and Learning in Psychology, 3/1,* 1-14

Macke, C., Taylor, J., & Taylor, J. (2013). Using team-based learning to teach social work research, human behavior, and policy. *The Journal of Baccalaureate Social Work, 18,* 64-75

Macke, C., Taylor, J., Taylor, J., Tapp, K., & Canfield, J. (2015). Social work students' perceptions of team-based learning. *Journal of Teaching in Social Work, 35,* 454-470

Michaelsen, L. & Sweet, M. (2011). Team-based learning. *New Directions for Teaching and Learning, 128,* 41-51

Schweifach, J. & LaPorte, H. (2009). Group work in foundation generalist classes: Perceptions of students about the nature and quality of their experience. *Social Work with Groups, 32/4,* 303-314

Simon, S. & Kilbane, T. (2014). The current state of group work education in US graduate schools of social work. *Social Work with Groups, 37/3,* 243-256

Stein, R., Colyer, C., & Manning, J. (2016). Student accountability in team-based learning classes. *Teaching Sociology, 44/1,* 28-38

Steinberg, D.M. (2004). *The Mutual-aid approach to working with groups.* (2nd Ed) Binghampton, NY: The Haworth Press

Sweet, M. & Sweet, L. (2008). The social foundation of team-based learning: Students accountable to students. *New Directions for Teaching and Learning, 116,* 29-40

Taylor, J. & McLendon, T. (2013). Using elements of team-based learning in an introductory social work course. *The Journal of Baccalaureate Social Work, 18,* 233-240

Travis, L., Hudson, N., Henricks-Lepp, G., Street, W., & Weidenbenner, J. (2016). Team-based learning improves course outcomes in introductory psychology. *Teaching in Psychology, 43/2,* 99-107

Venema, R., Meerman, J., & Hossink, K. (2015). Experiential, team-based learning in a baccalaureate social work research course. *Journal of Teaching in Social Work, 35*, 471-492

Yalom, Irvin & Leszcz, Molyn (2005). *The Theory and practice of group psychotherapy (5ᵗʰ Ed.)* 19-52. New York, NY: Basic Books.

Teaching appreciation for differences via intergroup dialogue (IGD)

Carolyn Gentle-Genitty, Corinne Renguette, and Dan Griffith

Introduction

There are many ways to teach appreciation for differences. Most often, this involves a one-and-done session with little room for continued growth or monitoring of skill development. To be effective, however, the method used to teach concepts around differences must recognize the personal and communal pain, hurt, shame, and vulnerability that marginalized groups feel resulting from the dominant culture's lack of awareness of and sensitivity to diversity and inclusion. Recognizing these aspects helps individuals respond to feelings of unworthiness and inadequacy. The difficulty is that people often attribute blame to others and think the responsibility for change belongs to someone else. Intergroup dialogue offers an interactive four-stage model that can help teach appreciation for and sensitivity to differences.

This chapter presents and defines inter-group dialogue (IGD) and shares information about some of the skills generated from using IGD. These skills can help participants gain awareness and foster action and can help educators teach appreciation for differences, integrate the model into their courses, and measure the outcomes. It is through awareness and action we author our own endings and advocate for social justice. The IGD four-stage model is a face-to-face facilitated learning experience that brings together different social identity groups over a sustained time to:

1. build trust by creating boundaries for communicating about difficult topics
2. share and understand commonalities and differences while

---

examining the nature and impact of social inequalities;

3. dialogue about difficult topics; and
4. explore ways of working together toward greater equality and justice (IGD in Higher Ed, 2007, p. 2).

This chapter will begin to explore these ideas and how they can help inform teaching.

Teaching appreciation for differences via intergroup dialogue

Campus communities are engaging in meaningful, yet difficult, conversations pertaining to race, gender, sexual orientation, religion, and other social identities. Indiana University-Purdue University Indianapolis (IUPUI), an urban university with approximately 30,000 students, adapted the four-stage intergroup dialogue model from the University of Michigan's Program on Intergroup Relations to help with this practice (The Trustees of Indiana University, 2017). Intergroup dialogue (IGD) has gained popularity among college campuses as a rigorous pedagogical tool to help students, faculty, staff, and leaders grasp how to communicate and lead when called upon to discuss the sensitive topics related to diversity and social, economic, and environmental justice.

Recent national events demonstrate the need for leaders to thoughtfully and effectively work in multicultural environments and who can help others navigate the inherent conflicts and tensions that emerge. For instance, advocacy for same-sex marriage, the right to use public bathrooms based on gender identity rather than birth gender, and other LGBT rights are perceived by some religious groups to infringe on their religious freedoms. *Black Lives Matter* highlights the long-standing frustration within the African-American community towards law enforcement, the justice system, and the need for corrections over issues like police stops, police-action shootings, sentencing guidelines, and mass incarceration. Fears of international terrorism and debates about immigration adversely influence the rights and freedoms of many U.S. citizens, lawful aliens, and others seeking lawful entry and protection within U.S. borders that have no association with terrorist activities. These and many seemingly less dramatic issues and events based on differences in cultural values and social identities negatively impact the ability of individuals and groups to communicate and to work and live together in many settings, including the workplace, community, neighborhoods, schools, churches, and public spaces. While IGD can benefit any undergraduate or graduate student, it will particularly benefit those seeking a greater awareness and practice with skills in civil discourse, intercultural communication, conflict resolution, and leadership.

The IGD teaching model contrasts markedly from traditional diversity educational approaches. Research demonstrates that learner comprehension of, engagement with, and willingness to converse on such topics are significantly enhanced through this model (Dessel & Rogge, 2008). The traditional diversity educational approaches introduce controversial topics absent from structured, thoughtful efforts to establish group norms, foster cohesiveness, and form trusting relationships beforehand. IGD, on the other hand, focuses on creating those relationships from the beginning. General expectations when using IGD are for students to gain transferrable skills for multicultural work, personal, and professional life settings including, but not limited to intercultural listening, conflict resolution, promotion of empathy and equality, and an increasing understanding of and appreciation for cultural differences. These experiences are essential to prepare students to discuss issues and topics around race or other social identities, to help them identify ways to engage in and promote issues of social justice, equity, and inclusion, and to foster multicultural communication and understanding in their future endeavors as both students and professionals in their chosen fields.

IGD competencies

Once an instructor has used the IGD training in their course, students may quickly demonstrate leadership capabilities to support others through intergroup conflicts and to help them better function as teams, corporate citizens, and community members. Specifically, the students will be able to implement the five core steps of IGD in personal, professional, and social settings. These steps include:

1. Create a space for dialogue [a negotiated space and time to

truthfully share];

2. Create rules and structure for the dialogue;
3. Set boundaries for one group to talk and the other to listen and reverse this process before drawing conclusions as a group;
4. Prepare to build community through shared space and engagement;
5. Draft plan of action for change with their voice and within their comfort zone. (Zuniga, 2003)

For all educational institutions, especially those in higher education, incorporating IGD into the environment can help to advance the intellectual growth of its citizens through research, creative activity, teaching and learning, and civic engagement. IGD aids in promoting educational, cultural, and economic development through a demonstrated commitment to diversity while offering concrete activities for co-curricular learning. The interactive nature of the sustained in-class dialogues and the development of dialogue facilitation skills provides students high impact curricular and co-curricular experiences supported through cross-cultural knowledge and civic responsibility centered on social justice. As some may argue, this is where art and science meets, in that through the lived experiences of students, we can interpret perspectives understood differently from personal realities to change meaning and interpretations of difference, creating a culture that fosters inclusivity.

IGD defined

There are many ways to teach appreciation for differences. Most to now have involved a one-and-done session with little room for continued growth or monitoring of skill development. To be effective, however, the method used to teach concepts and change thinking about differences must recognize the personal and communal pain, hurt, shame, and vulnerability that marginalized groups feel resulting from the dominant culture's lack of awareness of and sensitivity to diversity and inclusion. Recognizing these aspects helps individuals respond to feelings of unworthiness and inadequacy. The difficulty is that people often attribute blame to others and think the responsibility for change belongs to someone else. This chapter presents the skills generated from IGD to teach participants about how to bring awareness and foster action. This chapter highlights IGD as evidence-based practice, which can help educators *teach* appreciation for difference, integrate the model into their courses, and measure the outcomes. It is through awareness and action we author our own endings and advocate for social justice.

Intergroup Dialogue was developed in the 1980s by the University of Michigan Ann Arbor during campus racial conflict (University of Michigan, About, 2017). The IGD four stage model is a face-to-face facilitated learning experience that brings together different social identity groups over a sustained time to 1) understand commonalities and differences, 2) examine the nature and impact of social inequalities, and 3) explore ways of working together toward greater equality and justice (IGD in Higher Ed, 2007, p. 2). IGD is not a diversity training model. It does not espouse to define or teach to diversity, though an outcome of engagement in IGD is that of better diversity outcomes. IGD explores, in a safe space, with both groups present, power relations, problem solving, and dialogic interactions (time in session for discussion). As its tenets IGD, unlike diversity trainings, explores the history and current differences of the topic under exploration and fosters conversation based on earned trust, authentic connections, and dialogues. As a best practice, it integrates cognitive learning about i*dentity, difference, and inequality* with affective involvement of *oneself and others* through shared intimate personal reflections and meaningful critical dialogue to build relationships. Through relationships, sustained change and appreciation can occur. The intentional omission of the one-and-done mentality is one of the hallmark principles of IGD, relying on the belief that we can better appreciate difference if we have time to learn about and from each other while reserving judgement. It brings to life the statements we hear often in defense of "I am not... (fill in the blank)...because I have a friend who...(fill in the blank)". It presumes that if through the investment of time we cultivate relationships where we are able to see beyond the "fill in the blank" to call someone a friend then we should be able to use the micro example to make a macro impact.

IGD Four Stage Model (developed by the University of Michigan)

Stage 1: Group Beginnings: Forming & Building Relationships (2-3 sessions)
Goal: To support the formation of a dialogue-building relationship across differences. Establish group norms and rules for behavior during the process.

Stage 2: Exploring Differences & Commonalities of Experiences (3-4 sessions)
Goal: To explore meaning, increase awareness, improve listening skills, and promote understanding through relationship building.

Stage 3: Exploring & Dialoguing About Hot Topics (3-4 sessions)
Goal: To support and challenge risk-taking in communication about sensitive issues

Stage 4: Action Planning & Alliance Building (2 sessions)
Goal: To acknowledge contributions and celebrate collective efforts with action

Literature review

Through IGD, we prepare to build community and affect change by creating a space for dialogue. This becomes a negotiated space for truth where a group can create rules for dialogue, allow clear boundaries for one person to talk and the other to listen (and reverse) before drawing conclusions. Brene Brown in her book *Daring Greatly* offers the following inspiration for this type of risk-taking communication:

> When we spend our lives waiting until we're perfect or bulletproof before we walk into the arena, we ultimately sacrifice relationships and opportunities that may not be recoverable, we squander our precious time, and we turn our backs on our gifts, those unique contributions that only we can make. Perfect and bulletproof are seductive, but they don't exist in the human experience. (Brown, 2013, TEDx Houston)

IGD assumes that we will be imperfect. It is through this imperfection that we can learn more about ourselves and build community together. Research has shown that sustained intergroup dialogue processes like these, which support both cognitive and personal experiential learning, foster greater commitment among students to issues of diversity and social justice upon graduation compared to more traditional diversity education programs.

The four-stage model was evaluated for validity through a Multi-University Intergroup Dialogue Research Project, assessing student learning through intergroup dialogue programs at nine institutions (Gurin, Nagda & Zúñiga, 2013; Nagda, Gurin, Sorensen, & Zúñiga, 2009). Researchers compared the effects of intergroup dialogue on three categories of learning outcomes between traditional content courses on race and gender and similar courses that included an intergroup dialogue component. First, regarding intergroup understanding, students in dialogue courses showed a "greater increases in awareness and understanding of both racial and gender inequalities and their structural causes" than their counterparts in traditional content courses. Second, regarding intergroup relations, students in dialogue courses demonstrated "greater motivation to bridge differences and greater increases in empathy." With respect to the third category involving intergroup collaboration and engagement, these students felt "greater responsibility for 'challenging others on derogatory comments made about groups' and for participating in coalitions to address discrimination and social issues." They also "expressed increased motivation to be actively engaged in their post-college communities by 'influencing social policy,' 'influencing the political structure through voting and educational campaigns,' and 'working to correct social and economic inequalities" (Nagda, Gurin, Sorensen, & Zúñiga, 2009, pp. 5-6).

With respect to secondary education, in a study on the "Mix it Up program" sponsored by Study Circles and the Teaching Tolerance Project, three-fourths of the educators involved reported that "students said dialogues were a positive experience, and that students held honest discussions and evidenced more respect and were more willing to cross social boundaries" while half of these educators observed conflict in school decrease which they attributed to the dialogue program (Dessel & Rogge, 2008). In a study of 178 eleventh graders in two multicultural Midwestern high schools, participation in intergroup dialogue "increased critical social awareness and new friendships with students with different social identities, students' belief in the importance of building relationships before stereotyping, increased knowledge of different social identity groups, and increased awareness of prejudice and decreased prejudice" (Dessel, 2010b, pp. 417-18). These results indicate that IGD is a rigorous pedagogical tool that can and should be used in educational settings at all levels to promote an inclusive culture and climate.

In a study of empirical literature on intergroup dialogue outcomes, Dessel and Rogge (2008) found that participants across academic, community, secondary education, and interethnic settings generally report positive experiences with respect to improving intercultural communication and understanding and intergroup collaboration. In an academic setting, both students of color and white students participating in race dialogues reported feeling a greater sense of commonality with students from the other group (Dessel & Rogge, 2008; Gurin, Peng, Lopez, and Nagda, 1999; Gurin, Nagda, and Lopez, 2004). In pre-experimental and qualitative studies of student participation in dialogues, students reported "increased learning about the perspectives of people from other social groups, development of analytical problem solving skills, valuing new viewpoints, understanding the impact of social group membership on identity, gaining increased awareness of social inequalities, and raised awareness of racial identity for both white students and students of color" (Dessel & Rogge, 2008, p. 224). Again, these results indicate positive outcomes for using IGD in many different types of settings.

Infusing IGD in a course

Because of the excellent work of the founders and evaluators of IGD, infusing it in a course is simple. First, identify how much time is available to incorporate the work into the course schedule. Ideally the minimum amount of time would be four class sessions of at least three hours per session over four weeks or four weeks of two shorter sessions per week. Longer is always preferable because of the depth of the content and the time it often takes to build trust within the group. In our courses, we designed the course schedule to meet these minimums. Once you have the time identified, divide the four-stage model into a structure that works well for your students. For example, in our three-hour long class session, stages one and two occurred on the same day, stage three occurred in weeks two and three, and stage four occurred in week four of the dialogue structure.

Since Stage 1 is about building relationships and fostering trust, on the first day of the dialogue work, we had students brainstorm and create a list of rules for behavior (using some samples to get them started). They came up with rules like "be authentic" and "what happens in this room stays in this room" among others that were appropriate for these particular groups. During the Stage 2 portion of the class, they explored their differences and commonalities with activities where they could share details about their own identities by completing a social identity wheel (e.g. https://sites.lsa.umich. edu/inclusive-teaching/2017/08/16/social-identity-wheel/) and about their cultural backgrounds by bringing a *culture box* with items that represent something about their culture. In Stage 3, skilled facilitators helped students dialogue with each other about student-generated difficult topics and navigate the safe space of our classroom. In Stage 4, students listed actions they were comfortable seeing themselves taking in the future for how to become an ally and continue to expand the work they began in this class.

Going back to the five objectives mentioned earlier, we met these objectives by helping students to create a safe space where they can share their truths with negotiated rules and structure for the dialogue fostered by skilled facilitators. Guided active listening activities in pairs helped build trust, and since the courses were roughly split in half, one half of a class was able to talk and the other to listen by using a group activity where an inner circle would talk about a given topic and an outer circle would actively listen, and then the group as a whole debriefed about the process. We helped students engage with each other and build community in many aspects of the class interactions, and students were able to leave class with a draft of their own action plans that they created within their comfort zones and using their own voices.

One major challenge with infusing this model into a course is finding facilitators who know the IGD stages and have experience participating in dialogues so they can bring facilitation skills to the classroom and foster the type of environment that is necessary for this depth of sharing. In the original model, peers are facilitators. However, at our institution, because we are early in the implementation stages, we do not often have enough trained students to participate in peer facilitation. The University of Michigan offers a week-long summer Institute to learn more about IGD, and some of our faculty have attended this Institute and participated in several dialogues on campus, so we have well-trained faculty members who can facilitate (in lieu of students for now) and teach this type of course. We have recently created an IGD certificate program and have developed several courses where students can experience a deeper level of IGD principles and practices and even learn to become peer facilitators (and do just that in their capstone course) to help meet this challenge.

Another challenge is that students sometimes miss class, which can create a problem if they miss the relationship-building portion of the course. We minimized this challenge by stating the mandatory dialogue dates early so students would know when to be sure not to miss, but there is always someone who is ill or cannot make it.

Yet another challenge is to be certain to leave enough time for debriefing and reflection about the process and the learning, which is where a large amount of growth occurs. For the example herein, we used the four-week, three-hour class schedule, and we added a fifth week for debriefing, which helped meet this challenge.

Methods

Prior to the course start date, we administered a short questionnaire to learn about our students and determine a topic to use for the dialogue so we could, as equally as possible, split members of the class into two groups (see sample in appendix). Once determined, we discussed the resulting topic with the class to get their agreement and modifications. We then shared materials on IGD, the stages, and other definitional information to guide the discussions and allow for comfort with the process. To get specific assessment information from our students, prior to the dialogue days, we identified the characteristics we wanted to measure. Factor-loaded questions with noted reliability and validity through Cronbach's alpha were identified to develop a pre and post-test. Five traits were measured 1) empathy, 2) awareness of social inequality, 3) beliefs about inequality in society, 4) capacity to engage in dialogue, and 5) communication regarding differences.

Sample questionnaires for assessment

<u>**Comfort in Communicating With People of Other Groups (race/gender) (pre**</u> α =.696; <u>**post**</u> α =.732)

*a. I find it hard to challenge opinions of people in other racial/ethnic (gender) groups

b. I am able to respect and interact positively with people in other racial/ethnic (gender) groups whose views on social issues differ from my own

*c. I have difficulty expressing myself when discussing sensitive issues with people in other racial/ ethnic (gender) groups

e. I feel comfortable asking people of other racial/ethnic (gender) groups about their perspectives on issues involving their groups

*f. I avoid conversations with people of other racial/ethnic (gender) groups who hold really different perspectives from my own

*h. I worry about offending people from a different gender/race when I disagree with their points of view

A qualitative and quantitative mixed method design was used. Both focus groups and pre-posttests were employed. The instrument was a 45-item survey for pre- and posttests. The posttest included two open-ended questions.

Preliminary results

Undergraduate students in their first year of their major in a program at a Midwestern university in both fall and spring semesters participated in this study. The total sample size was 127 students in seven sections. Originally, eight sections were scheduled to participate in the study (all different instructors, six in fall, two in spring) with three instructors not using the IGD intervention and five using IGD; however, one of the classes that did not use IGD was unable to complete both the pre and posttests, so was eliminated from the data set, so only two sections that did not use IGD are represented in the data. One instructor used IGD in the first four weeks, one used it in the last four weeks, and three used it spread over the semester. For this chapter, we looked only at the pre and posttest results for two of the areas: empathy and awareness of social inequality. Overwhelmingly, the four instructors who used the IGD intervention in their courses showed the most improvement in the 13 questions about empathy and awareness of social inequality (10/13, 11/13, 10/13, 13/13), whereas the instructor who used it in the first four weeks and the instructors who did not use IGD all showed improvement in only 7/13 questions. The students who were not exposed to IGD and those who were exposed during the first four weeks had similar results, indicating that students may need more time to experience the IGD concepts more fully.

This study focused on five traits: empathy, awareness of social inequality, beliefs about inequality in society, capacity to engage in dialogue, and communication regarding differences. For this chapter, we looked only at the pre and posttest results for the first two: empathy and awareness of social inequality, which indicates a positive relationship with infusing IGD in a course. Further results and analysis will be reported soon.

Discussion and conclusion

Preliminary data suggests that students who used IGD in class throughout the semester (not in the first four weeks) were better able to develop their awareness of issues surrounding social justice regarding empathy and awareness of social inequalities. The quantitative data in this study begins to show trends toward a better understanding of differences and communication, confirming that appreciation for differences via IGD is worth spending additional time on for implementation and study. Additional work will include looking at the other questions in the remaining three areas, looking at qualitative data in depth, making course changes to help improve outcomes, and looking at additional courses that incorporate IGD across this campus.

Intergroup dialogues are prevalent in community, government, civic, social, and political settings at municipal, state, and national levels, suggesting the need for professionals from public affairs, law enforcement and related disciplines to lend their dialogue facilitation skills and expertise to support such initiatives. Walsh (2006) has identified over the course of 15 years more than 400 cities in 46 states and the District of Columbia that have implemented intergroup dialogue programs to improve race relations. Past undergraduate student participants in intergroup dialogue programs report direct benefits from and application of the skills, knowledge, and abilities developed through such programs to their current academic and career pursuits (Gurin, Nagda and Zúñiga, 2013).

Infusing IGD into academic courses makes sense for students and for our communities. While outcomes may differ from course to course and among institutions, students and communities will be better for having participated. We must provide all our students with more opportunities to learn how to communicate with our growing diverse world. If we continue to offer IGD-infused courses, collect and analyze data from those courses, and improve our course development and share best practices, we can also continue to improve the outcomes, speak to program successes, expand assessment, and, in so doing, disseminate more information, as additional work is needed to conduct more comparative assessment. All of these tasks are imperative to help develop awareness and continue to promote a culture and climate of inclusivity.

References

Brown, B. (2013, 2015). *Daring greatly.* New York: Avery.

Brown, B. (2010). The power of vulnerability. TEDx Houston. Retrieved July 2017 from: https://www.ted.com/talks/brene_brown_on_vulnerability

Dessel, A. (2010a). Effects of intergroup dialogue: Public school teachers and sexual orientation prejudice. *Small Group Research, 41*(5), 556-592.

Dessel, A. (2010b). Prejudice in schools: Promotion of an inclusive culture and climate. *Education and Urban Society, 42*(4), 407-429.

Dessel A. & Rogge, M. (2008). Evaluation of intergroup dialogue: A review of the empirical literature. *Conflict Resolution Quarterly, 26*(2), 199-238.

Gurin, P., Nagda, R., Lopez, G. (2004). The benefits of diversity in education for democratic citizenship. *Journal of Social Issues, 60*(1), 17-34.

Gurin, P., Nagda, B., Zúñiga, X. (2013). Epilogue: Intergroup dialogue in a changing world. In *Dialogue across difference: Practice, theory, and research on intergroup dialogue,* 355-376. New York: Russell Sage Foundation.

Gurin, P., Peng, T., Lopez, G., and Nagda, B. (1999). Context, identity and intergroup relations. In D. Prentice and D. Miller (eds.), *Cultural divides:*

Understanding and overcoming group conflict. New York: Russell Sage Foundation.

Nagda, B. Gurin, P. Sorensen, N., & Zúñiga, X. (2009). Evaluating intergroup dialogue: Engaging diversity for personal and social responsibility. *Diversity & Democracy, 12,* 4-6.

The Trustees of Indiana University (2017). IUPUI Rankings. Retrieved September 26, 2017. https://www.iupui.edu/about/rankings-statistics. html

University of Michigan (2017). About. Retrieved August 11, 2017. https://igr. umich.edu/article/igr-history

Walsh, K. (2006). Communities, race, and talk: An analysis of the occurrence of civic intergroup dialogue programs. *The Journal of Politics,* 68 (1), 22-33.

Zuniga, X. (2003). Bridging differences through dialogue. *About Campus.* http://people.umass.edu/educ202-xzuniga/downloads/ ZunigaAboutcampus.pdf

Welcome the stranger: Group work and hospitality in a fearful era

Lorrie Greenhouse Gardella

Introduction

How does group work welcome the stranger? Does the religious and cultural value of hospitality have a place in social work or social work with groups? Three recent experiences have raised my awareness of the relationship between group work and hospitality and I'd like to share these stories with you today.

Story #1: The picture party

West Haven Community House is a settlement house in a small working class city just outside New Haven, Connecticut,USA. Founded as the Group Work Council of West Haven (Gardella, 1997), the ramshackle Victorian house is where I had my introduction to group work as a day camp counselor and adolescent volunteer. Last summer, in preparation for its 75th anniversary, the Community House had a picture party. Anyone who had ever been involved with the Community House was invited to help sort through boxes of unlabeled pictures and to try to name the people in the pictures and the events that were going on.

A variety of people showed up at the picture party on a Saturday afternoon. They came from all over the state and from all walks of life – firefighters and first responders, teachers and social workers, business people and community leaders, homemakers and volunteers. I was able to identify some people in the pictures. I even found myself! What was particularly striking was that intermingled among the Community House photos were family pictures belonging to the longtime executive director, Sid Silverberg. Mr. Silverberg had saved mementos from his children's birthday parties and bar mitzvah celebrations alongside those of Community House board meetings and groundbreaking ceremonies. For Mr. Silverberg, who taught me and other young volunteers the essential values and skills of group work, there was very little distinction between professional and family life. The Community House was the community's house – and to some extent, as suggested by the turnout at the picture party, it still is.

Story #2: Publishing Edith

One of my research areas is social work history, and I had the privilege of conducting an oral history interview with a retired group worker named Edith Stolzenberg. Edith Stolzenberg was the first woman to be hired as a full-time social worker in Hartford Public High School in Hartford, Connecticut. I met with Ms. Stolzenberg in her West Hartford home, where floor-to-ceiling bookcases were filled with books and family photos. Upon closer inspection, I found that the family pictures included those of Ms. Stolzenberg's former students, who now were grown up with children of their own. The most surprising part of our oral history interview – and I did my best to hide my amazement – was that Ms. Stolzenberg brought students home to live with her. When children had run away or lost their families to a disaster, she gave them a temporary home.

I have been trying to publish the oral history of Edith Stolzenberg's career, but versions of the paper have been rejected by several journals so far. Although reviewers consistently have praised the quality of the writing and the thoroughness of the research, they have recommended against publication, because Edith Stolzenberg took unacceptable risks and set a poor example for social workers today.

Story #3: Lawn signs

The American Academy of Social Work and Social Welfare recently launched an initiative called "The Grand Challenges for Social Work" (AASWSW, 2016; Padill & Fong, 2016). The Grand Challenges initiative identifies twelve priorities for social work research and practice. Various national social work associations, such as the National Association of Social Workers (NASW) and the Council on Social Work Education (CSWE), have endorsed the Grand Challenges as a policy agenda for the profession. What is strangely missing from the Grand Challenges, however, is any explicit reference to the global refugee crisis.

In responding to the needs of immigrants, refugees, and asylum seekers, including undocumented persons in the United States, it is not the profession of social work, but rather the grassroots coalitions of churches, civic groups, legal clinics, and immigrants themselves that are taking the lead in advocating for asylum, offering sanctuary, and assuming the costs and risks of taking in strangers (United We Dream, 2017). During the past few weeks, families throughout the United States have set out lawn signs with a message in English, Arabic, and Spanish that reads: "No matter where you are from, we are glad that you are our neighbor." There are many versions of these signs, such as those available from: www.welcomeyourneighbors.org.

Ethics and values

These stories evoke for me the complicated relationship between the profession of social work and the value of hospitality. Hospitality is a value that dates from ancient times, when the custom of extending the protection of one's household to travelers made it possible for persons to travel long distances by themselves (Hobbs, 2001). At the turn of the 20th century, hospitality inspired early social workers to establish settlement houses that welcomed the immigrant poor (Addams, 1910; Kendall, 2000). In seeking professional status, however, social workers needed to differentiate their activities from domestic caregiving or charitable good works (Flexner, 1915; Gitterman, 2014). Although hospitality today is a value in nearly all religions and cultures, (Ahmed, 2000; Lashley, Lynch, & Morrison, 2007; Siddiqui, 2015), the word "hospitality" is not found in the *IFSW Statement of Ethical Principles* (2012), *NASW Code of Ethics* (2008), or the *NASW Standards and Indicators for Culturally Competent Practice* (2015).

Hospitality is a challenging value for social workers, because it opens a doorway between professional and personal life. Social workers have specified hours, while hospitality is always on call. The roles and responsibilities of social workers are defined by professional ethics. We are charged with promoting human rights in the roles of "controller" and "helper" (IFSW, 2012), and we are warned against "dual or multiple relationships with clients" (NASW, 2008, Section 1.06c). In contrast, hospitality as a value and voluntary practice is limited only by the conscience and capacities of the community (Gupta, Featherstone, & White, 2014; Moosa-Mitha, 2016).

West Haven Community House, when it began, was open to everyone for free or nearly free of charge. The porch light was always burning. Funded by philanthropies, such as the Community Chest (today, the United Way), Community House programs were staffed by volunteers who led activity groups under the supervision of a social worker. I was aware of at least one staff member who, escaping family violence, was allowed to make an apartment in the Community House basement and to live there for a time, probably in violation of zoning and housing codes. Such an open door and open access policy is no longer a sustainable business model for the Community House or for other nonprofit social services.

Safety and risk

School social work also has changed Edith Stolzenberg's day. Social workers no longer take clients home to live or even drive them in our own cars. In an effort to minimize risk, we tend to interpret professional ethics from an individualistic point of view. We are advised, particularly if we are women, to care for ourselves by balancing work and family and by separating our professional and personal lives (Bianchi & Milke, 2010; Gerson, 2010; Jackson, 2014).

Edith Stolzenberg would not have followed this advice. Guided by religious values and Jewish social tradition, she accepted the risks of hospitality and the inevitable the power disparities between host and guest ((Derrida, 2005; Eyal-Lubling & Krumer-Nevo, 2016; Hamington, 2010). In a professionally formative position at the New York Association for Jewish Children, Ms. Stolzenberg was introduced to the idea that social workers are communal servants. The community is obliged to care for its members, and social workers step in where social institutions, such as families or schools, are failing (Freid, 1968;

Jewish Child Care, 2017; Zucher, 1968). A similar sense of community obligation was held by social workers dedicated to African American, immigrant, LGBTQ+, and other communities that were not being well-served – or served at all – by mainstream social agencies (Carlton-Laney, 2001; D'Augelli, 1989; Gardella & Haynes, 2004).

Social calling

In the 1930s and 1940s, some German Jewish social workers who escaped or survived the Nazi Holocaust immigrated to the United States. Louis Lowy, Hans S. Falck, Gisela Konopka, and others were attracted to social work with groups work as an opportunity to restore social values that National Socialism had nearly destroyed (Kalcher, 2004; Konopka, 1988; Wieler, 1995). Despite their vivid awareness that societies can and do fail, these group workers believed in the positive course of human history, and they understood social work with groups as an instrumentality for human progress, democracy, and the social good (Gardella, 2011). Louis Lowy and Gisela Konopka periodically returned to Germany to reintroduce social work with groups to formerly Nazi-occupied countries.

In his early career, Louis Lowy, like Edith Stolzenberg, practiced social work with groups in Jewish sectarian agencies, such as the Bridgeport Community Center in Bridgeport, Connecticut. Social work with groups, Lowy found, enhances individual and social development by providing opportunities for social participation and lifelong learning (Lowy, 1960; Lowy, 1976). Group work with persons of any age prepares them for individual and community self-determination and political engagement in a democracy. In Lowy's view, secure families provide the basis for democratic societies, and mindful of hospitality, he called upon group workers to assure that isolated persons or persons in institutions had access to a family life:

> For those who lack families nearby, we must think of developing surrogates, people who volunteer or are trained to give the same kind of comfort and show the same kind of concern as family members; who can provide the individualized and personal attention for which there is no substitute (Lowy, 1980, p. 214).

Hans S. Falck shared Lowy's hospitable point of view. Hans Falck proposed "the membership perspective" as a general theory of social work that considers social membership to be the fundamental human condition (Falck, 1988; Falck, 1989). The membership perspective offered an alternative paradigm to the "dual focus" of social work that distinguishes between clinical and community practice. To Hans Falk as to Louis Lowy, the community could not be separated into social workers and clients, insiders and outsiders, or us and them. There is only "us," the human community.

The teachings of Louis Lowy and Hans Falck are significant for group work with immigrants, refugees, and other displaced or traumatized populations. In the words of Holocaust scholar Dori Laub: "A home can never be a home again after trauma, and an erased relationship can never provide safety" (Laub, 1998, p. 799). Group work offers opportunities for survivors to speak the unspeakable, to form empathic relationships, and to realize the possibility of home. By sharing memories – and by creating the memory of memories (Rakfeldt, 2015) – groups provide safety in the present, a secure social base for building hope, and a bridge to the future (Bowlby, 1988; Shorey & Snyder, 2005). Ultimately, group work and hospitality share a hopeful purpose. In the words of sociologists Jennie Germann Molz and Sarah Gibson:

> Hospitality is not just about the gift of repose, but also about the gift of hope. Making the guest feel at home is not just about seeing to his or her physical comfort or embodied needs (though these are certainly important); it is also about instilling the guest with a feeling of hope and a sense of being propelled forward (Molz & Gibson, 2007, p. 15).

Hopeful purpose

Perhaps more than any other field in social work, it is social work with groups that can realize the value of hospitality. Group workers promote social justice by bringing outsiders in, by mediating between "us" and "them," and by advocating for self and others (Ellerbrock, 2016). Group workers maintain a continuous balance between safety and risk, controlling and helping, and responding to individual and social needs. Group workers reconcile professional ethics with religious and cultural values, including our own values and those of group members.

Whether in our formal positions or as volunteers, group workers extend hospitality in many ways. We create welcoming spaces, such as school-based health centers, where we serve children and families regardless of their ability to pay (Rutgers, 2017). We provide places of safety through trauma-informed care (NCTSN, 2017). We reach beyond time-limited, evidence-based protocols to meet clients' needs (Galinsky, Terzian, & Fraser, 2006). We take political action with and on behalf of communities (Cohen & Mullender, 2006; Cifuentes, 2017).

As we enter a time of rising populism, nationalism, economic disparity, and terror, and as austere social policies exclude our most vulnerable populations, we have the potential to step in as group workers where social institutions are failing. Group workers can help people of all ages to live in safety and happiness with their families and in their homes; and we can help protect those who are at risk of losing their families or homes. We can commit to serving displaced persons and displaced communities all over the world.

Social workers in earlier generations practiced group work during perilous times, and they assumed risks and obligations beyond their formal job descriptions or codes of ethics (Levinas, 1994). For social workers such as Sid Silverberg, Edith Stolzenberg, Louis Lowy, Hans S. Falck, and Gisela Konopka, group work was not just a career; it was an identity and social calling. Today, group workers are being called again, and our responses will determine the hopeful and hospitable purpose of group work in a fearful era.

Postscript

Soon after this presentation, my oral history of Edith Stolzenberg was published (Gardella, 2017); and my "Welcome Your Neighbors" lawn sign was stolen from the front lawn.

References

Addams, J. (1910). *Twenty years at Hull House with autobiographical notes.* New York: McMillan.

Ahmed, S. (2000). *Strange encounters.* London: Routledge.

American Academy of Social Work and Social Welfare (2016). *Grand challenges for social work.* Retrieved from: http://aaswsw.org/grand-challenges-initiative/.

Bianchi, S. M. & Milkie, M. A. (2010). Work and family research in the first decade of the 21st century. *Journal of Marriage and Family, 72*, 705-725.

Bowlby, J. (1988). Attachment, communication, and the therapeutic process. *A secure base: Parent-child attachment and healthy human development,* 137-157.

Carlton-LaNey, I. B. (Ed.), (2001). *African American leadership: An empowerment tradition in social welfare history.* Washington, DC: NASW Press.

Cifuentes, M. (2017, June 10). Group intervention with immigrants at risk of deportation: A response to U. S. government terror. Paper presented at the *39th Annual Symposium, International Association for Social Work with Groups.* New York, NY.

Cohen, M. B. & Mullender, A. (2006). The personal in the political: Exploring the group work continuum from individual to social change goals. *Social Work with Groups 28*(3-4), 187-204.

D'Augelli, A. R. (1989). The development of informal helping resources for lesbian women and gay men: A case study in community psychology. *Journal of Community Psychology, 17,* 18-29.

Derrida, J. (2005). Principle of hospitality. *Parallax, 11*(1), 6-9.

Ellerbrock, K. (2016, June 15). German social group work with asylum-seekers.Paper presented at the *38th Annual Symposium, International Association for Social Work with Groups.* New York, NY.

Eyal-Lubling, R. & Krumer-Nevo, M. (2016). Feminist social work: Practice and theory of practice. *Social Work 61*(3), 245-254.

Falck, H. S. (1989). The management of membership: Social group work contributions. *Social Work with Groups 12*(3), 19-32.

Falck, H. S. (1988). *Social work: The membership perspective.* New York, NY: Springer.

Flexner, A. (1915, May). Is social work a profession? Paper presented at the *42nd Annual Session, National Conference of Charities and Correction.* Baltimore, MD.

Freid, J. (Ed.) (1968). *Judaism and the community: New directions in Jewish social work.* Cranbury, NJ: Thomas Yoseloff.

Galinsky, M., Terzian, M., & Fraser, M. (2006). J. (2004). The art of group work practice with manualized curricula. *Social Work with Groups, 29*(1), 11-26.

Gardella, L. G. (1997). Prime mover: Pauline Roney Lang. *Journal of Baccalaureate Social Work 2*(2), 22-42.

Gardella, L. G. (2017). Social work and hospitality: An oral history of Edith Stolzenberg. *Journal of Religion and Spirituality in Social Work: Social Thought.* DOI: 10.1080/15426432.2017.1350124.

Gardella, L. G. (2011). *The life and thought of Louis Lowy: Social work through the Holocaust.* Syracuse, NY: Syracuse University Press.

Gardella, L. G. & Haynes, Karen S. (2004). *A dream and a plan: A woman's path to leadership in human services.* Washington, D.C.: NASW Press.

Gerson, K. (2010). *The unfinished revolution: Coming of age in a new era of gender, work, and family.* New York: Oxford University Press.

Gitterman, A. (2014). Social work: A profession in search of its identity. *Journal of Social Work Education 50*(4), 599-607.

Gupta, A.; Featherstone, B.; & White, S. (2014). Reclaiming humanity: From capacities to capabilities in understanding parenting in adversity. *British Journal of Social Work.* Retrieved from: http://bjsw.oxfordjournals.org/content/early/2014/1122/bjsw.bcu137.

Hamington, M. (2010). *Feminism and hospitality: Gender in the host/guest relationship.* Lanham, MD: Lexington Books.

Hobbs, T. R. (2001). Hospitality in the First Testament and the "teleological fallacy." *Journal for the Study of the Old Testament, 95,* 3-30.

International Federation of Social Workers (2012). *Statement of ethical principles.* Retrieved from: *http://ifsw.org/policies/statement-of-ethical-principles/.*

Jackson, K. (2014). Social worker self-care – The overlooked core competency. *Social Work Today, 14*(3), 14.

Jansson, J. S. (2016). Moral distress in social work practice – When workplace and conscience collide. *Social Work Today, 16*(3), 18.

Jewish Child Care Association of New York (2017). History. Retrieved from: http://www.jccany.org/who-we-are/history/

Kalcher, J. (2004). Social group work in Germany: An American import and its historical development. In Caron, C. J.; Fritz, A. S.; Lewis, E.; Ramey, J. H., and Sugiuchi, D. T., (Eds.), *Growth and development through group work* (pp. 51-71). Binghamton, NY: Haworth.

Kendall, K. A. (2000). *Social work education: Its origins in Europe.* Alexandria, VA: Council on Social Work Education.

Konopka, G. (1988). *Courage and Love.* Edina, MN: Burgess Printing Company.

Lashley, C., Lynch, P. & Morrison, A., eds. (2007). *Hospitality: A social lens.* Oxford, England: Elsevier Books.

Laub, D. (1998). History, memory, and truth: Defining the place of the survivor. In Berenbaum, M. & Peck, A. (Eds.), *The Holocaust and history: The known, the unknown, the disputed, and the reexamined* (pp. 799-812). Bloomington, IN: Indiana University Press.

Levinas, E. Kelly, (1994). The rights of man and the right of the other. In *Outside the subject.* Palo Alto, CA: Stanford University Press, pp. 116-126.

Lowy, L. (1976). *The function of social work in a changing society: A continuum of practice.* Boston, MA: Charles River Books.

Lowy, L. (1960). Social work and social statesmanship. *Social Work, 5*(2), 97-104.

Lowy, L. (1980). *Social policies and programs on aging.* Lexington, MA: Lexington Books.

Molz, J. M. & Gibson, S. (2007). *Mobilizing hospitality: The ethics of social relations in a mobile world.* Burlington, VT: Ashgate.

Moosa-Mitha, M. (2016). Geography of care: Syrian refugees and the welfare state. *Affilia 3*(3), 281-284.

National Association of Social Workers (2008). *Code of ethics.* Washington, DC: National Association of Social Workers.

National Association of Social Workers (2015). *Standards and indicators for cultural competence in social work practice.* Washington, DC: National Association of Social Workers.

National Child Traumatic Stress Network (2017). Working effectively with military families: Ten key concepts all providers should know. Retrieved from: http://www.NCTSN.org/.

Padill, Y. C. & Fong, R (2016). Identifying grand challenges facing social work in the next decade: Maximizing social policy engagement. *Journal of Policy Practice, 15*(3), 133- 144.

Rakfeldt, J. (2015). Home environments, memories, and life stories: Preservation of Estonian national identity. *Journal of Baltic Stuidies,* DOI: 10.1080/01629778.2015.1075137.

Shorey, H. S., & Snyder, C. R. (2005). Hope for adolescence: Social goals, attachments, and transitions into adulthood. *Focal Point, 19,* 15-18.

Siddiqui, M. (2015). *Hospitality and Islam: Welcoming in God's name.* New Haven: Yale University Press.

Rutgers University Based Health Care (2017). School-based programs. Retrieved from: http://ubhc.rutgers.edu/services/children_family/schoolbased.html

United We Dream (2017). Immigrant youth building a movement for justice. Retrieved from: https://unitedwedream.org/news/.

Welcome your Neighbors (2017). Retrieved from: https://www.welcomeyourneighbors.org/

Wieler, J. & Zeller, S. (Eds). (1995). *Emigrierte Sozialarbeit: Portraits vertriebener Sozialarbeiterinnen nach 1933* [Emigrant social workers: portraits of social workers exiled after 1933]. Freiburg, Germany: Lambertus.

Zucher, M. (1968). The mutual responsibilities between communal servants and the community. In Freid, J. (Ed.), *Judaism and the community: New directions in Jewish social work* (pp. 88-93). Cranbury, NJ: Thomas Yoseloff.

Index

abstraction
    slavery as 23–4
    social work as 21–3
accreditation, US 63–4
action-reflection-action cycle 221
Action Research cycle 85–7, 89, 93–4
Adequate Education 82
adult education, creative writing 13
ako 154
Allen, G.J. 183
American Academy of Social Work and Social Welfare (AASWSW), Grand
        Challenges initiative 266–7
Anderson, D. 56
anti-oppressive perspective 171–2
Aotearoa New Zealand *see* Māori student study
appreciation for differences *see* intergroup dialogue (IDG)
art therapy 140
asylum law, undermining 4
austerity policy, effects of 5

BaFá BaFá
    Alpha culture 66–7
    Beta culture 67–70
    culture comparison 70
    debriefing 74–5
    observation of 'other' 70–4
    overview 64–5
    student explorers 65–6
    summary and conclusions 75–6
Balkanroute, closures 4
Battered Spouse Waiver (BSW) 102
BBC News 4
Brown, A. 56
Brown, B. 256
bullying 82, 83–4
Burris, M. A. 138–9
Button (badge), Social Work in 40 Objects project 28–9

Canada *see* diversity; Practicing Gratitude
caregiver study
    case scenario 126
    context and overview 126
    coping strategies 129
    discussion 134
    diversity 130–1

ethnicity 130–1
financial effects on carers 128
interventions for caregivers 131
Latino population group 133
multifamily psychoeducational groups 132–3
population aging 127
psychoeducational groups 132–3
social isolation 127–8
stress and coping theory 128–9
see also elders
Carr, W 85, 86
Cauvain, Simon 32
Charmaz, K. 56
Chee-Phung, Tuck 31
children
in war 10–11
see also Ukraine
Chun, M. 130–1
City University of New York (CUNY) 103
civic commitment, and group work 7
Clarkson, T. 23–4
Clarkson's box 23–4
cognitive behavioral therapy (CBT) 184
Cohen, Carol 28–9
cohesiveness 179
collective trauma 13
colonization, Aotearoa New Zealand 153
commonalities, group composition 116–17
conflict
and diversity 37–8
as normal 7
connection 179
coping strategies, caregivers 129
creative writing
additional writing 17
adult education 13
children's attitudes 14
collective 17
conclusions 19
context and overview 12
development in schools 13
exercises 16–17
new writing 18
practice 16–18
re-writing 16–17
results 18–19
teacher-student relationship 15
theoretical background 12–16

creativity
    benefits of 140
    as resource 13
    self-expression 144–5
credibility 56–7
crisis of trust 220
Croft, Suzy 26
cultural exchange
    Alpha culture 66–7
    BaFá BaFá 64–75
    Beta culture 67–70
    context and overview 62
    culture comparison 70
    debriefing 74–5
    observation of 'other' 70–4
    Social Work 220 Understanding Diverse and Oppressed Populations 64
    student explorers 65–6
    study location 63
    summary and conclusions 75–6
    see also diversity
cultures and objects 24–5
Curtis, E. T. 151
cyber-bullying 83–4

Dalek 29–30
Daring Greatly (Brown) 256
David, Enakele Seun 26–7
Deggendorf Displaced Persons Center 6, 8
deportations 4
Dessel, A. 258
diagnoses, in education 82
disability, social model 30
displaced persons, global refugee crisis 1–2
diversity
    caregiver study 130–1
    conceptualization 42–4
    and conflict 37–8
    context and overview 37–9
    data analysis 40–1
    data collection 40
    defining 37
    discussion 53–6
    emergence in groups 44
    within and between groups 38
    implications of study 55
    interviews 40
    limitations of study 56–7
    macro-level factors 48–9
    methodology 39–40

participant characteristics 43
participants and settings 41–2
power dynamics 46–8, 55–6
professional uses of self 49–50
redefinition 54
relational experience 44–5
relational understanding of 54–6
responding to 51–2
results 42–52
in social work 38–9
social work education 63–4
summary and conclusions 57–8
themes 42–52
vignette 53–4
working with 54–5
see also cultural exchange; intergroup dialogue (IDG)
divide and rule politics 4–5
Doel, M. 13–14
Doyle, R. 37, 38

early infant objects 24
ecological system theory 175
education
    Adequate Education 82
    higher education as group work context 152
    popular education 104–5
    and schooling 85
    social work 153
        see also cultural exchange
elders
    abuse of 128
    housing preferences and care needs 127–8, 131
    social isolation 127–8
    see also caregiver study
*Emigrant Social Workers: Portraits of Social Workers Who Were Exiled after
        1933* (Weiler & Zeller) 5
empowerment 6, 156, 171, 178
Epston, D. 176
ethics, and values 267–8
ethnicity, caregiver study 130–1
ex-prisoners *see* P.RE.TURN project
experiential learning *see* cultural exchange
Experiential Learning cycle 85–7, 90–3

Falck, Hans 270
Folkman, S. 128
food 28
Freire, P. 15, 104, 154
Freud, S. 12–13

Gandarilla, Marie 208
Gardella, L.G. 3
gender
    defining 118
    see also group composition
George, U. 37, 38
Germann Molz, J. 270
Germany, role in refugee crisis 4
Gibson, S. 270
Gill, Jean 207–8
global refugee crisis 1–2, 4
Gonyea, J. G., 133
Grand Challenges initiative 266–7
gratitude *see* Practicing Gratitude
Gray, Freddie 195
grounding 141
group composition 116–17
    attitude to male staff 120
    context and overview 116–17
    differences 122–3
    discussion 121–2
    learning/corrective experience 119
    limitations of study 123–4
    non-judgmental stance 120
    other themes 120–1
    participants 119
    practice example 118–19
    practice implications 122–3
    purpose of group 118–19
    setting 118
    summary and conclusions 124
    themes and responses 119–21
    worker experience 120
group work
    and civic commitment 7
    global 21
    member-worker relationships 117
    role and significance 10–11
    and Social Work in 40 Objects project 30–2
    student experiences 240
    teaching as 80
    volunteers 7
group workers, self-awareness 117
groups
    diversity 38, 44–5
    rehabilitative function 2

Haley, W. E. 128
Halton, C. 220, 224

healing 19
Hlavka, H. 175
hope 270
   hopeful purpose 270–1
   role of 3
hospitality 267–8, 270
human rights 267–8

IASWG Southern California Chapter
   Cake Pop Fundraiser 212–14, 215
   context and overview 206
   discussion and implications 214–15
   history 207–8
   Hope for the Holidays 210–12, 214–15
   leadership 214–15, 216–17
   limitations of study 216
   meet and greet 209
   meetings 209–11
   overview of chapter 206–7
   planning 214–15
   recommendations 216–17
   revitalization 209–13
IFAT 243–4
Ileke ibile 26–7
immigration, effects on social work 5
Indiana University-Purdue University Indianapolis (IUPUI) *see* intergroup
      dialogue (IDG)
individual readiness assurance test (iRAT) 243–4
inductive data analysis 40–1
intergroup dialogue (IDG)
   aims 255
   assessment questionnaires 260–1
   assumption of imperfection 257
   benefits of 254
   challenges 259–60
   competencies 253–4
   context and overview 251–2
   core steps 253–4
   defining 254–5
   development 255
   discussion and conclusions 262–3
   expectations 253
   focus of study 262
   four stage model 256
   intergroup understanding 257
   literature review 256–8
   meeting objectives 259
   Mix It Up program 257–8
   as part of a course 258–60

preliminary results 261–2
sample 261
secondary education 257–8
study methods 260–1
teaching appreciation for differences 252–5
vs traditional approaches 253
internationalism 21
intimate partner violence (IPV) 100–2
see also VAWA/U Visa Self-Prep Course (VAWA SPC)
Ireland *see* professional identities

Jean Tweed Centre *see* Practicing Gratitude

Kelley, P. 176
Kemmis, S. 85, 86
Konopka, Gisela 269
Kramatorsk 16
Kurland, R. 214–15

labelling, in education 82
language
    challenge of 68
    te reo Māori 156
    Ukraine 16
Latino population group, caregiver study 133
Laub, D. 10, 270
Laub, J. 174
lawn signs 266–7, 271
Lazarus, R. S. 128
learning, experiential *see* cultural exchange
Lee, Cheryl 207–8
Leff, J. 132
LePeau, L. A. 192
Leszcz, M. 183
Lewin, K. 80, 85–6
Lin, I-F. 129
listening 176–7
loneliness 128
Lowy, Louis 269–70
    advocacy 2
    biography 2
    role and significance 8
Lumpkin, A. 163

MacGregor, N. 24
managerialism 220
Māori people 149
    worldview 153–4
Māori student study
    aims 151

Aotearoa New Zealand context 153–4
background to study 150
"being on the same page" 158
cognitive disequilibrium 158
commitment and participation 160–1
competence 156
connection 158–9
context and overview 149–50
dominant/negative peers 161–2
findings and analysis 155–8
future practice 157
group composition 159–60
higher education context 152
implications of study 165–6
knowledge application 157
methodology 151–2
negative experience 159–63
peer influences 160–3
positive experience 158–9
recommendations 166
research rationale 150–1
social interactions 155
social work education context 153
student preferences 163–4
summary and conclusions 164–5
te reo Māori 156
teachers' role 162–3
understanding course content 155–6
working with clients 157
Marksberry, M.L. 15
Martin, Trevor 193
McCallion, P. 133
McLean, K. C. 176
McWilliams, N. 177
meaning-making 175–6
Meitheal Model 221ff
Memory jar 26
Michaelsen, L. 238ff
migrants, work opportunities 5–6
Mind the Gap 31
mindfulness 141
Mistry, T. 56
Mix It Up program 257–8
Mouthpiece to a french horn 32
Muhlhausen, D. B. 174
multifamily psychoeducational groups, caregiver study 132–3

narrative reconstruction 176
narrative therapy 176–7

Ndrecka, M. 174
neo-liberal policies, effects of 5
Netherlands *see* primary education study
New Zealand *see* Māori student study
Niemöller, Martin 196–7

Obama administration 193
    deportations 109
objectification, of abstraction 22
objects
    and cultures 24–5
    early infant objects 24
    evocative 24–5
    evoking social work 25
    see also Social Work in 40 Objects project
originality 57
O'Toole, F. 24
overcrowding 6

Palmer, Jill 29–30
Park, C. L. 176
pedagogical gap 62
peer evaluations, team-based learning (TBL) 244–7
peer support, team-based learning (TBL) 246
Pelled, L. H. 38
Perry, Joan 207
Petersilia, J. 175
photovoice 138–9
politics, divide and rule 4–5
popular education 104–5
population aging, United States 127
power dynamics, and diversity 46–8, 55–6
practical action research 85
Practicing Gratitude
    art therapy 140
    challenges 146–7
    connections to community 144
    context and overview 136
    creative self-expression 144–5
    evaluation methodology 143
    evaluation responses 143–4
    focus on strengths 145
    gratitude 139–40
    group mural 145–6
    implementation 141
    Jean Tweed Centre 136–7
    learning 146–7
    literature review 138–40
    location of study 136–7

methodology 138–9
mutual support 145–6
photovoice 138–9
purpose and intentions 137–8
sample themes 142
session format 142
structure 141–2
summary and conclusions 147
Supportive Housing Program 137
Pratt, M. W. 176
Praxis 178, 180–2
Praxis of Revenant's Empowerment and Transcendence Using Re-Narrations
    (P.RE.TURN) *see* P.RE.TURN project
P.RE.TURN project
case example 180–7
change process 178–9
context and overview 171–2
existing provision 171
group approach 179–80
limitations of re-entry programmes 174–5
Praxis 178, 180–2
re-entry experiences 173
re-entry population 172–3
Revenant's Empowerment 178, 182–4
summary and conclusions 187–8
theoretical perspectives 175–7
Transcendence Using Re-Narration 178, 185–7
primary education study
Action Research cycle teachers 89, 93–4
bullying 83–4
complaints to inspectorate 82–3
context and overview 79–80
defining groups 80–1
Dutch primary education 82–3
expectations of education 79–80
Experiential Learning cycle pupils 90–3
findings 88
focus of study 83–4
implications of study 95–6
individual plans 82
method 88
methodology 85–7
outcomes 94
recommendations 95–6
social media use 83–4
summary and conclusions 95
teacher responsibilities 82
teacher's role 88–9

principles for professional practice 222–3
prisons *see* P.RE.TURN project
professional identities
    boundary management 231
    building learning communities 226–7
    challenge 232
    collective working 230–1
    conflict resolution 224–5
    context and overview 219
    developing 227
    emerging themes 231–3
    facilitation 231–2
    focus on work not worker 232
    group processes 232–3
    life long learning 229
    Meitheal Model 221ff
    norming and facilitation 224
    outcomes 233–4
    ownership of practice 225
    practice frameworks 227–8
    practitioner voices 220
    practitioners' repertoires 228–9
    principles for professional practice 222–3
    process 223
    process deconstruction 226–30
    recording 233
    self-assessment 225–6
    social work supervision 220–1
    study rationale 221
    summary and conclusions 234–5
    supporting alternative paradigms 229–30
    trust and self-discovery 223–6
psychiatric trauma 12–13
psychoeducational groups, caregiver study 132–3
publishing Edith 266
pupils, Experiential Learning cycle 90–3

recipes for inspiration 18
reflection 220, 230–1
Refugee Convention 1951 4
refugee work, requirements and demands 6–7
relational theory 177
resource orientation 6
restorative practice stance 172
Revenant's Empowerment 178, 182–4
risk, and safety 268–9
Rogge, M. 258

safety

and risk 268–9
team-based learning (TBL) 241, 246–7
Sampson, R. 174
Schippers, M.C. 38
Scholar, H. 25
schooling, and education 85
schools, creative writing 13
secondary advantage 219
self-advocacy, VAWA/U Visa Self-Prep Course (VAWA SPC) 102
self-awareness, group workers 117
self-determination 6–7
self, professional uses of 49–50
self-reflection 50
Shaffer, Vanessa 208
Shippensburg University *see* Teach-in about Racial Justice
Shirts, R. G. 64ff
Silverberg, Sid 265–6
slavery, as abstraction 23–4
social calling 269–70
social constructionism 176
social isolation 127–8
social model of disability 30
social work
    as abstraction 21–3
    as contested 23
    definition 22–3
    diversity 38–9
    effects of immigration 5
    opportunities for migrants 5–6
    requirements and demands 6–7
    US accreditation 63–4
Social Work 220 Understanding Diverse and Oppressed Populations 64
Social Work in 40 Objects project
    abstraction 21–3
    book 33–4, 36
    Button (badge) 28–9
    Clarkson's box 23–4
    collections 33
    conclusions 34–5
    context and overview 21
    contributor stories 26
    Dalek 29–30
    evocative objects 24–5
    evoking social work 25
    exhibiting 33–4
    food 28
    and group work 30–2
    Ileke ibile 26–7

membership 31–2
Memory jar 26
Mind the Gap 31
Mouthpiece to a french horn 32
stories 26–32
traffic sign 27–8
website 36
socio-political context 270–1
Sokhela, Dudzile 28
Sorensen, S. 131–2
spiral of inquiry 14–15
Stolzenberg, Edith 266, 269
stranger stories
    context and overview 265
    ethics and values 267–8
    hopeful purpose 270–1
    lawn signs 266–7, 271
    the picture party 265–6
    postscript 271
    publishing Edith 266
    safety and risk 268–9
    social calling 269–70
    socio-political context 270–1
    Stolzenberg, Edith 266
    West Haven Community House 265–6
stress and coping theory 128–9
supervision 220–1
    see also professional identities
Support Our Law Enforcement and Safe Neighborhoods Act 193

taboos 117
Teach-in about Racial Justice
    aim 197
    content 200–2
    context and overview 192
    costs and benefits 202–3
    design and implementation 198–9
    historical context 192–5
    impetus 195–7
    study location 195
    summary and conclusions 203–4
teach-ins 197
teachers
    Action Research cycle 89, 93–4
    as group workers 80
    responsibilities 82
    role 162–3
team-based learning (TBL)
    adaptations to model 241–7

application phase 239
cohesion 245–6
context and overview 237
goals 242–3, 247
group rules 242, 247
and group work 240–1
heterogeneous groups 240–1
icebreakers 241–2
IFAT 243–4
individual readiness assurance test (iRAT) 243–4
interpersonal relationships 247
overview of approach 238–9
peer evaluation 239, 244–7
peer support 246
readiness assurance 238–9
safety 241, 246–7
scope of use 238
strategically formed permanent teams 238, 240–1
students with disabilities 242
subgrouping 245–6
summary and conclusions 248
team names 241–2
team readiness assurance test (tRAT) 243
the picture party 265–6
therapeutic factors, of group experience 179
theses 3–7
Thompson, Sue 27–8
Toseland, R. W. 133
traffic sign 27–8
Transcendence Using Re-Narration 178, 185–7
trauma 12–13
healing 19
trauma-informed approach 137, 140, 141
Trump administration 195–6
anti-immigration stance 109–10
tuakana-teina 154
Tuckman, B. W. 65–6, 69
Turkle, S. 24

U Visa 102
see also VAWA/U Visa Self-Prep Course (VAWA SPC)
Ukraine
context and overview 10–11, 12
language 16
see also creative writing
UNICEF 19
United Nations High Commissioner for Human Rights (UNCHR) 1–2, 4
United Nations Refugee Agency 1
United States

fatal shootings 194–5
incarceration rate 172
population aging 127
see also caregiver study; P.RE.TURN project; Teach-in about Racial Justice
University of Michigan 255–6
us-and-them relationships 7

values, and ethics 267–8
van Knippenberg, D. 38
VAWA Self Petition 102
VAWA/U Visa Self-Prep Course (VAWA SPC)
    adaptation of model 106
    client screening 109
    context and overview 99–100
    innovation/adaptation 107–8
    interdisciplinary group model 103–4
    legal remedies 101–2
    political environment and U Visa prep group 110–11
    practice implications 111–12
    restrictions on services 106–7
    risk of re-traumatization 103–4
    self-advocacy 102
    social group work theory in agency context 108–9
    socio-political and organizational contexts 106–8
    socio-political context 109–10
    summary and conclusions 111–12
    theoretical framework 104–5
    vulnerability of immigrant women 100–1
    see also intimate partner violence (IPV)
Video Interaction Counselling 88
Visher, C.A. 174
volunteers, in group work 7

Walsh, K. 262
Wang, C. 138–9
war
    trauma of 13
    writing about 18
West Haven Community House 265–6, 268
WhatsApp 83–4
White, M. 176
Wieler, J. 5
Wilberforce, W. 23–4
Wu, H-S. 129

Yalom, I. 179, 183, 247
Yeager, D. S. 176